D1101428

THE GARDENING WHICH? GUIDE TO

SMALL GARDENS

THE GARDENING WHICH? GUIDE TO

SMALL GARDENS

RUTH CHIVERS

WHICH?
BOOKS

CONSUMERS' ASSOCIATION

Which? Books are commissioned by
Consumers' Association and published by
Which? Ltd, 2 Marylebone Road, London NW1 4DF

Distributed by The Penguin Group:
Penguin Books Ltd, 27 Wrights Lane, London W8 5TZ
First edition 1995

Copyright © 1995 Which? Ltd

British Library Cataloguing in Publication Data
Chivers, Ruth
The Gardening Which? Guide to Small Gardens
I. Title
635

ISBN 0 85202 587 4

No part of this publication may be reproduced or transmitted in any form or by any means,
electronically or mechanically, including photocopying, recording or any other information
storage or retrieval system, without prior permission in writing from the publisher.
This publication is not included under licences issued by the Copyright Agency.

Credits
Editorial consultant: Alistair Ayres, Editor *Gardening Which?*
Cover photographs: Heather Angel, Pat Brindley
Cover design: Eve White
Design: Eve White, Type Technique
Typesetting: Type Technique, London W1
Colour reproduction: FMT Colour, London SE1
Printed and bound in Great Britain by Scotprint, Musselburgh

Gardening Which? magazine

You can find up-to-date information on all the latest plants, gardening products
and techniques in *Gardening Which?* magazine, which regularly carries out tests
and trials of plant varieties and suppliers, as well as gardening equipment and
sundries such as composts and fertilisers. Each issue is packed with ideas,
practical advice and results of the magazine's independent evaluations.

Gardening Which? magazine is available by subscription only. For details and
free trial offer, write to *Gardening Which?*, Consumers' Association,
Freepost Hertford X, SG14 1YB or freephone 0800 252100.

Where to see the *Gardening Which?* theme gardens

Gardening Which? magazine has created a collection of small gardens at
Capel Manor, just north of London. The gardens illustrate affordable
solutions that can be put into practice anywhere.

You can visit the *Gardening Which?* theme gardens at Capel Manor,
Bullsmoor Lane, Enfield, Middlesex EN1 4RQ
Phone 0181-366 4442 for details of opening times.

CONTENTS

Introduction   6

WORKING OUT PRIORITIES

How much money?   8   •   How much maintenance?   18
Gardens for disabled people   26   •   Play areas for children   29
Allowing for pets   32

ASSESSING YOUR GARDEN

Existing features   34   •   Soil and climate   39   •   Wildlife   43
Legal considerations   46

DESIGN IDEAS

Balcony gardens   48   •   Cottage gardens   52   •   Exposed gardens   58
Family gardens   60   •   Formal gardens   64   •   Front gardens   68
Long, thin gardens   74   •   Low-maintenance gardens   80
Noisy gardens   84   •   Patio gardens   86
Plant-lovers' gardens   88   •   Roof gardens   94   •   Shady gardens   98
Sloping gardens   100   •   Tiny gardens   104
Wildlife gardens   110

MAPPING OUT YOUR PLANS

Measuring up   114   •   Working to scale   117

GETTING STARTED

Making a schedule   124   •   Preparing the site   128

HARD LANDSCAPING

Boundaries   134   •   Paths and patios   142
Raised beds   152   •   Garden buildings   156   •   Trelliswork   160
Arches and pergolas   164   •   Water features   168

PLANTING

Planning a scheme   176   •   Seasonal interest   190
Lawns   200   •   Plants to be wary of   205

OPTIONAL EXTRAS

Ornaments   206   •   Containers   210
Garden furniture   212   •   Lighting   214   •   Compost bins   216
Garden security   217

Index   218

INTRODUCTION

Many people are awestruck – and inspired – by the small exhibition gardens constructed specially for the major garden festivals held in spring and summer each year: bare plots transformed over the course of a few weeks into delightful outdoor idylls. Often it seems that the smaller the plot, the more creative the garden designers have been. Inspiration may also come from other people's gardens seen on television or visited through the National Gardens Scheme. Small gardens have certainly had more coverage in recent years than ever before – and deservedly so, considering that about 75 per cent of British gardens are under 125 square metres. Many small gardens shown in magazines and books could be described as works of art, vividly demonstrating that a small space need be no limit to the imagination.

But when we look at our own small garden, we may see something that falls well short of being a work of art. Is it because it is a difficult shape, completely in shade or overlooked by a block of flats? Does it demand more time and effort than we have available to keep it looking good? Does utilitarian clutter such as bins and bicycles detract from the overall picture? Sometimes we do not know exactly why our gardens disappoint us: for instance, we may be so used to certain ugly or awkwardly sited features that we no longer notice their presence.

The aim of this book is to show how good looks and practicality can be combined in small gardens of every type. It will take you through the entire design, construction and planting process, helping you to work through each stage in the same way as a professional garden designer would. They look first at function – what you would like from your garden: a pleasant view from the house; a place to relax in summer; somewhere that produces a range of rewarding and attractive plants, perhaps including fruit, vegetables and herbs; somewhere that will encourage birds and other wildlife; somewhere that provides an interest and not-too-strenuous activity for someone elderly with time to spare, a play area for children; and a place that can cope with mundane matters such as hanging washing, storing refuse or the activities of household pets.

Certainly, there are variable factors. Every small plot has its own set of microclimates, for instance. But, as the book shows, through judicious planning you can arrive at a successful garden design that will please and delight all year round, has the facilities you and other garden users need, and will not prove arduous to maintain.

Throughout, the approach is step-by-step. The first two chapters concentrate on the early stages of planning, in which you clarify your basic needs and aspirations and assess what is in your garden already. 'Design Ideas' shows how you might deal creatively with challenges such as having a sloping or a long, thin garden, or how to emulate a particular style, such as a cottage garden, without losing out on practicality. You should then be able to map out your plans on paper and produce a design that incorporates everything you could wish for within an attractive whole.

The book does not stop at theory. The chapter called 'Getting Started' will help you draw up a schedule and prepare your plot. 'Hard Landscaping' covers the construction elements – everything from erecting a fence to establishing a wildlife pond. 'Planting' explains how to devise a planting scheme and create a 'backbone' structure of plants, and how to choose and use trees, hedging, climbers and other plants to achieve year-round interest in terms of colour, shape and fragrance. The final chapter, 'Optional Extras', shows how accessories such as garden furniture and lighting can increase the amenity of a garden, and includes the security features which, sadly, have become so necessary in recent years.

Many of the small gardens in this book were created by the Gardening Which? team at Capel Manor, in Enfield, Middlesex (and can be visited). Others shown have been chosen to illustrate specific design principles or plants. Without exception, these gardens have been designed for real people with practical requirements, but who also have a desire to enjoy a glorious outdoor environment that happens to form an extension to their home.

WORKING OUT PRIORITIES

The first step to take when planning to alter a garden is to identify the basics: your budget; the amount of time you or others want to spend in maintaining it; and what essential facilities might have to be included in the new design, such as access for a wheelchair user or a safe play area for a child.

HOW MUCH MONEY?

The earlier you give thought to the amount of money you are prepared to spend on revamping your garden, the better, as you will be able to plan and design the details to suit. As a very rough guide, the total cost of implementing a major new plan for a small garden – including hiring contractors, site preparation, new paving and so on – can be compared with the total cost of redesigning and kitting out a kitchen. As there are many ways to design an indoor living space, each offering the main features in different price ranges, so a new garden design can be realised at different levels of expenditure. Adjusting ideas to fit budgets need not compromise your favoured design, but it is best to think about likely costs from the outset rather than waiting to calculate figures from your final plan. You might think about substituting less expensive man-made paving materials for higher cost natural stone, or grassing over an area until you can afford to pave it. Alternatively, during the planning and designing stages you might decide to spend a lot on a particular feature and economise on other elements, having weighed the relative costs and benefits of each part of your design. Whatever your budget, keep costs down by researching and shopping around for materials.

LABOUR

Who builds your new garden will greatly affect the overall cost of the project. The largest part of the construction price is usually swallowed up by hard landscaping – paving, walls, fencing – including the labour costs involved. You can obviously keep this cost down by doing some of the work yourself. Basic site preparation is easy for unskilled but energetic and enthusiastic novices – such work can include breaking up old concrete from paths and patios, grubbing out unwanted plants and weeds, digging foundations and levelling the ground. However, your costs may then be in the hiring of a skip to dispose of debris and in the hiring of specialist machinery, either to do the job faster or to do the job at all. For instance, moving earth for ponds and the foundations of walls can be made easier by hiring a mini excavator, small enough to pass through an average doorway. More advanced site preparation, for example regrading a sloping site into stable natural contours, may best be carried out by a contractor experienced in this type of work.

Once the site is cleared and the foundations are dug, you can make even greater savings if you have the necessary skills and time to carry out the construction work yourself. If the only real hard landscaping is going to be a paved patio, the task of laying this is relatively simple. In terms of equipment needed, you may be able to do the job using a makeshift tamper for awkward corners, and hiring a vibrating plate compactor for a really firm base. You will also need to use one of these if you are laying block paving. The importance of choosing the right type of paving unit for the size of your patio or paths will be hammered home when it comes to the practicalities of splitting or cutting large slabs to fit the area. This is a source of added expense when using a contractor as well.

Cutting can be avoided by using preformed slabs which come in varying radii to form circular or curved areas of your paths and patios. This rules out the need for hiring an angle-grinder to cut curves. Block and slab splitters can be hired in a range of sizes. Laying concrete, mortaring paving joints or building walls will be easier if you hire a cement mixer. It will also be worth hiring a heavy-duty wheelbarrow at the same time if you do not already have one.

If your time is more precious than money, you might hand over to a landscape contractor or builder for the construction part of the project. Front gardens can be a top priority if you are going to be faced with negotiating a mound of rubble and weeds each day. It can be a false economy to tackle projects beyond your level of competence, certainly where safety is an issue. Walling and step building may well be beyond the level of your skill and they require high-cost skilled labour from contractors. Retaining walls and free-standing structures in particular require skilled design and execution. Any reputable contractor will be covered by insurance should problems arise. Another point

Above: preformed slabs can be cheaper than bricks, and the range of styles that are readily available is enormous.

Left: wooden decking can be one of the most expensive options for a surface, even in a very small garden. Recycling old wood can reduce costs.

Right: transform the bleakness of paving slabs with hand-thrown terracotta pots planted with bright flowers.

Above: though not cheap materials, brick and stone can complement each other handsomely.

in favour of hiring a contractor may be the competitive quote offered based on the contractor's savings on bulk orders of materials.

You may want to take charge of preparing areas for planting once the contractor's building work is finished. Powered rotovators make easier work of this than back-breaking digging but they can require a certain amount of operator strength. Compacted soil generally needs to be rough dug first.

PAVING

A paved patio is important to most people, but it is also frequently the most expensive feature of a garden. If you have a low budget set aside for the garden and a paved area already exists, you may as well keep it. Old slabs can be relaid to form a new shape, or the paving can be extended with a contrasting material such as

gravel. If old slabs look a little grimy, pressure washing gives good results. Gravel is a cheap material but may not be a suitable choice of surface for a main seating area. Furthermore, it will usually have to be contained by an edging, and the stones are irresistible to young children. The next cheapest paving option is in-situ or poured concrete. Concrete can be given different textured finishes – notably with the aggregate exposed, or imprinted and colour-tinted – and it can easily be formed into curves.

Paving costs can be kept down without losing out on style by using ordinary materials in an extraordinary way. Concrete slabs can be 'lifted' by the way in which they are laid. For little extra money, you might lay bricks with them in a pattern that suits the area. A cheap paved surface can be edged with a more expensive one – for example exposed aggregate concrete edged with granite setts. You may have decided that only the mellow tones of old natural stone slabs such as York will produce the results you want. Even if you do the work yourself, this material is beyond the bounds of most budgets. However, the range of reconstituted stone slabs on offer now includes convincing York-coloured lookalikes.

Joints affect both the look and cost of paving. Normally, natural stone is butt-jointed – without mortar – and man-made slabs can be laid likewise. However, some slabs and patterns are enhanced by the mortar or finish given to the joints. Whatever the type of paving chosen, you will have to excavate a hole and install a sub-base at least 75-100mm deep. When comparing d-i-y costs with a contractor's estimate, remember to take into account the cost of getting heavy materials on to the site. If you live in a terraced house, extra time – and thus money – may apply due to the logistical problems of getting materials and machinery into the back garden.

BOUNDARIES

Boundary treatments can be another major item of expenditure in a small garden. You may be lucky enough to inherit sound walls, fences or kempt hedges which will form the framework of a new design. If not, hedges are the cheapest option, followed by fencing, then, at the top of the scale, walls. The style of garden you want to create may dictate the material you should use, as may existing materials to be found in your own house and other buildings and hard surfaces in the surrounding area. Hedging can be appropriate in both town and country gardens and is a suitable treatment for a number of different garden styles – wildlife (hedgerow), cottage (either deciduous or evergreen hedging, sometimes clipped into topiary), formal (evergreen closely trimmed). But hedges can take five years or so to get established and when they do may take up valuable space in a small garden. They also require ongoing maintenance.

Timber fencing comes in many different guises to suit most situations and budgets and is a

Timber fencing is a popular choice as a boundary. It is easy to install and comes in many shapes, sizes and styles.

BOUNDARY TREATMENTS
Hedging
Advantages:
Good wind filtering;
Range of planting options.
Disadvantages:
New ones can be slow to grow;
Need ongoing maintenance;
Take up valuable space in a small garden;
Take nutrients from surrounding soil.
Fencing
Advantages:
Quick and relatively easy to put up;
Range of different types;
Effective windbreak provided by slatted styles;
Can be temporary.
Disadvantages:
Shorter lifespan than hedges or walls;
Require access for regular maintenance;
Less effective than walls at reducing noise and pollution levels.
Walls
Advantages:
Long lasting; Good shelter;
Excellent reduction of noise and pollution.
Disadvantages:
Do not filter wind;
Expensive and difficult to construct;
Matching materials can be difficult.

popular boundary treatment for small gardens. Old fences can be rejuvenated by being painted with wood stain – lots of colours are available. With a limited budget, trellis panels can be attached to unattractive closed boarded fences, or added to fence panels to give extra height. Around 1.8m is usually enough height to provide privacy; any boundary fence over 2m in height will require planning permission as well as being a drain on a budget. A boundary wall, the most expensive option, will require planning permission above a mere 0.9m high. Always check your house deeds and with your neighbours before altering a boundary.

DIVISIONS

Dividing up even a small garden is a good way to add interest and intrigue, or, for purely practical reasons you may want to create a utility area out of sight in a convenient corner. Boundary treatments can be used as dividing structures, but you may not want the solidity of these materials, nor have the money and space to spare. Trellis panels are cheap and take up little space. They can be semi-permanent, planted or left as decorative structures in their own right, and range from the rustic half-pole type, ideal for a cottage garden, to the manicured, fine-gauged variety that sits happily in a formal town courtyard. You could design and build your own trellis to economise even further. Willow or hazel hurdles have made a resurgence in garden use in recent years – they are easy to install, and do not take up a lot of valuable space, but are very expensive. For a different look, there are nylon-coated steel tube dividing panels that can be linked together in the same way as timber trellis. If you already have metal gates in the garden, bespoke metal panels to match would link different parts of your garden but they can be expensive.

Other useful dividing structures can be created if you place timber posts in the ground (75x75mm minimum diameter, by, say, 2.5m finished height) and link them either with swags of thick rope or crossbeams of timber. Using cheap posts and rope is a traditional way of training climbing roses. If funds and space allow, you might use 'brick-and-a-half' pillars instead, or natural stone ones if these match other materials in use in the garden.

CHEAPEST OUTLETS FOR MATERIALS

Paving and bricks: builders' merchants. With some types, if using a lot, try direct from manufacturer. Specialist stone companies and quarries for natural stone.

Gravel and loose materials: builders' merchants for large quantities delivered loose or to be picked up with a trailer. Small quantities – d-i-y superstores.

Bark mulches: specialist suppliers for very large quantities – delivered loose, or can be bagged. Extra cost still makes it cheaper than garden centres.

Fencing, trellis, hurdles etc: specialist fencing companies for different fencing types. Timber yards, builders' merchants – former can make trellis to size.

In a small garden a timber
trellis can be a useful
dividing structure, a
support for climbing plants
and an attractive feature
in its own right.
The blue trellis shown here
was home-made and so
cost only as much as the
wood used.

RETAINING STRUCTURES

Simple changes in level add interest to any garden, but coping with steep slopes can add greatly to construction costs. Creating a level area in a very uneven garden by installing a retaining wall may be an unavoidable expense. Budget materials for simple retaining structures include railway sleepers and treated timber logs, available in a range of sizes. Both of these materials can be used vertically or horizontally and with any appreciable slope behind them must be firmly secured into the ground. Crib walling, also known as gabions, are available in metal or timber versions and look like open boxes filled with stones and rocks. They may be a little industrial for the small garden, but scaled down, lighter versions of both these and sleepers are now available.

Brick, stone and concrete walls require good design and professional construction if they are to retain a steep slope. Raised beds should also be constructed with care. Costs can be kept down by using concrete blocks and facing them with bricks or stone to match the rest of the house and garden. A rendered finish can also be used; this is cheaper but less durable and is likely to fall off and need replacing. Rendering can be textured and painted to suit the location. Height, length and the coping or top finish given to a retaining wall all affect the overall cost.

DECORATIVE FEATURES

There is a multitude of ready-made garden features in a range of materials and decorative finishes. Making decorative features yourself is, of course, the cheapest option, and will suit you better if you regard garden design as an

Above: old railway sleepers can be a cheap and efficient surround for a raised bed.

Right: this small garden has a large paved area and so was expensive to build.

opportunity to indulge arts and crafts skills. The cost of timber arches and pergolas varies according to the type of wood, ranging from softwood, which needs to be pressure-treated, through to imported hardwoods and oak. With both of these features, the supporting pillars can be constructed from brick or stone, which would be a more expensive option again, even if you do the work yourself. As they are tall structures they require strengthening: the crossbeams might be formed from either timber or metal, which has an advantage in that it can be bent into a curve.

Obelisks and similar features for formal gardens can be made simply and cheaply from treated roofing laths. Inexpensive traditional salmon putchers and fan-shaped plant supports made by willow hurdle-makers are good ideas for informal gardens. Bamboo, willow or hazel sticks can be bound together to form simple temporary features.

Large features such as summerhouses, gazebos and playhouses may be beyond modest budgets when bought ready-made, as well as possibly unfeasible in a small garden, but a competent carpenter can bring them within reach. It is possible to include water in a small garden in a number of ways, from a simple container or half barrel, either sunken or above ground, to a formal pool with water spouts. The amount of your total budget that a suitable water feature takes up will depend on the style and the quality of the materials used in its construction. A raised pool can be made from treated timber, a liner and, if required, a pump for a fountain, without the expense or effort of excavation.

RELATIVE COSTS

Arches, pergolas and arbours

	d-i-y	'Off the peg'	Bespoke
Timber	££	££ – £££	£££ – ££££
Metal	££	££ – £££	££££
Nylon-covered steel (e.g. Agriframes)	–	££ – £££	–
Brick or stone pillars	£££	–	££££

Obelisks and columns (trellis) etc

	d-i-y	'Off the peg'	Bespoke
Timber	£	££ – £££	££££
Metal	££	££-£££	££££
Nylon-covered steel (e.g. Agriframes)	–	£££	–
Metal shapes for instant topiary	£	££	–

UTILITIES

In ascending order of cost, greenhouses are available with metal, plastic-coated metal (UPVC) and timber frames – the latter can be built with a brick half-wall base. Old sheds, if weatherproof, can add character to a garden and form a sympathetic background to planting. It is worth repairing and retaining them where possible. New sheds are usually made from timber, the price depending on the size, quality of the timber, and options such as windows and stable-type doors. If you need workshop space as well, you will probably want to consider a larger, stronger building, which will cost more than the basic garden shed.

A conservatory can be regarded as a utility if it provides extra living space. Adding one to a small garden requires careful planning, especially if it takes up an area of space previously used as a patio. Providing a new paved area beyond the conservatory will further add to the cost of installation. They range from the inexpensive metal framed 'bolt on', through UPVC framed structures with half brick walls, to bespoke state-of-the-art period-

Above: you can brighten up an existing shed with a coat of paint. Don't be afraid to experiment.

Right: a garden with a lawn, such as this one, is far cheaper to construct than the paved garden shown on the previous page. You will need to spend a lot of time mowing, though.

RELATIVE COSTS

Containers	
Wire (basket)	£
Plastic	£ – ££
Ceramic	££ – £££
Timber	£ – £££
Terracotta	££ – £££
Reconstitued stone	££
Stone	£££
Cast iron or lead	£££ – ££££
Fibreglass	££££

style 'glass houses'. Designing your own for either yourself or professionals to build can be cost-effective when compared with 'off the peg' solutions of the same size.

Other important factors that affect the cost of a conservatory are getting the temperature right within it by balancing light and shade, a specialist area that should be researched thoroughly. 'Maintenance-free' UPVC will not require painting but cannot be repaired in the same way as wood should it get damaged.

LAWNS, PLANTS AND CONTAINERS

Soft landscaping – planting – is nearly always the cheapest element of a garden. If you have a bare garden, however, buying everything at once for even a small space can still add up to a serious bill. Unless it is in a really terrible condition, an existing lawn takes little time to restore using a combination of selective weedkillers, then patching, levelling, scarifying and mowing. Power rakes and rollers can be hired to take some of the hard work out of this process. So if you already have grass, however tatty it may seem, keeping it may be the best bet for a modest budget. For new areas of lawn, seeding will be much cheaper than turfing. Moreover, sourcing good quality turf can be a problem.

It is a waste of money buying large deciduous hedging plants such as beech, as they should be cut back to a low level after planting. Keep existing trees to save money – buying large-sized specimens can be done, but at considerable cost. If you have planned one or two new plants as strong focal points, consider buying much larger than normal specimens for an instant effect, but avoid wasting money on large specimens of naturally fast-growing varieties.

Splitting a large project up into small areas on which to work enables you to plant each area separately and budget accordingly. Working this way, it is possible to save money by propagating herbaceous perennials for other parts of the garden. Planting that is visible from the house should be given priority even if you have a limited budget. Grow plants from seeds or cuttings where possible, starting them off on windowsills in the house if necessary. Containers for plants, preferably large, give instant results, with your outlay on them ranging from modest for plastic to extreme for cast iron. Many people utilise old household objects as containers – buckets, saucepans and so on – which, of course, costs nothing, but be sure to make holes for drainage in such receptacles.

Rare varieties and delicate, exotic plants can be many times more expensive than plants commonly found at local outlets, although this may not be a barrier to the plant hobbyist. Mail-order special offers are a relatively cheap way to build up plant stocks, but the size of plants will invariably be smaller than those bought from a nursery or garden centre. When buying herbaceous plants, larger specimens can often be divided to give you two or three smaller ones. You will get a better 'drift' effect by planting in groups than single plants. Once you have drawn up planting plans for your new design, resist the temptation to in-fill between young plants with temporary gap-fillers. The money may be better spent on a weed-suppressing mulch. Specialist flower markets, held in some cities once a week or so, can be a good source for quality plants, with prices often about two-thirds of the shop price. It may be wise to resist impulse buying, though, making fewer visits to garden centres, nurseries and markets and buying only the plants on your planting list.

RELATIVE COSTS

Planting	
Trees	££ – £££
Shrubs	£ – ££
Hedging and edging	£ – ££ a metre
Climbers/wall plants	££
Annuals/biennials	£
Bulbs	£
Herbaceous perennials	£ – ££

HOW MUCH MAINTENANCE?

As you think about what you want from your garden, how much work the gardeners of the household are willing and able to put into routine maintenance is an important factor that will affect your design solution. Consider this factor *realistically* before you plan the details. That there may be a therapeutic element to routine chores is also worth considering by all members of your household at this stage – even if the idea of any benefit is quickly discarded. For instance, weeding for many might be the outdoor equivalent of the chore of washing dishes, but others may love the opportunity to uproot and hoe. What you want to avoid though, is a garden that is difficult to look after.

Some styles of gardens and planting are naturally more labour-intensive than others. For instance, cottage gardens, fruit and vegetable growing, rock gardens with alpines, and rose gardens planted predominantly with hybrid teas all fall into this category, so avoid these kinds of gardens if you want to devote no more than an hour or so each week to gardening.

In rock gardens such as this, a lot of time can be wasted keeping invasive and vigorous plants under control.

CHECKLIST

● Who looks after the garden now? Will this be the same in the future?

● How much time do you and others want to spend on routine chores; on relaxational pottering – hobbies and tasks of your own making; in sitting and enjoying the garden?

● Will the time available increase or decrease in the foreseeable future?

There are a number of features that can be installed to reduce the need to mow, weed, water and so on, which can be of benefit to both full-time and once-a-fortnight gardeners. It makes sense to consider such methods as part of a new garden design, so that the time,

expense and effort of installing them is absorbed into that of the construction of the whole. Design ideas for purely low-maintenance gardens can be found on pages 80–83.

MOWING

Most small gardens have lawns, and, even allowing for a less than immaculate sward, cutting grass is a significant task for a good half of the year for many people. The task of caring for a lawn is perceived by gardeners in different ways. Some will be happy with a basic green patch that includes daisies and other intruders and will willingly leave areas of grass to grow quite long. Others, perhaps of the same household, will not be able to relax unless the lawn is closely clipped with mowing stripes

An intricately shaped lawn can be time-consuming to mow.

Here, the edges are smoother, and pond and tree are out of the way.

clearly visible. For these people, getting the lawn into this condition can be an enjoyable part of gardening. As a guide, cut a rough and ready lawn at least 10 times each year. For a finer lawn, cut at least 30 times a year, fertilise in spring and spike and scarify each autumn too.

Doing away with grass altogether is a good solution for someone who does not relish the thought of having to mow regularly, and this may also free up valuable space in the small garden. A small town garden lends itself perfectly to hard landscaping, where there may be limited light, in any case, to grow a lawn successfully. Minimising the area of lawn is also an idea, but consider that although a tiny area of lawn may not take much time to cut, the time spent regularly hauling out the grass-cutting equipment may itself prove infuriating.

By mowing little and often, total time spent caring for a lawn over a season may be significantly reduced: the resulting fine

Install a 'mowing strip' to allow your lawnmower to catch those last blades of grass.

clippings can be left on the grass as a moisture-retaining mulch. As another solution, letting the grass grow quite long is well suited to some styles of garden. A 'wildlife' corner of the garden, where grass can be left longer than elsewhere and perhaps naturalised with bulbs and wildflowers, may be an ideal compromise for a household whose members want different things from grass.

Coping with corners and awkwardly shaped edges with a lawnmower always slows down the work. The solution to this has to be at the design stage: make the edges of the lawn straight or at least into sweeping curves. Replacing corners with curves will help ensure

TIPS FOR AN EASY-CARE LAWN

● Design a simple lawn shape. Do not create awkward corners that are difficult to reach.

● Include a mowing strip.

● There is a good range of lawnmowers for small gardens. Keep blades sharp for an easier task.

● When sowing a new lawn, use a durable seed mixture that does not include the more vigorous strains of grass such as rye grass.

● Do not spend time watering grass during a drought – it will soon recover in the autumn.

that there are no patches of unmowable grass. Trees can be problematic to mow around – the ground is often bumpy because of the tree roots and the grass itself very patchy. Again, leaving patches of grass to grow longer around trees may be the solution.

A 'mowing strip' can be an excellent labour-saving feature. Instead of having to snip the grass overhanging borders as a separate task because the lawnmower misses it, lay a line of paving slabs or bricks level with or just below the height of the lawn so that the mower blades don't catch. The initial expense and time spent installing the mowing strip may further repay you because areas of grass will not die back as a result of overhanging plant growth.

CARING FOR PLANTS

Bedding (seasonal displays), varieties of herbaceous plants that require frequent division, mixed borders and shrub borders without ground cover all require lots of work. For the plant-lover, nurturing plants is the best part of gardening. However, even if you are skilled at growing difficult plants and have more than the odd hour here and there to devote to your hobby, keep sight of practical considerations. Having a host of semi-hardy herbaceous perennials in a border may be attractive now, but even the keen gardener can become demoralised by borders that are so big that a schedule of tasks, such as a whole afternoon of dead-heading, is impossible to adhere to. It is a fair rule of thumb to design borders at a maximum of 3.5 to 4m in width, and to break them up into manageable sections, perhaps with stepping-stone maintenance paths. Check what type of soil your garden has (see page 39)

Left: after many hours of your labour, bedding plants will look glorious.

Below: a shrub such as this Choisya ternata *will make few demands on your time.*

to avoid wasting time on plants that just do not stand a chance of surviving, such as ericaceous plants in limy conditions, the soil registering a high pH value.

Bedding displays

Caring for summer bedding plants involves preparing the beds, watering, weeding, deadheading and getting rid of the plants at the end of the year – all of which takes up a lot of time. One way you can cut down the work is to plant a permanent edging around annual beds using low-growing evergreen shrubs. The edging will give some interest throughout the year as well as seasonal interest at certain times. In addition, you can use shrubs as dot plants in the beds.

You can then still use bedding plants for that bright splash of colour in summer, but you won't need nearly as many.

Fruit and vegetables

It is entirely possible to grow sufficient quantities of fruit and vegetables in a small garden to supply your household, so long as you are aware from the outset that the cycle of sowing, planting out, hoeing and watering for a good crop will require a high investment of your time for best results. However, by growing vegetables in raised beds and using horticultural fleece to keep out pests, you can avoid jobs such as digging and spraying. Harvesting the crop will be the most enjoyable task.

Gravel beds

Growing plants in gravel beds can be an attractive way to set off foliage and flowers, and, if the beds are properly prepared, it can be virtually maintenance-free. Getting rid of weeds from the start is the main way to ensure this.

Groundcover plants

Low-growing groundcover plants can be used as a low-maintenance alternative to a lawn and to fill any patches of bare earth between taller plants. Steep grass slopes take extra time to mow, but lend themselves well to groundcover planting. The front garden may be an area that you want to spend less time in than the back garden, so groundcover and shrub planting instead of lawn and herbaceous planting may be more appropriate there, too.

The golden rule is to get rid of all traces of weeds before you start. After clearing the ground wait several months before planting to ensure weeds are out. This may sound unnecessary, but trying to control weeds like couchgrass and ground elder growing among groundcover is very difficult. It is also important that you match the vigour of the plant to the area you want to cover. For example, *Cotoneaster dammeri* grows more than 60cm a year. If you have to keep cutting

Roses such as 'Angela Rippon' (bright pink) do not need quite as much maintenance as old-fashioned varieties.

the plants back, it defeats the purpose of low-maintenance planting. In a restricted area, *Cotoneaster salicifolia* 'Repens' would be a better choice. If you are aiming for quick groundcover, do so with a minimal number of plants: closely packed ones can soon outgrow their allotted space.

Hedging

Traditional hedging, such as beech, privet or *Lonicera*, requires trimming at least once or twice a year. To make shorter work of this laborious task buy an electric trimmer. Low-maintenance hedges include *Rosa rugosa*, *Berberis* x *stenophylla* and *Pyracantha*.

Herbaceous borders

Staking, dead-heading, cutting back, dividing and weeding can make herbaceous borders one of the most labour-intensive areas in the garden. But a lot depends on your choice of plants. It is usually the traditional favourites like delphiniums, lupins and Michaelmas daisies that demand the most work. Foliage plants such as hostas and non-invasive ornamental grasses (like *Hakonechloa macra* 'Albo-Aurea', *Helictotrichon sempervirens*, *Miscanthus sinensis* 'Gracillimus' and *Stipa gigantea*) are invaluable in a border as they give a very long season of interest for very little effort.

Make dead-heading easier, particularly in wide borders, by providing stepping stones to enable you to get at the plants at the back. If you do not have time to dead-head all the plants, concentrate on those that seed all over the place if not caught in time, like alliums and *Alchemilla mollis*.

Mixed borders

In a mixed border, with so many different types of plants growing at different rates, problems can occur when some plants start shading others out or invading their space. You can then be caught in a seemingly never-ending cycle of cutting back and moving plants in an attempt to maintain a good-looking border. To make life easier, it pays to put annuals and perennials that need regular dividing or plants that may need spraying near the front of the border. At the back of the border, try and use plants that are unlikely to need any attention such as shrubs and long-lived perennials. Take care to give these plants space to grow to their final size and move apart any long-term plants that are likely to compete with each other for the same space. In the short term, you can fill the spaces in between with annuals or short-lived plants that grow quickly.

Roses

Roses are extremely popular, but there is no point in growing large-flowered or cluster-flowered (floribunda) types unless you are prepared to give them a lot of attention. They need annual pruning, feeding in spring and summer, spraying at least every two weeks during the growing season, daily removal of dead flowers and regular checking for suckers and over-vigorous water shoots. If you do not

Choose Rosa rugosa *for a hedge that will look good with little effort on your own part.*

have time to do this, the bushes are likely to look a mess with unhealthy leaves and blown flowers.

Modern shrub roses such as 'Fountain' (crimson) and 'Penelope' (creamy pink) produce bushes no more than 1.5m in height or spread and require little or no pruning, apart from removing dead or damaged wood. Similarly, miniature roses do not require any regular pruning but they vary a lot in disease resistance. You could grow 'Angela Rippon', 'Easter Morning', 'Little Flirt' or 'Starina' without spraying.

Shrub borders

Provided you do not plant shrubs too close together or are prepared to move any that become overcrowded, a shrub border can be virtually maintenance-free. A couple of rectangular beds, no more than one metre wide, planted with shrubs that do not require

Above: forest bark mulch is the perfect complement to many border plants.

pruning and a selection of low-growing plants, preferably evergreens, will look good virtually without help. You could extend seasonal interest by incorporating bulbs into the border.

SUPPRESSING WEEDS

Weeding offers the opportunity to really get to know your garden from the ground up. However, any garden owner with little time or inclination to devote to its maintenance will reap the rewards of effective methods of weed suppression. When preparing soil prior to planting, perennial weeds should be eradicated as far as possible. If you have inherited a serious weed problem such as a patch of ground elder right in the middle of where you plan to put your main area of planting, it pays to use a systemic weed killer – probably several applications will be required. The ground should be left fallow until you are satisfied that the problem has been solved. Just before planting you can cover the cleared ground with old carpet or black plastic to stop annual weeds from seeding into the soil.

Eliminate weeds by eliminating the empty spaces where they can grow. Mulches and groundcover planting are the main ways of doing this. Materials for mulches include gravel, bark, wood

This Potentilla fruticosa *'Red Ace' is surrounded by a gravel mulch.*

chips, grass clippings and cocoa shells. Not only do they discourage weed seedlings from appearing, they also help to conserve moisture around the roots of fresh planting.

In a border, having removed most of the weeds, apply a 5cm layer of bark chippings in early spring to prevent annual weeds from growing and make it easier to pull out perennial weeds that reappear. Top up the mulch every spring after applying fertiliser to the border.

At the back of the border, under shrubs and trees or where weeds tend to invade from next door, lay strips of black polythene over as much of the ground as possible. Cover the polythene with a 3cm layer of bark chippings, gravel or even pebbles both to hide it and hold it in place. Where pieces or strips of polythene meet, overlap by 10 to 13cm to reduce the chance of weeds growing through gaps. Where you want to grow bulbs or herbaceous plants between shrubs, use a 5cm layer of bark or gravel instead of black polythene.

If you have a gravel path, a non-chemical way to stop most weeds is to lay heavy-duty black polythene beneath the loose topping. However, make small holes in the polythene to allow water to drain through.

To be successful with groundcover, you need to dig out all the weeds thoroughly before you start and use a 5cm deep mulch of bark chippings to prevent further weed growth while the groundcover plants are establishing.

Don't discard grass clippings: use them as a weed-suppressing mulch.

WATERING

Watering plants in the ground should not prove to be a major task if you have chosen ones that will thrive and survive in your soil type. If it is sandy, for instance, choose *Cistus, Helianthemum,* lavender, rosemary, *Caryopteris, Santolina.* If you spend a lot of time away from home either avoid containers or grow in them plants such as geraniums, succulents and cacti, which will survive a drought more easily. Using the right compost will further reduce the need to water: you need a multi-purpose one for seeds and young plants, and John Innes Nos 2 and 3 for larger, established plants.

Where plants require minimal watering, a lightweight watering can should be sufficient in the small garden; if not, install an outside tap and use a hose on a reel to save time. You can also take measures that may get rid of the task of watering altogether, for instance if you mulch beds, use water-retaining gels in container compost, and line terracotta containers. If you want lots of containers but not the work of watering them, try installing an automatic drip system or 'leaky-hose system' in the garden.

Left: mulch a newly planted tree with black plastic and bark.

Growing plants in greenhouses is not really a good idea for the weekend gardener, and even the enthusiast may find the watering rather time-consuming. Shade a greenhouse to conserve moisture. Automatic vent openers and irrigation systems such as timers for taps, overhead misters and capillary matting may all help to reduce the need to water.

GARDENS FOR DISABLED PEOPLE

Many of the maintenance-reducing tips discussed on pages 18-25 are relevant for disabled people. You do not necessarily have to be severely disabled to find gardening a major problem. If you have back problems, install any device that will reduce the need to lift and carry, such as an outside tap, or re-think your planting altogether so that heavy jobs, such as watering lots of containers, are no longer necessary. Good access from paths to all parts of the garden is an essential feature for people with restricted mobility. Decide if slopes need steps, or if steps need ramps. Raised beds should be considered by wheelchair users and anyone with bending problems. Likewise, conservatories or greenhouses can be appropriate because plants can be placed in them at a height to save backs, knees and hips from aches and strains. Do not forget that there are a number of tools on the market that are positively designed to counter such problems as lack of grip, restricted reach or back weaknesses.

A tranquil corner to rest with the fragrance of flowers will be appreciated by a blind person.

IMPORTANT MEASUREMENTS
Actual widths
Wheelchair 80cm
Zimmer frame 86cm
Person on crutches 95cm
Minimum widths for wheelchair access
Openings 90cm allowing for a straight approach
(No manoeuvring can be attempted within
2.5m of an opening)
Paths 120cm
Corners 110cm
Ramps and slopes
Gradient 1:12 for short runs only 1:20 for longer runs
The surface should be non-slip, and surface water should
drain across the width of a ramp
Handrails for steps and slopes
Ideally two handrails 75-100cm height
Place handrail before first riser or start of slope, end at
the last riser or the slope end

LAWNS

Bumpy lawns with unexpected holes can be a problem for people with impaired movement. For those confined to wheelchairs, in particular, the surface of a lawn can be too soft, causing the chair to sink. The following specialist products are available for frequently used areas of grass, such as paths. They redistribute the weight from wheelchairs and feet, reduce resistance to wheelchairs and protect the lawn from being broken up by wheels, but they do have a few disadvantages.

Netlon Pathguard is a dark green polythene mesh, available in 1x30m rolls, which is laid straight on to the area, ideally in spring. This allows grass to grow through but does not interfere with mowing. It is relatively cheap but, of course, visible on the surface for most of the year. It also needs regular maintenance – pegs must be firmly in place – which involves bending. The more expensive *Netlon Advanced Turf* is laid beneath the surface and so is invisible. Under supervision, existing turf is removed to a depth of 100mm, and the area is covered with a mixture of sand- and loam-based growing medium and the system's polypropylene mesh. The ground is then re-seeded or re-turfed with a suitable grass mixture. A similar product, using a sand-based growing medium and reinforcing plastic fibres, *Fibreturf* has the advantage of being relatively cheap and invisible, but it does require expert installation.

By contrast, *Notts Sport VHAF GR700* is both cheap and easy to install. This system's polypropylene fabric is laid on to a soil surface, followed by the sowing of a special seed mixture, which penetrates the fabric and roots beneath. The roots are thus protected and will recover quickly from any damage, while the fabric acts as a load distributor. It does have a couple of disadvantages, though – the fabric can become visible where grass is very worn, and you need to mow at a higher setting, which reduces the rolling resistance benefit.

RAISED BEDS

For gardeners in wheelchairs or with bad backs or bending problems, raised beds will bring plants up to a height at which it is comfortable to work. Raised beds also add interest to flat gardens, but when planning them make sure they do not dominate the line of vision, cutting out pleasing vistas and focal points seen from wheelchair level. The view through the winter months is particularly important, as is the view from downstairs windows.

DIMENSIONS OF RAISED BEDS FOR GARDENERS WITH RESTRICTED MOBILITY
Height
60cm for wheelchair gardeners
90cm for ambulant gardeners
Width
60cm if one-sided access only
120cm for access from two sides
Distance in and around beds
120cm min

A raised bed can accentuate the interest of plant shapes as well as making maintenance easier.

PLANTING FOR BLIND PEOPLE

Choose plants that will produce perfume in different seasons from one another

Spring
Clematis armandii (evergreen clematis)
Ribes (flowering currant)
Viburnum carlesii (Korean spice viburnum)

Summer
Jasminium officinale (jasmin)
Nicotiana (tobacco plant)
Philadelphus (mock orange)

Autumn
Cercidiphyllum japonicum (katsura)
Clerodendrum
Elaeagnus x *ebbingei*
Myrtus communis (myrtle)

Winter
Daphne odora (winter daphne)
Mahonia japonica
Lonicera fragrantissima (winter honeysuckle)

Include plants with foliage that releases a scent when brushed or crushed

Chamaemelum (chamomile)
Eucalyptus gunnii (gum tree)
Helichrysum italicum (curry plant)
Rosmarinus officinalis (rosemary)
Salvia officinalis (sage)
Thymus (thyme)

Include bamboos and large grasses, which make noises in the wind, and big-leaved plants that make a pleasant sound when rain falls

Acanthus (bear's breeches)
Briza (quaking grass)
Darmera (umbrella plant)
Gunnera (prickly/giant rhubarb)
Rheum (ornamental rhubarb)

Raised beds do not have to be box-like: vary height according to need, and be creative with shape, perhaps incorporating sheltered spots to sit. The walls of the beds have to contain the weight of the soil, so their foundations are constructed in the same way as for other kinds of retaining walls. The concrete foundation is usually twice the thickness of the wall. Whatever material is used for construction, the top of the wall should be finished with a smooth surface. If using bricks, choose a chamfered engineering brick or a bull-nosed coping brick. With timber, any cut edge should be angled for water to run off, and the top should be slightly rounded to avoid snagging and injury when working on the bed. Handles and handrails can be securely incorporated into brick and concrete walled beds.

FEATURES FOR BLIND PEOPLE

For blind or partially sighted people, plant for fragrance – think particularly of fragrances acting as landmarks in a large area. Partially sighted people will appreciate bold shapes and colour contrasts, while contrasts in the surface underfoot, for example from gravel to grass, can be a useful way to signal important changes such as a slope in the ground. Changes in path direction can be marked with texturally contrasting paving or by distinctive planting – small trees or shrubs – or a garden feature such as a timber arch. Steps

that will be used by a blind person should ideally be given a handrail that extends along the path by a minimum of a metre. Also consider edging borders with a low kerb to act as a guide both for moving around the garden and for identifying the position of plants.

HARD SURFACES

A network of paths leading to all parts of the garden makes gardening easier and safer at all times of the year for disabled people, but the material makes a big difference. Smooth surfaces such as stone and wood tend to attract moss and algae, and can become very slippery when wet. Rather than replace any such existing surfaces, treat them with a non-slip paint, such as the kind used on boat decks. Loose surfaces such as gravel and chipping can be frustrating for people who find walking difficult, and even a surface of gravel that is firm enough to walk across easily can be impassable to wheelchair users, as the stones prevent the wheels from gripping. Self-binding gravel or hoggin provide a more suitable flexible surface. The best solution, however, is to choose textured paving and lay it on a slight gradient so that it sheds water. Always secure loose slabs, which can cause loss of footing. Ensure that your patio or path has a well-compacted hardcore base. Set slabs on motor dobs so that they do not subside in years to come, causing a hazardous, uneven surface.

As we grow older, level paving, solidly constructed seats and raised beds become all the more important.

PLAY AREAS FOR CHILDREN

Gardens provide a wonderful opportunity for imaginative and creative children's play and children often develop a lasting interest in plants, natural history and gardening. There are several factors that should be considered if you are re-designing a garden that is going to be used by a child. Make sure that your design is simple and that the features you use are robust and safe.

A patio by the house may prove better than a lawn for young children to play with their toys; small toys can be lost easily in grass. A patio is also a good spot for sandpits and paddling pools where you can keep an eye on toddlers and not have to trek backwards and forwards so much.

Paddling pools and sandpits can be bought ready-made – which can be an advantage as they can be moved into sun or shade as required – but you could consider building them into your garden as bespoke items that will have a useful life after your children have grown out of them.

For instance, as a raised structure, a sandpit or paddling pool is easily built from materials matching those used in the rest of your garden; later, when the child loses interest in sand play, the feature can be transformed into a raised flower bed.

A sandpit that is excavated from the ground can later be lined with a butyl liner and filled with

A sandpit can provide years of fun for small children.

POISONOUS PLANTS

These plants will poison young children if they try to eat them.
For a list of irritant plants see page 205.

Aconitum (monkshood)
Aesculus (horse chestnut)
Agrostemma githago (corncockle)
Aquilegia (columbine)
Arum (lords and ladies)
Atropa (deadly nightshade)
Brugmansia (angels' trumpet)
Caltha (marsh marigold)
Catharanthus roseus (rose periwinkle)
Colchicum (autumn crocus)
Convallaria majalis (lily of the valley)
Daphne laureola (spurge laurel)
Daphne (all other species)
Datura (angels' trumpet)
Delphinium
Dieffenbachia (dumb cane, leopard lily)
Digitalis (foxglove)
Euonymus
Euphorbia (except poinsettia)
Gaultheria (checker berry)
Gloriosa superba (glory lily)
Hedera (ivy)
Helleborus (hellebore)
Hyoscyamus (henbane)
Hypericum perforatum
Ipomoea (morning glory)
Iris
Juniperus sabina (juniper)
Kalmia (calico bush)
Laburnum
Lantana
Ligustrum (privet)
Lobelia tupa
Lupinus (lupin)

water and plants to form a pond. Bear the eventual use in mind at the planning stage.

Keep sandpits and paddling pools covered when not in use to protect them from family pets and other animals. Sand used in pits should be silver sand, not builders' sand, as this stains clothes.

Paved paths of any material can provide circuits for trikes, bikes, roller skates and other forms of wheeled items. Gravel paths, although cheap and easy to install, are best avoided in gardens where children under ten play. Not only can gravel cause nasty injuries and get embedded in cuts, but few young children can resist throwing it around.

Older children will enjoy having secret corners in which they can create their own dens and hidey-holes away from adult eyes. So, if your garden has the scope for being divided into distinct areas, either by screens such as trelliswork, or by plants, incorporate this into your design. These secret corners can double as quiet, shady places for you to sit in, too.

There is a huge range of specially manufactured garden play equipment, such as climbing frames, swings and slides. Greater flexibility is offered by the movable, modular types, and repositioning them every now and then in different parts of the garden will give your lawn time to recover.

However, it is not always necessary to buy special play equipment. In a small garden consider using features such as arches and pergolas as dual-purpose items. Old, sturdy trees can be used for climbing practice. Providing the structure is sound, an old shed can take on a new lease of life as a play house.

You may want to use safe surfaces in children's play areas. These can include wooden decking, impact-absorbent paving and bark. Remember that bark will appeal to pets as a potential toilet area, so cordon off area.

Lawns provide a safe, soft surface for general play and ball games. For budding sports-persons, they should not be obstructed by washing lines or trees. Lawns can have miraculous powers of recovery – choose a hard-wearing, all-purpose seed mixture if you are

GARDEN SAFETY FOR CHILDREN

● Keep spiny plants away from paths.

● Avoid staking with canes. If you must, be sure they are capped.

● Try to prevent pets – yours and neighbours' – using the garden as a toilet.

● Remove rusty nails.

● Ensure that statues and containers are secure. Make sure they are firmly cemented in position. Never perch them on top of walls.

● Do not leave pools of standing water uncovered where children under five play. Consider safe water features for the sound of water (see pages 173-5).

● Avoid the most poisonous plants (see boxes opposite), but keep your precautions in perspective: teach children not to eat any plant in the garden without asking first.

● Avoid skin-irritating plants (see page 205).

● Do not leave sharp tools or electrical machinery unattended – even for a moment.

● Store garden chemicals well above reach, ideally in a locked cabinet. Never keep such chemicals in anything other than their original containers: it is illegal to do so. Do not keep solutions in sprays – pour away the excess.

re-seeding and keep mower blades set to cut at 3 to 4cm. Fleshy herbaceous planting is not so tolerant. Choose hardy shrubs that will withstand missiles and trampling. Thorny shrubs should be kept away from play areas as they puncture young skin and footballs. Bear in mind that nobody will get much relaxation if a lawn used for family play is positioned close to a greenhouse or your herbaceous border full of prize plants.

Children can be encouraged to help voluntarily with garden tasks (worms and composting are attractive from an early age). Encourage experiments in the garden by leaving children a patch of earth to dig. Scaled-down versions of gardening tools can be put to good use by children in a garden of their own making. In a very small garden a container will suffice for this purpose. Choose plants that are fun to grow, for example, colourful annuals, fast-growing vegetables and sunflowers. Children may also be interested in collecting very small plants such as alpines – these are particularly suitable as they survive periods of drought and neglect.

POISONOUS PLANTS

Narcissus (daffodil and narcissus)
Nerium oleander (oleander)
Ornithogalum (star of Bethlehem)
Pernettya
Phytolacca (poke weed)
Polygonatum (Solomon's seal)
Prunus laurocerasus (cherry laurel)
Rhamnus (buckthorn)
Rhus radicans (poison ivy)
Rhus succedana
Rhus verniciflua
Ricinus communis (castor oil plant)
Scilla
Solanum dulcamara (woody nightshade)
Taxus (yew)
Thuja
Veratrum (false helleborine)
Wisteria

Above: choose gaily coloured and fun-shaped plants for children to nurture, such as bulbs, cornflowers, French beans, nigella, sunflowers, thymes and tomatoes.

Left: don't let your children talk you into growing pumpkins as they can take up far too much space!

ALLOWING FOR PETS

You may need to accommodate your own pets in the garden or wish to deter visits from neighbours' cats and choose plants and materials with that in mind.

Dogs can cause damage to your garden – most commonly lawns can acquire brown dead patches caused by female dog urine. Borders can be reduced to piles of earth by dogs determined to dig. Try training your dog not to do this. There are harmless chemical deterrents on the market, but surrounding plants with a mesh supported by canes may prove to be a better solution. Dogs have strong territorial behaviour and will patrol the perimeters of a garden, charging straight at the boundary if there are any 'intruders' such as a cat or an unfamiliar noise. Remember to consider your neighbours: a dog may scare people in the next garden if there is only chicken wire as a fence, and a dog that barks a lot is annoying to all. Most dogs are generally only a problem as puppies and can be trained to respect the garden.

Both cat and dog faeces carry a health risk and should be disposed of without direct handling. Either bury them deep, wrap in newspaper and place in a dustbin, or incinerate. Choose mulches with care: bark chippings and fine gravel may attract pets as a toilet area. Cocoa shells are reported not to attract cats and stone chippings are usually left alone. For cats, provide a 'toilet area' of fine soil, sand or ash in a hidden corner and train the animal to use it – ideally from kitten stage.

Cats can cause considerable damage to the stems and trunks of plants when they use them as scratching posts. They use patches of bare earth as toilet areas and like sunny spots to lie in. Thus, they can be a problem when seeds are sown in situ and young seedlings are freshly planted out. Protect seeds by surrounding them with twigs or netting stretched above the soil. This has to be removed before young plants get too big. There are chemical deterrents based on aluminium ammonium sulphate, which is repellent to cats but not humans, and there are some physical deterrents in the form of plastic spikes (trade name *Catscat*), which can be placed around plants that exert a strong appeal. Keeping seed beds moist may also deter cats, because they prefer dry soil. A traditional deterrent to neighbours' cats is to keep a dog, but then they are not garden-friendly either.

Catmint (*Nepeta*) is loved by domestic felines: they will use it as a rolling ground. Planting this in a designated area of the garden may distract them from trampling over your prize plants. However, it will also attract every cat in the neighbourhood.

Dogs, especially puppies, can wreak havoc in the garden by digging.

It is possible to house a dog permanently outside if you have the space and you introduce it to outdoor life when it is a puppy. A dog run should have a minimum width of 1.8m and be at least 1.75m high. The fencing should be made from a material that cannot be tunnelled under or clawed to bits. To conserve body heat, the kennel should be only slightly larger than the dog it will house, and it should be sited away from prevailing winds. The area must receive sun and also some shade, and have good drainage and ventilation. Choose a surface that is easy to clean. An added benefit is close proximity to an outdoor tap and hose.

et rabbits will eat your plants and dig burrows everywhere if you do not provide a secure hutch and an adequate run. They are also highly prone to attack by dogs, foxes and cats, so it is a good idea to enclose their area completely.

Guinea pigs are grazing animals, so build them an enclosure that can be moved around the lawn as they munch through it. Avoid using lawn chemicals. Other domestic pets have specific requirements which may necessitate making adjustments to features in your garden.

In terms of garden safety, you will need to take into account both pets and children if you plan to use chemical treatments on weeds or pests in your garden. All chemicals should be kept out of reach of both animals and children and applied only when they are safely indoors. Check manufacturers' advice about any period of toxicity after application. Avoid using poisonous plants if you have pets in your garden, as it has been known for animals to ingest plants such as monkshood (*Aconitum*) with dire results.

Some cats love lying in the sun. If you do not want your tubs or plants squashed you could consider planting catmint elsewhere.

Cats will rub their scent over various objects in order to claim the garden as their own.

ASSESSING YOUR GARDEN

Look at your garden as it is now. Identify what you should keep and perhaps highlight, and what you want to get rid of, or disguise, in your new scheme. Find out about any legal restrictions within which you will have to work. Now is a good time, too, to find out what creatures are using your garden and what kind of soil you have.

EXISTING FEATURES

The traditional advice for people who have moved to a house with an established garden is to wait a year before doing anything major to it. This allows you to see exactly what there is through the seasons and stops you unwittingly disposing of bulbs and herbaceous plants at times of the year when there is little showing above the ground.

If you intend to wait a year, then take photographs of the changing views in your garden and its plants throughout the months. A series of shots taken from the same spot through a sweep of 180 degrees each time gives you the advantage over professional designers who see a garden only in one season. Make notes to keep for the time when you draw up or lay out your plan. If you have lived with your garden for some time and are unhappy with it but not certain what the problems are, a second opinion from a horticulturally minded friend may be worthwhile.

MATURE PLANTS

For most people, a policy of wholesale clearance will deprive their gardens of the character given by mature planting. A single old fruit tree can add instant character to an otherwise new design. Buying in mature specimens can be done, but at great cost. So unless trees are diseased, unsafe, or planted uncomfortably close to the house, it is usually worth keeping them. You may have to keep one, in any case, if there is a tree preservation order (see pages 46-7). Trees and plants may have suffered years of neglect or inappropriate pruning prior to your arrival. Pruning can reinvigorate even the most unpromising subject, and many trees can be given a new lease of life as a support for climbing plants. Deciduous trees and shrubs can drop their leaves in winter to reveal an interesting form and lovely views beyond. Mature plants can be used as focal points or key plants in the new layout. On the other hand, you may conclude that old trees

This garden has been neglected for a few months, but the wall is sound. You could dig over the whole corner after moving any interesting perennials to a temporary location.

WHICH PLANT TO KEEP?

Retain to preserve mature appearance

● Old trees such as apple with gnarled branches – don't have to bear fruit: they could provide a beam for a swing, somewhere for children to climb, or support for newer climbing plants such as roses.

● Planting that is performing a function well, such as screening an ugly view or framing a good view outside the garden.

● Structural or backbone planting – both evergreen and deciduous types – either around perimeter, or within garden as a form of division.

● Particularly good specimens of old established trees – if they are of an appropriate size – and shrubs, especially those that are rare or unusual.

● Good weed-free clumps of perennials.

Plants with better modern equivalents

● Michaelmas daisies are notoriously prone to mildew – *Aster* x *frikartii* 'Mönch' is a good modern mildew-resistant variety.

● *Lavandula angustifolia* 'Hidcote' is less leggy (more compact) than the old English variety.

● Substitute David Austin English roses for old-fashioned shrubs and damask types that are prone to mildew and disease.

---

shrubs and flowers are using all the available space in your small garden and taking too many nutrients and water from the soil.

Leyland cypress hedging is a notorious culprit once left to grow without the restraint of pruning at the right time. The result is towering dark walls that take light, water and nutrients away from your small garden that it can ill afford to lose. It is difficult to cut back and get a Leyland cypress to regrow successfully from old wood, so a neglected hedge like this may have to be one of the first things to go.

To judge the condition of any plant you need to establish its identity. If it does not produce flowers, fruit or foliage, try remedial treatment. Clumps of herbaceous perennials can take on a new lease of life after being lifted and divided. If they still do not perform, getting rid of them is the only solution, particularly if they inhabit key areas. However, many old varieties of shrubs and perennials have been superseded by newer introductions. These may be more appropriate for your garden in terms of compactness of growth, flower and fruiting quality, and

resistance to pests and diseases. Some plants are naturally short-lived: for example, *Lavatera*, *Buddleia davidii*, lavender, brooms and some roses. Others are more responsive to a good pruning: for example, *Philadelphus*, *Deutzia*, cotoneaster and *Viburnum*.

CONDITION OF PATHS AND PATIOS

Loose or broken slabs are an obvious hazard. If the paved area is in generally good condition apart from one or two slabs, new ones can be 'patched' in. If the damage is in a prominent part of the area, it is a good idea to repair the bad patch with original slabs from a less prominent part of the area, so that the new slabs will be less obvious in their place. The same applies to brick paving.

Broken paving is both ugly and dangerous.

Concrete can crack and generally look rather grim in time. Expanses of plain concrete are never appealing, but replacement entails digging up the old surface. One option is to patch it up and then use the surface as a base for tiles or other unitary paving. When you assess the condition of hard materials, take into account location. A certain amount of wear and tear may be acceptable in a secondary seating area or a side path, provided the surface is even.

It is a common fault of garden paths to be in the wrong places or too narrow, causing flower beds to be trampled on and bare patches to be worn in lawns. Patios, too, are often undersized, leaving a shortage of space for sitting and eating at a table, or to manoeuvre around a corner with a full wheelbarrow. Take the opportunity to extend paved areas of this kind.

CONDITION OF TIMBER AND METAL STRUCTURES

You will probably want to retain, either in-situ or in a different part of the garden, any existing fences, rose arches, trellis work, pergolas or gazebos, as these add height and often struc-tural interest to a garden (see page 38). However, look for rot in timber, especially if it is not known to have been pressure-treated. This includes the wood above and below ground level. Posts should not move, even when firmly pushed. A fresh application of preservative is always wise with any wooden structure prior to re-use, though it won't cure or prevent rot. Metal items should be checked for signs of corrosion. Much depends on the function these features are to perform – the weight of planting they must support, or related structures with which they may form a weak link.

EYESORES

In small gardens, boundaries can be only too obvious. Seeing beyond them is difficult, and what can be seen may be the blank wall of a neighbour's garage or something even more utilitarian. You may have inherited sound but ugly fencing which your budget will not allow you to replace. Screening bad views beyond your boundary as well as the boundary itself can be best achieved by planting groups of conifers or evergreens near to the house. Screens along the rear boundary need to be very tall to block out unsightly buildings and other eyesores. Creating a focal point within the garden will focus attention inside rather than letting the eye be drawn to what lies beyond. Focal points can be created with plants (see page 184) and ornamental features such as containers (see pages 206-13).

Areas of the garden that are less obvious from the house can be earmarked as possible sites for utility areas and other potential eyesores, but you need to take into account ease of access, frequency of use, and suitable aspect. If you are

retaining mature trees or shrubs where little grows behind them, this may be a good place for your utility items (see also 'Garden Buildings', pages 156-9). A shed can dominate a small garden, particularly if it is dilapidated. One next to a building will be less obtrusive, or you can paint it to match the house, garage, or nearest paintwork. You can also plant a boring shed with a quick-covering climber such as *Clematis montana*. Alternatively, abandon any form of disguise and instead enhance the garden shed so that it looks like a much grander structure, in keeping with the style of your garden.

Greenhouses are available now that combine practicality with good looks. Wooden frames look softer and can be decorated with finials. You can disguise the outline of a metal greenhouse with planting, and an arch placed in front of it can take the eye away from the structure. The colour of the frame makes a difference – white stands out more than green or black. Inside, use bamboo or wooden slatted blinds, or dark mesh, to screen from the sun. You can also make your greenhouse sit more happily in the plot by surrounding it with paving slabs matching those used elsewhere in the garden.

The damage to the wall of this border has been caused by people taking a short cut from the back door to the lawn. Plant tall plants to deter visitors and yourself from doing this or, better still, provide a path at this point.

The presence of laundry can detract from an otherwise pleasant garden. Rotary washing lines can be folded away when not in use. Setting its socket in paving near the back door helps to prevent a bare patch in grass in summer and mud in winter. Putting the rotary line behind a screening trellis is another option. It can also be part of a secondary seating area, a circular area of gravel edged with bricks with the socket in the centre. If you prefer a traditional line, retractable ones can be attached to a wall or fence. Wrap the posts of a permanent line in netting and train flowering climbers up them or attach hanging basket brackets from the top facing outwards. The posts can also be draped with wire to create ivy swags or spirals for an instant topiary feature.

Is your compost heap an eyesore? In small gardens it is worth buying one of the reasonably attractive wooden bins which can be placed next to a path and screened with evergreen plants. (For more about decorative compost bins see page 216.) Barbecues are generally sited prominently on the patio next to the house and can look unattractive. Consider building around one if this is the case, taking the opportunity to create storage space for barbecue accessories,

toys and games beneath the surface. Use the raised area to house small planted containers when the barbecue is not in use.

LOOKING FOR POTENTIAL

Many people find it much easier to list all the things they dislike about their gardens than to look for good points that might be highlighted.

Perhaps you feel you have an overall problem of garden shape or size. For instance, terraced houses often have long but narrow gardens, and many gardens are just a few metres square. Within our design ideas chapter (pages 48-113) are creative solutions for gardens in a wide range of dimensions, some also with problems such as being sloping or noisy.

Often, neighbours' gardens seem so much better. A small garden can, in fact, be extended in scope by 'borrowing' views or features from the surroundings, such as plants in neighbouring gardens or interesting roof lines and building details. The way your garden is laid out at the moment may actually produce this effect, so take care not to obscure views by careless siting of features. Such views can be framed effectively by planting trees and shrubs

Building a hut like this for a dustbin is a good idea, but why not screen it further by planting a shrub a few feet in front?

The tree in this garden might be worth keeping, but consider screening or moving the greenhouse, re-arranging the border (see pages 184-5) and brightening up the path (pages 142-51).

on either side, which usually makes a small garden appear larger.

As for good viewpoints in your own garden, perhaps there is a cacophony of colour in summer, but little going on at other times. To create a garden that is delightful year-round, it is often better to re-think the whole layout rather than patch the existing garden with the odd feature here and there. Your garden's overall size and shape, and any existing large features you want to keep should be the starting point for a new design. Look again at gardens you admire, and you will almost certainly find that they follow a basic pattern of simple shapes. Such shapes are formed by 'masses' (plants and structures) and 'voids' (the spaces between them, usually lawns and paved areas). Ask yourself if in your garden the voids over-dominate the masses, or vice versa. For example, a large lawn surrounded by narrow borders of low-growing plants will probably look out of proportion. To redress the balance, you could replant the borders with shrubs or small trees, or make the borders wider.

Look at the direction of any existing path, which often has a large impact on the eye as well as the route you take through the plot. If you often ignore the path and have worn away patches of lawn, the path is clearly in the wrong position. This does not mean to say you should

create a straight path from A to B instead, which may be far too severe. A gently curving path will create a relaxed feel. However, make it curve around an obstacle – a screen, flowerbed or feature, say – both to give a sense of purpose and to discourage the taking of short cuts.

Are you able to take in the whole of your garden from one viewpoint? Most plots are rectangular, and a common layout is of a rectangular lawn surrounded by beds rigidly following the boundaries. The vista of such a garden may be pleasing to your eye, but consider how much more interest could be added if you partition the garden into different areas, creating a sense of mystery as to what might be round the corner. You can do this by shaping masses and voids into bays and spurs. A sweeping curve or L-shape can be good solutions for a small garden. The main principle is to keep the shape simple.

Think about how your garden changes through the seasons. Perhaps when your favourite deciduous tree loses its leaves, the whole look of your garden is altered, seeming bare. The solution is to plant a backbone of plants that help give your garden its shape all year, complemented by other plants arranged so that different areas of the garden have colour in different seasons. For ideas on how to do this, see the 'Planting' chapter, pages 176-205.

Vertical elements are always important, helping to create masses, providing shelter and shade, and dividing the garden into sections. Existing boundary walls, fences or hedges, arches and pergolas, trees and tall shrubs will be providing much-needed vertical interest, so think twice before discarding, even if the feature is not quite right. You may find a better solution is to transform such items in-situ or move to better locations.

We spend a lot of time looking at our gardens from inside the house. Think about the angles from which you view the garden the most: these may be quite different from those of the people who laid out the existing features. Give these sightlines priority when you are assessing the situation. You may well find you want to reposition some mature plants so that they feature more in your view from the window, or find a new site for a pergola or arch that effectively frames a view of the rest of your garden from your favourite chair.

SOIL AND CLIMATE

LAYERS OF SOIL

The soil in your garden will affect what you can grow, depending on factors such as its level of acid. You should be able to identify three distinct layers, namely topsoil, subsoil and bedrock. Within the crumbly topsoil, which might be about 45cm deep, there should be much organic matter and earthworm activity. This is the growing medium. The subsoil may be paler in colour, several metres deep, and have fewer roots and earthworms penetrating. Subsoil is not an ideal growing medium. Below this, you will hit the bedrock, which will be very stony. If for any reason you do not have topsoil (perhaps it has been removed in recent excavation), you will need to add some before planting.

SOIL pH

pH (potential Hydrogen) figures from tests show levels of acidity or alkalinity.

Alkaline soils are referred to as 'sweet', acid as 'sour'.

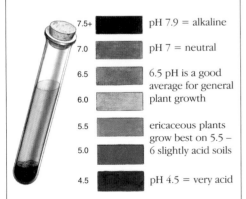

7.5+	pH 7.9 = alkaline
7.0	pH 7 = neutral
6.5	6.5 pH is a good average for general plant growth
6.0	
5.5	ericaceous plants grow best on 5.5 – 6 slightly acid soils
5.0	
4.5	pH 4.5 = very acid

● To increase the pH figure (increasing alkalinity), add lime.

● To decrease the pH figure (increasing acidity), add sphagnum peat or flowers of sulphur.

● Ericaceous, acid-loving plants include heathers, rhododendrons, azaleas and arbutus.

IS YOUR SOIL ACID OR ALKALINE?

Garden soil provides four means of sustaining plant growth: physical support; a supply of oxygen to roots; elements essential for plant growth; and a method of water storage. Acidity, structure and soil texture all determine what plants will thrive. The levels of acidity and alkalinity are expressed as pH figures and can be tested with a variety of inexpensive kits available from garden shops and plant centres. It is possible to maintain different levels of acidity in different parts of the garden, but this is a real chore. If you live on alkaline soil and want to grow ericaceous plants it is better to grow them in tubs, containers or raised beds. Growing vegetables successfully may require the addition of lime to the kitchen garden plot.

WHAT TYPE OF SOIL IS IT?

There are four main types of soil, which retain water to varying degrees, so affecting drainage in your garden. Peat retains most water, followed by clay, silt, then sand. To find out what sort of soil you have got, take a small sample and moisten. First, rub between your fingers. Does it feel gritty, sticky, or smooth and silky? Roll into a ball, then roll out into a thin cylinder. Try to bend it into a ring. Finally, rub it with a finger. Does it take a polish?

The major soil types based on texture are as follows:

Sand – gritty, can not be formed into ball. Will not take a polish.

Sandy loam – gritty, can be rolled into ball but not cylinder. Will not take a polish.

Silt loam – smooth, silky, can be formed into cylinder but makes only weak ring. Takes a slight polish.

Sandy clay loam – gritty and sticky, forms cylinder but not ring. Takes a polish.

Clay loam – sticky, forms cylinder but not ring. Takes a polish.

Clay – sticky, easily bent into ring. Takes a polish.

Peaty – dark brown or black containing a lot of decayed vegetable matter. Does not form cylinder or take a polish.

THE WATER TABLE

This is the natural level of water found in the ground. It will change with the seasons and may also vary through the garden with changes in ground level. To check, dig trial holes to a depth of 45cm in different parts of the garden, fill with water and note any changes in the length of time it takes to drain away. In free-draining soil the water should drain away before your eyes.

High water table Too much water will damage the root systems of plants – they literally drown – usually found with heavy clay soils.

Solution: Create soakaways to take water away from buildings; improve drainage of planted areas by adding organic matter and grit to open up texture of soil; adapt planting to suit. Trees take up a vast amount of water – hence felling of mature specimens may cause drainage problems. Plant moisture-loving plants.

Low water table Can cause plant starvation through lack of root access to water and soluble nutrients, usually found with sandy light soils.

Solution: Add bulk to soil texture to help moisture retention; adapt planting to suit. Grow drought-loving plants – alpines require well-drained soil, as do plants of Mediterranean origin.

THE WEATHER

The temperate climate of Britain makes it possible to grow a huge diversity of plants. In general, the west and higher areas receive more rainfall than the east. The Gulf Stream and warm wet winds produce winters that tend to be milder in the west but drier in the east. Town gardens will have higher temperatures than area averages because of the protection and heat generated by groups of buildings.

Most of Britian is moderately exposed to wind, but the areas where it will make gardening more difficult are on coasts and hills. It is worth taking steps to limit the effect of wind where rainfall is low, or where the growing season is long and warm, because you will see benefits very quickly. In high rainfall areas, heavy soils will be too wet to cultivate for much of the year, and waterlogging can be a problem. On light soil, heavy rain quickly washes out fertilisers and nutrients. In low rainfall areas, summer drought can be a serious problem, especially on light soils.

MICROCLIMATES

Microclimates are created by combinations of aspect, sun, exposure to winds and shelter provided by plants or barriers such as walls and fences. Your small garden presents a unique set of conditions across different areas allowing a variety of planting. The existence of microclimates helps to explain why some plants may thrive in a neighbour's garden but not your own. One garden may be enjoying the shelter of a slight hollow, sunny and protected from wind. The other may be shaded, with much cooler, damper conditions.

Use the shelter created by south-facing walls and fences to grow tender climbers, wall shrubs and trained fruit trees such as apricots. Mediterranean plants will not survive the conditions in the heavy soil at the bottom of a northerly slope but might thrive in well-drained soil near the base of a south-facing wall. Walls can create areas of drought at the foot of them because they shelter the area from rainfall. This is particularly true of west-facing walls receiving warm, wet, westerly winds.

Note the direction of prevailing winds when you assess your garden. Solid vertical barriers can create wind tunnels and eddying problems. Aim to filter winds by presenting them with permeable barriers and vary the type of planting with the situation. Deciduous trees can provide shade in summer yet allow winter sun to warm an area. The desiccation brought about by prevailing winds will affect plants as well as the siting of a seating area. The wind chill factor should be borne in mind. Cold air creates microclimates when it is trapped by walls and fences as it flows downhill.

Note any frost pockets in your garden: it is more usual for plants to be killed by freezing moisture in their systems than by dry, cold conditions. Also remember that heat is reflected by some materials better than others. Light-coloured paving and walls are good reflectors, but may be uncomfortably bright and cause leaf scorch and bleaching of flowers. Sunny slopes will warm quickly in spring to produce early flowers and crops. A raised bed in the right position can produce the same results. Plant shade-loving plants beneath mature trees and large shrubs (see pages 98-9). Bog gardens can be included where the ground is naturally always moist (see pages 170-2).

Rainfall

On heavy soils, the main problem will be waterlogging. On light soils, heavy rain will leach nutrients out of the soil.

On heavier soils, you may have some of the problems of the pale blue areas.

On light soils in dry summers, drought may be a problem.

Take steps to keep as much moisture in the soil as possible.

Drought is likely to be a problem in all but very wet summers.

Wind Exposure

Very exposed.

Exposed.

Quite exposed.

Sheltered.

1. *A solid, vertical fence or wall will affect the passage of a strong, prevailing wind by creating eddies in the formation shown. Roughly speaking, an area of calmer air as wide as the fence or wall is high will be created just in front of the barrier. However, the wind eddies will make it uncomfortable to sit out.*

2. *By contrast, a slatted fence diffuses (baffles) the passage of wind, rather than sending it into eddies. The wind is gentler over a wider area.*

3. *Light-coloured paving and walls reflect light and heat, which will act in your favour in an area of the garden that is otherwise too cool or dark. However, in an already warm part of the garden they may create an unbearable hotspot, with plants becoming parched and bleached in colour.*

4. *Dark-coloured paving and walls absorb heat during the day and release it at night. Consider using dark-coloured materials for your patio if you like to entertain outside in the evening.*

5. *Cold air sinks down slopes and can become trapped by retaining walls, creating potential frost pockets. Avoid siting your patio in a permanent cold spot.*

6. *A deciduous tree or planting on a pergola near your house will provide an area of cool shade during the hot summer months, while in winter, with the leaves gone, sun will be able to filter through and warm the area.*

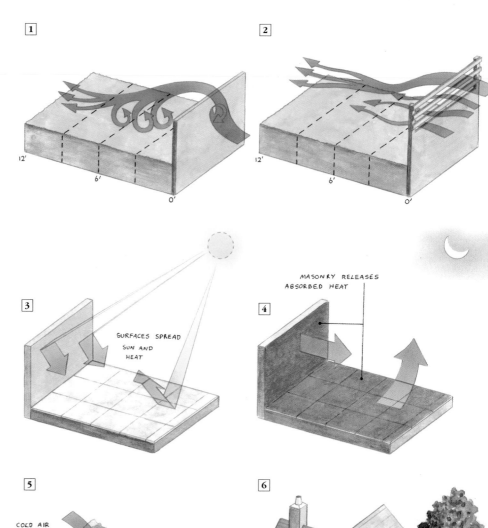

SURFACES SPREAD SUN AND HEAT

MASONRY RELEASES ABSORBED HEAT

COLD AIR

RETAINING WALL

PLANTINGS SHADE PATIO

WILDLIFE

Your garden will have residents and visitors of the wild variety. Even if you are not interested in designing a garden primarily to attract wildlife (see pages 110-13), it is useful to know how the creatures can be beneficial or destructive.

The most important garden animal is the earthworm. Be pleased if you find lots of these when you assess your garden, as they make a crucial contribution to soil fertility and assist in the processes of aeration and drainage. Centipedes are good too, as they feed off pests. Ants feed on insects, but their nests can be a problem and they may guard aphids against other predators in order to farm their sticky excreta. Holes in leaves and slime trails are signs of slugs and snails, who are definite foes. Aphids ruin leaves. Some moth caterpillars may eat roots and stems. Chemicals to control these common pests are widely available.

Butterflies and moths are some of the most colourful garden visitors and usually welcome. The garden pests among them are the cabbage whites who have developed a dietary preference for all cultivated forms of the cabbage plant family. They can be controlled by

destroying the larvae in autumn, or you could try growing your vegetables among flowers. Ladybirds should be encouraged by any gardener as they feed off aphids. Unfortunately, most chemical forms of aphid control also kill ladybirds.

Wasps and spiders suffer from an 'image' problem but are in fact useful as predators. Wasps dislike disturbance of their nests and professional help should be sought if you find one in a spot close to a well-used area of your garden or in a shed or other outbuilding. Although they become a particular nuisance in the fruiting season, they are less likely to sting if ignored, and will die when the first cold weather starts.

The environment of a pond contains its own set of creatures. Frogs and newts eat slugs in numbers and other pests. Some fish, such as sticklebacks, will eat small forms of aquatic wildlife; minnows will eat mosquito larvae.

The majority of birds are welcome visitors for their varied song and control of some pests – snails and aphids. However, you will have to use

Caterpillar damage to runner bean.

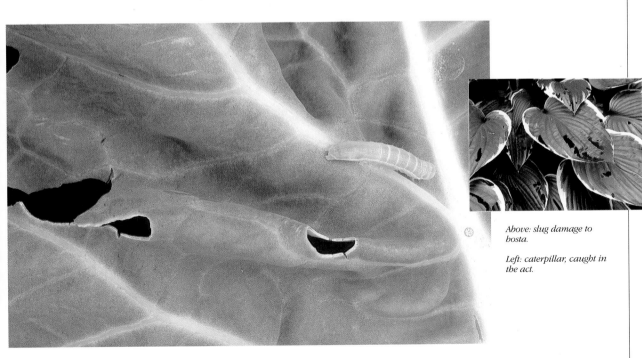

Above: slug damage to hosta.

Left: caterpillar, caught in the act.

Ladybirds are always welcome in the garden. This one is eating aphids.

Below: the white substance on this plant is actually a mass of woolly aphids.

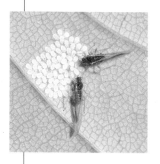

Above: aphids will have a whale of a time in a neglected garden.

fruit cages if you are growing fruit crops for human consumption. Site any feeders away from areas of vegetable-growing, as an increase in droppings is inevitable. Starlings and pigeons can be aggressive and frighten off other birds, while magpies can rob other nests at breeding time. Herons often take fish from ponds and you may have to resort to noise-making wire and other devices to discourage unwanted birds.

In rural areas (mostly), moles are predators of earthworms. Moles can also cause subsidence problems by tunnelling close to the surface of the ground. This, to say nothing of the devastation they can wreak on a lawn, makes moles potentially unwelcome visitors, although the tilled earth from molehills can be useful. *Euphorbia lathyris*, the caper spurge, might deter them and other mechanical devices are

also available, but the success rate is very low. You may have to hire a pest controller, who might put down strychnine-poisoned worms. Make sure pets are out of the way if you resort to this method.

Badgers, protected by law, are nocturnal visitors most likely to be found in country gardens. They have great strength and can destroy fences that lie along their paths. Whether you want to attract them or not, you may find the only way to stop your fence being regularly damaged is to include a special gate in it at the appropriate point.

Although not destroyers of plants, foxes can wear paths through a garden and create a mess when searching out easy sources of food. In recent years, they have become more frequent visitors to urban gardens, lured by the contents

Left: This vixen has just raided five dustbins.

of dustbins. They can kill domestic pets, such as rabbits, and poultry anywhere. Take precautions by building housing for bins, and protect any susceptible animals with proper caging.

Wild rabbits and deer are prolific grazers, which can destroy swathes of garden planting. This includes consumption of young herbaceous and vegetable growth by rabbits to bark stripping of mature trees by deer, both with equally dire results. Rabbits do leave nettles alone, an essential food source for other forms of wildlife such as butterfly larvae. There are rabbit- and deer-resistant garden plants, but you may find you need to create physical barriers. Make all fencing rabbit-proof if necessary by burying smaller-gauge fencing below the surface of the earth to a depth of 60cm. The buried mesh should be curled up at the bottom, on the rabbit side of the fence, to confuse the

animal, making it think it cannot dig any deeper. Trip wires above the fence line can deter deer.

Squirrels are amusing to watch but can be as destructive of property as any rodent, and they steal bird food from tables and feeders. Food for birds is best placed in squirrel-proof containers made from non-wood materials. Mice, voles, shrews and rats are all common garden visitors. Although the first three are rarely a problem, rats should be discouraged at all costs. If you find rats in the garden, seek professional advice about their extermination. Do not put any cooked food scraps on open compost heaps and keep other animal feeds and grains in gnaw-proof containers.

Hedgehogs are the perfect garden visitors. They feed off many garden foes including slugs, snails and numerous kitchen garden pests.

Above: moles will be anything but welcome if they do this to your lawn.

LEGAL CONSIDERATIONS

Laws relating to planning permission can be complex and not always clearcut, as they are constantly being reinterpreted. If your house is a listed building, or situated in a Conservation Area, a National Park or an Area of Outstanding Natural Beauty (AONB), then certain garden works are subject to legal constraints. Trees protected by preservation orders (TPOs), and some in conservation areas, are covered, as are boundaries. If you plan to incorporate more land into your garden currently used for other purposes it will pay to seek advice. 'Building works' in a small garden are unlikely to require planning permission. But if you live in one of those special areas above, or if the work includes building a shed, greenhouse, summer-house or other outbuilding that is near the boundary or takes up a prescribed amount of space, you may need consent. If in any doubt about whether any work involved in implementing your design requires permission, check with your local council before you start work.

BOUNDARIES

Changes to vehicular access into your property will usually require planning permission. Local authority highways departments have specific regulations governing installation and changes to drop kerbs. Ownership of boundaries is sometimes unclear. If in doubt, consult the land registry, or check title deeds if unregistered. If a leasehold property check the leasehold. A small 'T' by a boundary on any plan of the property indicates ownership. Owners may be under no obligation to repair unless this is covered by a clause in the relevant documents. But they would be liable for damage arising from the collapse of fences or walls.

Boundary walls, fences and gates under 2m in height do not require planning permission. This reduces to 1m for boundaries adjacent to a public highway. Existing structures higher than these limits can be altered without planning provided the original height is not exceeded. Restrictive covenants governing boundary treatments in some housing developments should be in the title deeds. Freestanding walls and fences in the garden are not covered by these permitted development rights, so check if

heights exceed the figures above. In Conservation Areas and AONBs, boundary materials and methods of construction may be subject to constraints. These may extend to the height and materials used for features inside the garden in some cases.

TREES

Planting of trees (or anything else) is not subject to planning permission, but may be of interest to a local authority if your garden is part of a Conservation Area. Pruning and felling of all trees subject to TPOs and trees covered by Conservation Area restrictions will require permission. If there are protected trees in your garden you can get a copy of the schedule relating to them from your local council. The owner retains responsibility for protected trees, their condition and damage they may cause. A TPO may cover individual trees, groups or areas of woodland and the schedule will make this clear. A 'tree' is generally defined as a plant with a single woody stem. Any pruning beyond light trimming with secateurs is an offence. Dead, dying or dangerous trees can be felled without consent and a replacement specimen planted. However, it is difficult to prove circumstances after the event, so get permission before doing anything that can be construed as major work to a tree protected by either method. Failure to do so can result in the imposition of heavy fines.

DRAINAGE

The disposal of surface water and foul sewage is subject to planning permission. In garden terms, you are not liable for natural rainwater flooding from your garden into your neighbour's, provided garden features have not been designed to do this deliberately. It makes sense not to create drainage problems for anyone when constructing garden features as they cause destruction and problems that can be expensive to rectify.

Excavation work in gardens is not subject to predefined limits but to a test of whether resulting construction is 'incidental to the enjoyment of the dwelling'. Extensive excavation and re-levelling involving heavy machinery may require permission, so check before you start. These works must be

accessible, have adequate capacity and have a level suitable for gravity flow. So excavation and paving of any type that affects public or private drains should have permission.

OTHER POINTS

You have no right of way across a neighbour's land without his or her permission, even to repair a boundary wall that you own. If the neighbour refuses, an order granting entry under the Access to Neighbouring Land Act 1992 must be applied for. Damage to your neighbour's land has to be made good, and this may mean extra insurance for you. No laws govern the tidiness of gardens nor do you have a right to a 'view'. However awful something may look in an adjoining garden, there is nothing that can be done unless it poses a nuisance or health hazard. In these cases local

Above and left: storm damage to boundaries (walls, fences and even hedges) can result in disputes over who takes responsibility for repairs.

councils have powers under the Town and Country Planning Act to order it to be cleaned up. The Weeds Act of 1959 lists certain weeds that have to be controlled, including spear thistle, broad-leaved dock and ragwort, but orders have rarely been served.

DESIGN IDEAS

Good garden design is about creating a harmonious scheme. Look at the area surrounding your garden and consider what texture, colour or shape might be repeated within it. Simplicity and unity should always apply to the overall layout, proportions and theme of a garden. In this chapter is a host of ideas for different styles and situations, all with an emphasis on harmony and practicality.

BALCONY GARDENS

Gardens that are a storey or more above ground level always have different climatic conditions. The temperature is often about five degrees centigrade higher than that at ground level. However, balconies that are sited along the gable ends of buildings close to neighbouring ones may suffer from excessive shading. Often, wind funnelling is a problem; the wind-speed factor on average is doubled at balcony level, causing much greater water loss from plants. Wind damage can sometimes go unseen for several seasons. In winter, the wind-chill factor comes into play, decreasing temperatures.

Hanging baskets and containers filled with colourful plants can turn even a tiny urban balcony into a little Eden.

Balconies really are an extension of the room from which they are accessed, so planning is very important. The position of windows, access doors and views visible from inside must all be plotted on a plan. With limited ground or floor space you will still need to plan path 'routes' that should be kept clear – to window box planting at the edge, or to a vantage point to enjoy the view.

Plan mobile or in-situ containers to suit your scheme. Choose appropriate plants, usually very hardy types. Use lightweight compost and add slow-release fertiliser in pelleted form. Make sure it is easy to water the plants, which will dry out much quicker than those on the ground. Even balconies can include largish plants as permanent backbones, but choose small forms of shrubs. Silver/grey leaved varieties can withstand wind and water shortages well, but harmonise plant colour with interior décor. Make seasonal changes by slotting in pots of bulbs and annuals into gaps in permanent planting. Insulate containers in very cold weather to avoid frost damage to plant roots.

THE NARROW BALCONY

The narrow balcony in this plan houses a collection of plants in small, movable containers and is a place for sitting out. A sense of unity is maintained in this small area by having containers of one kind of material. Extra shelter

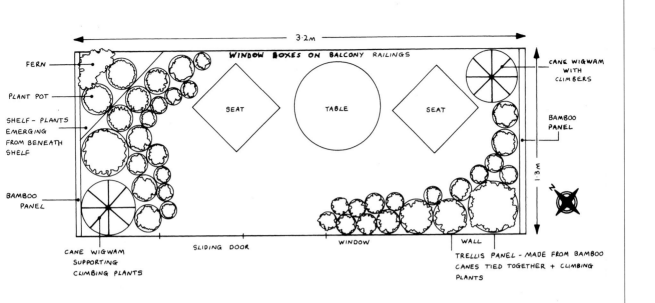

3.2m

FERN

PLANT POT

SHELF - PLANTS EMERGING FROM BENEATH SHELF

BAMBOO PANEL

WINDOW BOXES ON BALCONY RAILINGS

SEAT

TABLE

SEAT

CANE WIGWAM WITH CLIMBERS

BAMBOO PANEL

1.3m

N

CANE WIGWAM SUPPORTING CLIMBING PLANTS

SLIDING DOOR

WINDOW

WALL

TRELLIS PANEL - MADE FROM BAMBOO CANES TIED TOGETHER + CLIMBING PLANTS

Above: layout for a narrow balcony.

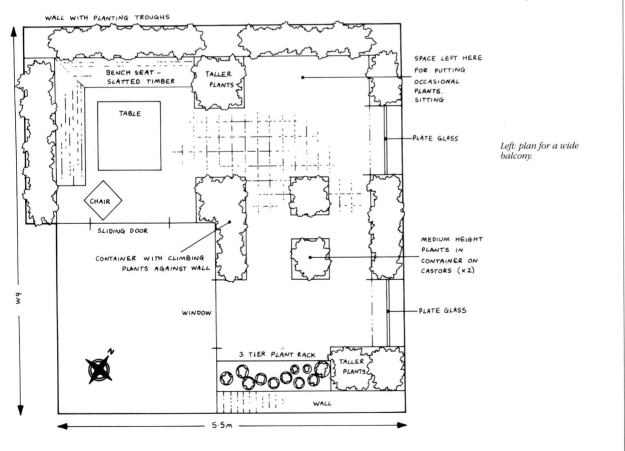

WALL WITH PLANTING TROUGHS

BENCH SEAT - SLATTED TIMBER

TALLER PLANTS

TABLE

CHAIR

SLIDING DOOR

CONTAINER WITH CLIMBING PLANTS AGAINST WALL

WINDOW

3 TIER PLANT RACK

TALLER PLANTS

WALL

SPACE LEFT HERE FOR PUTTING OCCASIONAL PLANTS. SITTING

PLATE GLASS

MEDIUM HEIGHT PLANTS IN CONTAINER ON CASTORS (x2)

PLATE GLASS

N

6m

5.5m

Left: plan for a wide balcony.

Right: if you regard your balcony as an extension of the room from which it leads you are more likely to use it as such.

Far right: a variety of containers at different levels can add a sense of depth and colour to your balcony.

and privacy is provided at the ends by bamboo panels – excellent wind filters. Window boxes are secured at both the top and bottom of the balcony railings to give maximum growing space, and the building walls are used to support climbing plants and hanging baskets.

Gardening on this scale need not restrict the variety of plants grown – varieties of delicious small tomatoes and beans have been chosen for this balcony and are attractive in their own right. Containers are kept out of the seating space – important in tiny areas – and the table and chairs are lightweight and collapsible for easy transfer indoors. The view of the street below and surrounding townscape can be enjoyed in comfort from the balcony.

THE WIDE BALCONY

A wide balcony really can be an outside room, as the plan on page 49 shows. The balcony is edged with a wall wide enough for built-in planting troughs and interspersed with toughened glass – a good way of providing shelter without losing a view or light. The line of sight from the window is kept clear so the vista can be enjoyed throughout the year. Seating is provided through a built-in L-shaped timber bench, which doubles as storage for gardening tools and outdoor articles – very useful where space is at a premium.

Right: the use of trellis, climbers and unusual ornamentation can transform a dull brick wall.

PLANTS FOR BALCONIES

*Climbers/trailers/
scramblers*
Clematis alpina
Clematis montana
Euonymus fortunei
Hedera (ivy – avoid very
vigorous types)
*Hydrangea anomela
petiolaris* (climbing
hydrangea)
Lonicera (honey suckle)
Parthenocissus (Virginia
creeper)
Tropaeolum majus
(nasturtium – annual)
Vinca minor (periwinkle)

*Architectural/
backbone*
bamboo (check
hardiness)
Berberis (Barberry)
*Chamaecyparis
lawsoniana* 'Columnaris'
(Lawson's cypress)
Fatsia japonica (fatsia)
Juniperus communis
(common juniper)
Juniperus 'Skyrocket'
(Rocky Mountain juniper)
Laurus nobilis (bay – clip
to shape)
Pinus aristata (bristle
cone pine)
Taxus baccata 'Standishii'
(yew-fastigiate form)

Other shrubs
Artemesium absinthium
(common wormwood)
'Lambrook Silver'
Caryopteris x
clandonensis 'Heavenly
Blue'
Cistus (rock rose)
Cytisus x *kewensis*
(broom-prostrate)
Genista (broom)
Rosmarinus (rosemary)
Salvia officinalis (sage)

IMPORTANT CONSIDERATIONS FOR BALCONIES

● Planning or legal constraints often apply.

● Establish the weight the balcony can take before installing features.

● Check drainage, particularly if you want large containers.

● On a small balcony choose lightweight flooring, furniture and containers.

● All fixings should be very secure.

● Choose plants that withstand wind.

● Harmonise style and colour of balcony with décor of adjoining rooms.

All of the rectangular containers are constructed from treated timber and stained to match the interior décor to provide a visual link between interior and garden. The two larger containers provide dividers, and, for extra intimacy, the smaller containers on wheels can be positioned to complete the 'wall'. The planting in the larger containers includes structural shrubs to give a permanent backbone to the scheme. A collection of plants in smaller containers is held on a tiered rack, giving maximum display area and height. This is placed against the end wall to allow plenty of clear floor space. The planting troughs at the edges contain a mixture of evergreen small shrubs and conifers with seasonal planting.

COTTAGE GARDENS

Cottage-style gardens remain popular despite the fact that few of us actually live in cottages or rural surroundings. Romantic images of thatched cottages with honeysuckle and roses climbing around doorways and gates, coupled with abundant, seemingly haphazard planting, strike a chord with many people.

TRADITIONAL COTTAGE STYLE

Numerous Victorian pictures depict cottage gardens, but the style can be traced further back. There were signs of it in Elizabethan times, but it really came to fruition in the eighteenth century. Underneath the luxuriant foliage the gardens were always functional plots: the main purpose was to provide food. Vegetables were grown in straight rows, with a strong emphasis on root vegetables to be turned into soups or cooked with meat, particularly bacon. Peas, beans and salad crops were grown in the summer.

Crops of apples, pears, plums, redcurrants, strawberries, gooseberries and other fruit were used for making wines and preserves. A large variety of herbs were grown for both culinary and medicinal usage, such as for herbal teas. Pigs were often kept in the gardens, being fed on corn, meal and surplus vegetables. Chickens usually had to find food for themselves. Bees and bee hives were also a common sight, with the honey being used as a sweetener. The presence of bees affected the planting: fragrant blue flowers are particularly attractive to the bee. Other planting was herbaceous, using both annuals and perennials.

The original cottage gardens were shaped not through notions of style or design but through necessity. They were enclosed behind low walls, hedges or fencing. A framework of straight paths defined the beds, which were shaped geometrically to make best use of the space. Close planting resulted in the profusion of plants spilling over the pathways and bursting through the boundaries. A path at the front of the cottage led straight from the front door to the road, and at the back there was a path straight down to the earth privy at the end of the garden. Any other paths would also be straight, following the shortest line from one point to another.

MODERN DESIGNS

As a style to be reinterpreted, the cottage garden lends itself perfectly as a low-budget solution for a small garden, but it does require more maintenance than other styles. If you are not totally committed, try transforming just part of your garden into a separate cottage-style 'room'. A front garden is appropriate, as many cottage gardens were to the front of the house.

The key to success in establishing this kind of garden is to start with a very formal geometric layout, with rectangular or diagonal paths linking all parts of the garden. For boundaries, use hedging (e.g. holly, hawthorn, hornbeam), picket fencing or willow hurdles. Paths were originally formed from compressed earth, mud, ash and stones found in the ground, but nowadays one of the cheapest materials to use is gravel. First put down a 75-100mm layer of hoggin (a gravel mixture containing an assortment of stone pieces to form a solid base), and tamp this down firmly into the ground before adding the surface layer of gravel or pea shingle. Edging to your paths is not essential if you want to keep costs down, but it will stop the gravel straying into the borders. A treated timber edging (e.g. gravel boards sold for fencing) held in place with wooden pegs will keep gravel in place, and this will quickly be obscured by the spread of planting at the edge of borders.

You may desire a paved area for sitting out and eating larger than was a feature in the past – if so, incorporate this with a little care so that it blends in with the rest of your cottage garden. To economise, lay cheap concrete paving slabs, leaving a thin gap between each to sow with grass to soften the effect. Alternatively, slabs can be laid with spaces left for low-growing plants such as thyme, chamomile and pennyroyal. Another possibility is to use riven slabs, which are now available in many different colours – including convincing York lookalikes – laid in a random pattern and interspersed with bricks.

Traditional cottage gardens did not have lawns, since this would have taken up valuable growing space for useful plants (and there were no mechanical lawnmowers available to the

Entrance to the Cottage Garden at Capel Manor, designed by Gardening Which?

Opposite: a timber bee hive is an appropriate accessory even for the modern cottage garden.

COTTAGE PLANTS

Low-growing perennials

Alyssum saxatile
(gold dust)
Arabis (white rock cress)
Aubrieta deltoidea
(rock cress)
Campanula carpatica
(bellflower)
Chamaemelum
(chamomile)
Erigeron karvinskianus
(fleabane)
Iberis sempervirens
(perennial candytuft)
Rosmarinus repens
(rosemary)
Saxifraga (saxifrage)
Sedum (stonecrop)
Thymus vulgaris (thyme)
Viola cornuta
(sweet violet)
Viola tricolor (heartsease)

Taller perennials

Alchemilla mollis (lady's
mantle)
Althaea rosea (hollyhock)
Aquilegia vulgaris
(columbine)
Astrantia major
(masterwort)
Dahlia
Delphinium
Dianthus barbatus
(sweet william)
Dianthus spectabilis
(bleeding heart)
Digitalis purpurea
(foxglove)
Erysimum (perennial
wallflower)
Geranium
Lavandula angustifolia
'Hidcote' (lavender)
Nepeta (catmint)
Helianthus annuus
(sunflower)
Limnanthes douglasii
(poached egg flower)
Reseda odorata
(mignonette)

Climbers

Hedera helix
(common ivy)
Jasminum officinale
(jasmine)
Lathyrus latifolius
(perennial sweet pea)
Lonicera periclymenum
(honeysuckle/woodbine)
Tropaeolum majus
(nasturtium)
Vitis coignetiae (Japanese
crimson glory vine)

small garden owner then!). If you have both a front and back garden, it could well be feasible to do away with the grass totally at the front, where it is less likely to be used, anyway. If you are keen to have some lawn, make sure that it is a useful size for recreational purposes. Any well-used pathway that already crosses an existing lawn can be defined by laying slabs as stepping stones. This kind of linking of different areas of the garden is in keeping with the functional aspect of cottage gardening.

A profusion of flowers in every direction is typical of the cottage style.

Vegetables can appropriately be grown in a separate kitchen garden, screened from the main area by rustic trellis or trained fruit trees. A kitchen garden can be given a formal layout in the style of a 'potager'. This is a plot divided into small beds (generally 1.2m wide for easy access from both sides) and paths; each area contains vegetables planted in a decorative way. The beds can be edged with dwarf box (though this harbours slugs), herbs such as chives or parsley, or step-over trained apples.

Greenhouses, coldframes, sheds and dustbins can look out of place in a cottage garden, so consider grouping such utilities in a separate area, screened off with hedges, hurdles or tall plants. If you need to dry clothes in a crowded cottage garden, string a traditional washing line between two trees or two posts planted with flowering climbers that are not too vigorous. The line need not always stay in place, and a slab path leading to it can be laid in a mixture of compost and gravel, into which you can plant low-growing plants. With a rotary clothes line, choose a position either close to the house or with other utility features and set the bottom socket flush with the surrounding surface.

PLANTING

When it came to planting, the original cottage gardeners did not agonise over colour co-ordination. Plants were acquired through propagation, gifts from fellow gardeners, and from material available from newer plants acquired by the wealthy landowners. The cottage gardeners had a plentiful supply of old varieties and can be thanked for the conservation of many of these. They were careful to plant sun-lovers in south-facing borders, shade-seekers in north-facing places. Planting closely to pack in as much as possible and allowing plants to self-seed in happy confusion were normal practices.

In order to mimic the cottage style, it is important that you do everything possible to improve your soil before planting, to enable it to hold plenty of nutrients and to safeguard it from drying out. Dig in at least a 5cm layer of organic matter (e.g. spent mushroom compost, farmyard manure), and for clay soils, include a 5cm layer of sharp grit too. Start by planting one or two trees or large shrubs in key positions – perhaps to frame a view, act as a centrepiece or hide an eyesore. Keep any old apple trees, particularly gnarled specimens, and hollies, yews, lilacs and shrub roses, as they provide an

ACCESSORIES FOR THE COTTAGE GARDEN

● Containers: half barrels, simple styles of terracotta and chimney pots. Utilise old china casseroles, old watering cans etc.

● Old-fashioned trugs – flat, wooden fruitbaskets – either for pure ornamentation or for use in collecting flowers and vegetables.

● Terracotta rhubarb forcers – stylish with or without the rhubarb.

● Willow hurdles for instant barriers, rose arches and plant supports.

● Sculptures and scarecrows woven from willow.

● Rustic-style timber for rose arches and furniture, and picket-style or rustic palisade timber for fencing.

● Timber bee hives – they don't *have* to house bees.

instant sense of maturity and cottage character to your re-shaped garden. In traditional cottage gardens shrub planting was minimal, however it is worth planting up to a third of a modern cottage garden with shrubs to reduce maintenance. Also include a proportion of evergreens and winter-flowering plants to provide year-round interest. Then, as now, plant 'treasures' or slightly tender exotics can be kept close to your house, perhaps in a collection of containers to be taken in for overwintering.

Climbing plants were traditionally grown against the walls of the cottage, and yew and fruit trees such as quince were trained into archways over

the entrance and pathways. These ideas are well worth including in the contemporary cottage garden. Willow and hazel twigs were used to create supporting structures for fruit, vegetables and plants. Nowadays, woven rustic style supports, hurdles and rose arches can be bought for an instant cottage look. Climbing plants such as clematises and roses were planted to curl and scramble through a supporting tree or hedge; this has been widely adopted into modern gardening practice. If you have an old unproductive fruit tree, consider using it as a ready-made support for climbing plants, rather than chopping it down.

Borders were sometimes given an edge of low-growing plants such as pinks or pansies, as well as the ever popular box. There is a wide choice of modern varieties of cottage garden plants that are disease resistant and compact, making them more suitable to small plots. When planting herbaceous plants, avoid the regimentation of traditional herbaceous borders. Aim to put tall plants in the middle of groups of smaller ones, and plant the odd clump of tall plants next to paths.

The ancient craft of topiary was practised by some of the original cottage gardeners, probably those gardeners who worked in the grounds of the large country houses. Where space is limited, container-grown topiary specimens can be moved around your garden for instant effects. They thrive all year round, and are particularly invaluable in winter when they can provide much needed structural interest. Ready-made topiary is expensive; it may be more fun for you to try pruning shapes yourself. Box, yew, bay and holly are the traditional plants for training, but you could also consider privet, Leyland cypress and *Lonicera nitida*. Ivy can be trained over metal frames or wire mesh to create the same effect as topiary.

Shrubs
Buddleia davidii (butterfly bush)
Coronilla glauca
Cytisus x praecox (Warminster broom)
Daphne mezereum (mezereon)
Deutzia
Fuchsia 'Mrs Popple' (hardy fuchsia)
Hebe
Jasminum nudiflorum (winter jasmine)
Kolkwitzia amabilis (beauty bush)
Laurus nobilis (bay)
Lonicera x purpusii (winter honeysuckle)
Mahonia
Myrtus communis (myrtle)
Philadelphus coronarius (mock orange/syringa)
Ribes sanguineum (flowering currant)
Rosa eglanteria (sweet briar/eglantine)
Syringa vulgaris (common lilac)
Viburnum carlesii (Koreanspice viburnum)
Viburnum opulus (Guelder rose)
Viburnum tinus (laurustinus)

Hedging, topiary and trees
Buxus sempervirens (box)
B. s. 'Suffruticosa' (dwarf/edging box)
Carpinus betulus (common/European hornbeam)
Crataegus monogyna (hawthorn)
Cydonia oblonga (quince)
Ilex aquifolium (holly)
Laburnum x watererii 'Vossii' (golden chain tree)
Ligustrum ovalifolium (privet)
Lonicera nitida (boxleaf honeysuckle)
Malus 'Golden Hornet' (crab apple/fruiting crab)
Malus 'Rev. W. Wilks' (apple)
Malus sylvestris (native crab apple)
Prunus (cherry)
Pyrus calleryana 'Chanticleer' (ornamental pear)
Taxus baccata (yew)

THE GARDENING WHICH? COTTAGE GARDEN

This cottage garden, at Capel Manor to the north of London, has been built as a contemporary example based on traditional cottage gardening 'design' principles. The layout has been kept very simple to provide a geometric framework for luxuriant planting. A central path divides the plot in two, and the garden is further subdivided by a square turned through 45 degrees providing smaller paths through generous borders. Each end of the central path is framed by an arch. The arches are simple, coated metal frames that do not detract from the style of planting. Here, roses have been trained over the arches.

The picket-style gates and fencing give a traditional cottage feel. If you are creating a

the other end of a path. The paths are also wide enough to allow plants to sprawl and tumble over their edges yet remain practical as routes around the garden to features. A compost bin has been given an appropriate disguise in the form of a bee hive.

The plan and photographs of the cottage garden at Capel Manor clearly illustrate how very geometric, formal-looking borders on paper are transformed by intensive cottage-style planting. Purists may want to stick to old varieties of flowers, but the lists here include modern ones which are more compact and disease-resistant, making them suitable alternatives for modern cottage gardeners.

A tapestry effect has been achieved in the Capel Manor cottage garden by an informal mix of plant heights and types – some tall plants have been placed at the front of borders, and herbs, fruit, vegetables and flowers grow in happy confusion side by side. Care has been taken on positioning larger plants so that they do not swamp smaller ones or cast shade over sun-loving neighbours. Companion planting of, for example, marigolds among vegetable crops and roses helps to keep pests at bay.

The Capel Manor cottage garden when newly planted.

cottage garden in just a corner of your garden, trellis panelling would be a good boundary treatment, and low hedges of box or lavender can be sufficient to delineate a small plot. As with the cottage gardens of old, this one has no grass. Paths have been paved with bricks, the central one with a 45 degree herringbone bond turning into a running bond on the side paths. Both of these bonds give a sense of movement encouraging the visitor to discover what lies at

Planting list

1 Clematis Viticella
2 Macleaya 'Kelway's Coral'
3 Echinops 'Taplow Blue'
4 Anemone japonica
5 Trachelospermum asiaticum
6 Paeonia 'Festiva Maxima'
7 Rosa Iceberg
8 Sedum 'Autumn Joy'
9 Gypsophila 'Flamingo'
10 Rosa Iceberg
11 Sidalcea 'Elsie Heugh'
12 Rosa mundi
13 Geranium 'Johnson's Blue'
14 Polygonum atrosanguinea
15 Lavandula 'Hidcote'
16 Helleborus foetidus
17 Hemerocallis 'Stella de Oro'
18 Viburnum x bodnantense 'Dawn'
19 Rosa Iceberg
20 Rudbeckia 'Summer Sun'
21 Dianthus 'Doris'
22 Buxus sempervirens
23 Nigella White
24 Geranium 'Johnson's Blue'
25 Agapanthus 'Lilliput'

26 Chrysanthemum 'Bronze Beauty'
27 Geranium sanguineum
28 Alchemilla mollis
29 Papaver 'Harvest Moon'
30 Rosa 'Madame Alfred Carrière'
31 Rosa 'Emily Gray'
32 Rosa 'Sanders' White Rambler'
33 Rosa 'The New Dawn'
34 Rosa 'Buff Beauty'
35 Paeonia mlokosewitschii
36 Tiarella 'Hewitt's Double'
37 Hosta fortunei aureomarginata
38 Geranium sanguineum
39 Geranium albanum
40 Geranium sylvaticum albiflorum
41 Aster 'Brilliant'
42 Achillea The Pearl
43 Campanula glomerata 'Superba'

44 Scabiosa caucasica 'Clive Greaves'
45 Rosa Pearl Drift
46 Paeonia 'Festiva Maxima'
47 Thalictrum 'Hewitt's Double'
48 Papaver 'Helen Elisabeth'
49 Geranium sanguineum
50 Rosa 'Buff Beauty'
51 Heuchera Bressingham hybrids
52 Geranium renardii
53 Digitalis purpurea
54 Rosa 'Buff Beauty'
55 Crambe cordifolia
56 Agapanthus 'Golden Rule'
57 Agapanthus Headbourne hybrids
58 Rosa Pearl Drift
59 Polygonum atrosanguinea
60 Iris sibirica
61 Rosa Pearl Drift

Rudbeckia *above picket-style fencing.*

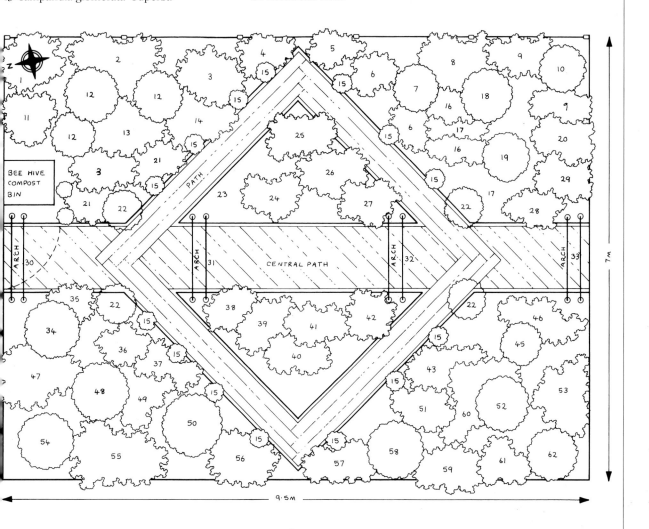

EXPOSED GARDENS

Strong prevailing winds can be a major problem for exposed gardens. At the same time, these gardens often enjoy good views that should really be framed as part of the design. Often, the best and easiest way to do this is to plant appropriate trees on either side of the view. The installation of hedging and fencing with spaces left here and there for the wind to be filtered is one such solution to the exposure problem. The creation of sunken areas within the garden is another method of providing shelter for both seating and planting. Using wind-resistant shrubs and perennials is, of course, essential. Coastal gardens, though windswept and with the additional problem of salt, provide a wonderful environment for growing plants that are difficult to care for inland.

As far as trees go, *Crataegus* and pine are appropriate for windswept coastal and inland areas. Choose *Crataegus monogyna* and *Pinus nigra* or *Pinus sylvestris* for cold, hilly, inland areas. By contrast, *Pinus nigra maritima* thrives by the sea.

Fucshia 'Riccartonii' is a hedge commonly found in coastal areas in Ireland and the south-west of England, and *Griselinia littoralis* will also flourish by the coast in the warmer parts of the British Isles. *Mertensia maritima* is a native plant, ideal for sandy soil. Lyme grass, a natural inhabitant of sand dunes, may invade your garden if you live by the sea.

The seaside garden shown in our plan uses an informal hedgerow along most of the windward boundary, giving way to a picket-type fence and gate. Choice of materials used in the garden reflects the seaside location. Simple pots have been made by forming ship's rope into a coil.

ADVANTAGES OF COASTAL GARDENS

- Mild winters – usually fewer and less intense frosts.
- Warmer climate on the western coasts of the British Isles owing to the Gulf Stream.
- Increased density of UV light causes wood of shrubby planting to ripen at a faster rate.
- Access to unlimited quantities of seaweed – good as a mulch or as a compost heap additive.

Fishing nets, shells and pieces of driftwood can all be collected and incorporated into the seaside garden as decorative features.

The seating area takes the form of a timber deck. Just below an upper stone terrace, it takes advantage of the slope of the site to provide extra shelter. The view of the sea is the focal point to be enjoyed from the 'deck', effectively framed by salt-tolerant shrubs and naturally wind-twisted pines on either side of the path leading up to the deck. Timber decking will dry quickly in sea breezes and it provides built-in seating. Shade from the sun is provided by

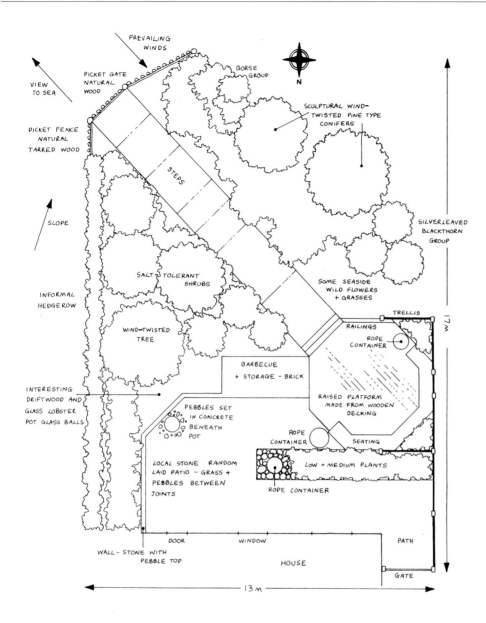

Diagram labels:

PREVAILING WINDS

VIEW TO SEA

PICKET GATE NATURAL WOOD

GORSE GROUP

N

SCULPTURAL WIND-TWISTED PINE TYPE CONIFERS

PICKET FENCE NATURAL TARRED WOOD

STEPS

SILVERLEAVED BLACKTHORN GROUP

SLOPE

SALT-TOLERANT SHRUBS

SOME SEASIDE WILD FLOWERS + GRASSES

INFORMAL HEDGEROW

TRELLIS

RAILINGS

ROPE CONTAINER

WIND-TWISTED TREE

BARBECUE + STORAGE – BRICK

RAISED PLATFORM MADE FROM WOODEN DECKING

17 M

INTERESTING DRIFTWOOD AND GLASS LOBSTER POT GLASS BALLS

PEBBLES SET IN CONCRETE BENEATH POT

ROPE CONTAINER

SEATING

LOCAL STONE RANDOM LAID PATIO – GRASS + PEBBLES BETWEEN JOINTS

ROPE CONTAINER

LOW + MEDIUM PLANTS

DOOR

WINDOW

PATH

WALL – STONE WITH PEBBLE TOP

HOUSE

GATE

13 M

PLANTS FOR COLD HILLSIDES

Trees
Acer pseudoplatanus (sycamore)
Betula pendula (silver birch)
Chamaecyparis lawsoniana (Lawson's cypress)
Crataegus monogyna (hawthorn)
Laburnum
Pinus nigra (Austrian or black pine)
Pinus sylvestris (Scots pine)
Sorbus – most
Taxus baccata (yew)

Shrubs
bamboo
Berberis – most (barberry)
Cornus alba (dogwood)
Corylus maxima (hazel, filbert)
Cotinus coggygria (smoke bush)
Cotoneaster – most (especially *C. horizontalis*)
Kerria japonica
Mahonia aquifolium
Potentilla fruticosa
Spartium junceum (Spanish broom)
Spiraea japonica
Ulex europaeus (gorse)
Viburnum – most

Perennials
Acaena (New Zealand bur)
Achillea (self-supporting in wind) (yarrow)
Anemone x *hybrida* (Japanese anemone)
Bergenia cordifolia (elephant's ears)
Coreopsis verticillata (tick seed)
Echinops ritro (globe thistles)
geraniums – most
Phlox – most
Persicaria affinis (knotweed)

timber arbours that support climbing plants. Another alternative would be canvas, unfurled along wires as a horizontal 'sail' to suit the season. The stone of the upper area is local, random laid with grass or low plants in the joints, reflecting the informal style dictated by the location of the garden. Large pebbles have been used loose at ground level with smaller ones set into mortar on top of the retaining wall. Vertical interest is provided by taller trees and shrubs, tolerant of and shaped by the salt-laden prevailing winds. This garden might belong to a holiday home where low maintenance is essential.

Selection of plants shown for seaside garden

Armeria (sea pink)
Atriplex halimus (tree purslane)
Cistus (rock rose)
Crambe maritima (sea kale)
Elaeagnus (Oleaster)
Eryngium maritimum (sea holly)
Euonymus
Geranium
Hebe
Juniper
Lathyrus japonicus (sea pea)
Lavandula (lavender)

Leymus arenarius (lyme grass, European dune grass)
Mertensia maritima (oyster plant)
Papaver somniferum (opium poppy)
Pelargonium peltatum (ivy-leaved geranium)
Phlomis fruticosa
Pinus negra maritima (Corsican pine)
Rosmarinus officinalis (rosemary)
Ulex europaeus (gorse)

FAMILY GARDENS

Tulips, hyacinths and tough shrubs in the family garden.

Brightly coloured trellis divides the lawn and vegetable garden.

Most family gardens are created on a limited budget. The layout of a successful family garden balances the needs and requirements of different members of the family, most of whom may look upon the garden primarily as a practical space for playing games, hanging the washing and so on. Often the best, and simplest, design solution is to create a large paved area, a lawn big enough for gentle ball games, and a utility area. There is enough room in most small gardens for these three basic areas. Optional extras, space permitting, might be a kitchen garden or other screened-off area mainly for adults, or a separate area for children's play, and trees for climbing.

The functional nature of the family garden is no barrier to good looks. Features such as pergolas and arbours may well be of greater aesthetic interest to adults than children, but all structures should be sturdily built to cope with being climbed by daring youngsters as well as being knocked about by balls. Plants should be easy-care, unless at least one member of the family is particularly keen and has time to spare, and does not expect the others to share the same enthusiasm. In general, it is best to have a

ryegrass mixture for the lawn, and robust flowers and shrubs which will recover quickly if trampled. For advice specifically about children and pets using gardens, including safety matters, see pages 29-33.

THE FAMILY GARDEN

The *Gardening Which?* family garden at Capel Manor shows how in a small garden features can be arranged for the benefit of various family members without losing out on style. A large patio within sight of the house is an important area for a family with young children. This patio enjoys the afternoon sun, while the pergola and summerhouse offer areas of shady seating. The paving consists of inexpensive standard concrete slabs, which are at an angle of 45 degrees to the lawn. This is a good tip for making an area of paving lead into the garden, rather than finish in a static straight line. As the layout involved cutting slabs, a tidy finish was achieved by edging the paving with a brick-on-edge detail. The edging forms a semicircular shape to tie the patio to the house.

Any bricks used in the garden should preferably match those used for the house, or be of a

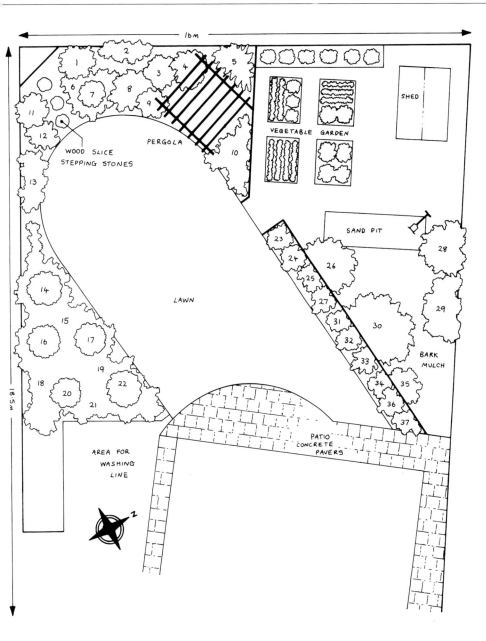

Above: home-produced vegetables help feed the family.

Planting list

1 Cornus alba
2 Solanum crispum
3 Berberis thunbergii
4 Phormium tenax
5 Bamboo
6 Potentilla 'Abbotswood'
7 Taxus baccata 'Fastigiata'
8 Lonicera 'Baggesen's Gold'
9 Prunus lusitanica
10 Rosa 'Golden Showers'
11 Elaeagnus pungens 'Maculata'
12 Hydrangea quercifolia
13 Viburnum opulus 'Sterile'
14 Mahonia x media 'Buckland'
15 Heliopsis
16 Choisya ternata
17 Euonymus alatus
18 Echinops ritro
19 Festuca glauca
20 Elaeagnus ebbingei 'Limelight'
21 Sisyrinchium striatum
22 Cotinus coggygria
23 Bronze fennel
24 Sedum 'Autumn Joy'
25 Lavandula
26 Buddleia davidii
27 Aster x frikartii
28 Bamboo
29 Buddleia davidii
30 Bamboo
31 Phlomis fruticosa
32 Santolina incana
33 Potentilla 'Daydawn'
34 Hebe pinguifolia 'Pagei'
35 Buddleia davidii
36 Rosa 'Compassion'
37 Clematis alpina

Right: a sandpit and logs for the children.

Main picture: patio and lawn view of the family garden.

contrasting colour as here. The same type of slabs has been used for the path to the utility area. Other paths in the family garden are formed from simple slices of tree trunk, providing an informal stepping-stone path through the wide border to the summerhouse and the gravel utility area.

The utility area takes up a sizeable corner, divided from the rest of the garden with timber trellis panels. These have been painted dark blue, usually a good colour to use in the garden, and both the summerhouse and the picnic-style table have been finished to match, giving a harmonious feel to the garden. The utility area houses functional features – a shed for garden equipment, five small beds for growing vegetables and also a play area for toddlers that includes a rectangular sandpit and a log pile set in a safe surface of bark mulch. Placing these last two features here means that when they are outgrown, their area could be changed to reflect new needs and interests – a self-built den might take their place, perhaps making way for a greenhouse in the future.

Below: a place to hang the laundry need not be boring.

The family garden's combination of functionality with good looks is again illustrated by the treatment given to the area for the washing line. This has been surfaced with textured concrete. Pavers have been used to divide the area into segments: the area is given more textural interest at the same time as making the concrete easier to lay. The size of the circle has

been matched to the diameter of the rotary clothes line.

The area of lawn in the family garden has been kept to as large a size as possible, but there is still plenty of border space. The borders have been planted for year-round colour and interest, using a selection of plants that are both resilient and easy to maintain.

TOUGH PLANTS FOR FAMILY GARDENS

Shrubs
Buddleia davidii
(butterfly bush attracts
butterflies)
Choisya ternata (e;
Mexican orange blossom)
Cotinus (smoke bush)
Deutzia
Escallonia (e; Jew's
mallow)
Kerria japonica
Osmanthus (e)
Photinia (e; willow)
Salix (small shrubby
forms)
Spiraea
Weigela
Viburnum (some e;
laurustinus)

e = evergreen

Herbaceous plants
Alchemilla
(lady's mantle)
Acanthus
(bear's breeches)
Anemone japonica
(Japanese anemone)
Crocosmia
(montbretia)
Epimedium
Geranium
Geum
Heuchera (alum root)
Nepeta (catmint)
Persicaria (knotweed)

and grasses including
Carex

The larger border to the left of the lawn includes a good mix of deciduous and evergreen shrubs that provide a backbone for the rest of the planting. The garden is beautiful all year round because of this planting. When the perennials come into bloom, the backbone planting acts as a backdrop. The size of the vegetable beds makes it possible to cultivate them using a low-maintenance raised bed system, edged with treated timber. Vegetables can be reached in these beds without trampling on the soil. An application of organic materials to the soil at the beginning of winter ensures help from worms with the work of 'digging' this in. This area might be developed as needs change to include decorative features, different planting and a quiet space to sit.

FORMAL GARDENS

Formal gardens are usually symmetrical about a central axis. A formal garden can be particularly appropriate if your house has a definite architectural style – Georgian, Queen Anne, Victorian etc. Many of the great gardens of country manors are formal, suiting the architecture of the house and linking it with the surrounding area. Modern housing, by contrast, tends to sit more happily with an asymmetrical, informal, design. For country or suburban gardens, it may be enough to incorporate a formal theme in one part of the garden. This might naturally be an area close to the house with other strong architectural features – paved patios, raised beds, steps and so on. If you have enough room, you can design your small garden to change character by 'unwinding' from a formal garden by the house into a softer, more informal style further away from the building.

HISTORY

The development of formal gardens in this country owes much to external influences. Elements of formal gardens like topiary and statuary can be traced back to the Romans. Features dating from the medieval period include elaborate trelliswork used to divide up the garden, and training plants against rails and over arbours for decorative and practical purposes. Knot gardens and mazes date from Tudor times. Over the next two centuries ideas were imported from the Netherlands, Italy and

A Victorian fountain forms the centrepiece of this formal garden.

Opposite: plan of a formal garden.

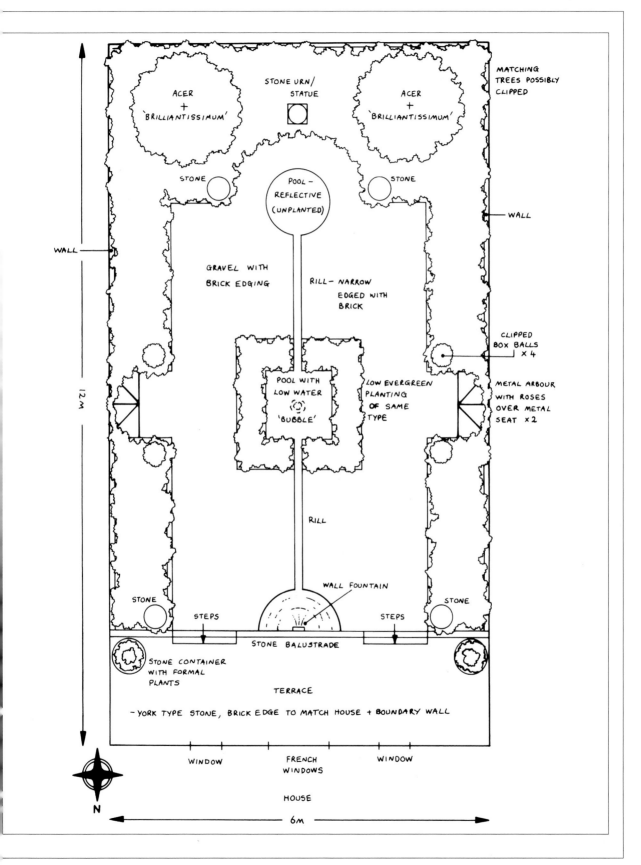

MATCHING
TREES POSSIBLY
CLIPPED

ACER
+
'BRILLIANTISSIMUM'

STONE URN/
STATUE

ACER
+
'BRILLIANTISSIMUM'

STONE

WALL

STONE

POOL –
REFLECTIVE
(UNPLANTED)

WALL

GRAVEL WITH
BRICK EDGING

RILL – NARROW
EDGED WITH
BRICK

12 M

CLIPPED
BOX BALLS
× 4

POOL WITH
LOW WATER
(☼)
'BUBBLE'

LOW EVERGREEN
PLANTING
OF SAME
TYPE

METAL ARBOUR
WITH ROSES
OVER METAL
SEAT × 2

RILL

WALL FOUNTAIN

STONE

STEPS

STEPS

STONE

STONE BALUSTRADE

STONE CONTAINER
WITH FORMAL
PLANTS

TERRACE

– YORK TYPE STONE, BRICK EDGE TO MATCH HOUSE + BOUNDARY WALL

WINDOW

FRENCH
WINDOWS

WINDOW

HOUSE

N

6 M

Below and right: matching pairs of clipped box on either side of a central path will give an instant formal effect.

INSTANT FORMAL EFFECTS

● Create an axis on which to place symmetrical features.

● Create focal points, either singly or as a series along the central axis of the garden – use classically shaped pots and urns (unplanted), sundials, armillary spheres.

● Place matching pots on either side of a door or opening, planted with topiary shapes cut from holly, box, yew or some of the faster-growing conifers.

● Make sure any lawn is close-clipped and weed-free.

● Alternatively, plant low-growing evergreen plants such as ivy, *Arenaria balearica*, *Leptinella squalida*, *Pachysandra terminalis*, thymes, chamomile – all perennials – instead of grass for green groundcover.

● Plant pairs of small trees or shrubs that can be clipped into formal shapes, e.g. pyramids, domes or spirals.

● Train wall shrubs such as *Pyracantha* to flank and form an arch over a door, or train other suitable trees (fruit) and shrubs.

● Trace patterns on the ground and plant with box for contemporary parterres – leave unplanted, or soften with planting without obscuring shape.

France, including straight axes, shaped beds and flowers from the Netherlands, parterres or elaborately patterned beds from France, and statues from France and Italy.

New homegrown thinking, whereby lines were regarded as unnatural and inappropriate in the garden, characterised the Landscape Movement, which started in the mid-eighteenth century. New gardens were developed, whole landscapes were changed in some cases and much of the formality of the gardens was swept away. Although formal gardens reappeared during the Victorian times, later approaches to garden design have led to the development of what is recognised as a typically English style, with formal lines softened by luxuriant planting, and in larger-scale schemes the natural lines of the landscape enhanced by informal planting.

FORMAL STYLES FOR SMALL GARDENS

Certain types of planting lend themselves to formal treatment, such as herb and rose gardens. Both can be laid out in a symmetrical arrangement of beds around a central feature such as a sundial or stone birdbath. These should be the right scale in relation to the space. In this way, a formal area can be included in a small garden, with the area or room enclosed by hedging, if space allows, or formal-style trelliswork.

The symmetrical nature of a formal garden results in a balanced layout. Geometrical shapes and proportions encourage an atmosphere of restful relaxation rather than fast movement through the space. The formal design shown in the plan on page 65 is divided into four roughly equal rectangles.

Boundary walls are a perfect element for a formal garden. Trellis or clipped hedging, preferably evergreen, are alternatives. The paved terrace in the plan runs the width of the house and is visually linked to it by a matching brick edging. York stone, or local stone to match house walls, is typically formal treatment. A cheaper reconstituted stone can duplicate this effect, with the slabs laid in a random pattern. The terrace is at a higher level than the rest of the garden, its edge defined by a stone balustrade of classic shape – again, reconstituted stone reproductions are low-budget alternatives but they have the disadvantage that they tend not to age.

From the terrace, the central axis of the garden is defined by a narrow rill that emanates from a water spout built into the terrace wall. This flows down to a central pool and then on to a plain reflecting pool at the far end. A classical urn provides a focal point or 'full stop', as it were, placed in the centre of the semi-circular apse, the two corners marked by stone balls.

Three steps lead down to the main part of the garden. Grass has been replaced by gravel edged with bricks to match the house and walls. Two metal arbours shelter matching seats in a shape that reflects the central axis. On either side of each arbour, clipped dwarf box balls define the edge of each niche. Four obelisks are placed in the side borders in pairs.

The essence of a formal garden is one of measurement and control. The lines of the garden are all-important and should be kept clear to give year-round structure. Planting in a formal garden can be stylised – such as with

Formal-style vegetable garden.

the matching pair of *Acer platanoïdes* 'Brilliantissimum' at the end of this garden, and borders edged with dwarf box. Or it can soften without obscuring. Choose plants for a formal garden from a restricted range of plants and palette of colours.

In the suggested plan for a formal garden, roses and fruit trees have been trained along the walls without obscuring the lines, and the obelisks provide structure and support to planting of roses and clematis, used to extend flowering interest. An edge of green around the central pool is provided by *Pachysandra terminalis*, a low-growing plant that provides an alternative to grass.

FRONT GARDENS

When it comes to drawing up a budget to cover garden works, a larger proportion is usually allocated to the back rather than the front of a house, the general rule being that back gardens are for private, recreational use, whereas front gardens are public spaces whose main function is to provide access to the house for pedestrians and, frequently, car-parking. It is worth considering breaking this rule if your front garden is larger than average or if it enjoys a more favourable aspect than the back of your house. Adopt the practices common in other European countries, especially those surrounding the Mediterranean. If your front garden enjoys long hours of afternoon and evening sun, take advantage of this by planning a pleasant place to sit. This can be as private or as open as you wish. Getting the work done quickly and keeping maintenance to a minimum are common priorities for the front garden.

WELCOMING AND FRAMING

Front gardens should be welcoming, user-friendly places for both you and your invited visitors. They should fit into the surrounding neighbourhood yet show some individuality. Ideally, front gardens should offer continuous interest. It is both practical and pleasant to add a 'landmark' or distinguishing feature to the site. This might take the form of a particular specimen tree, large shrub or man-made feature. A coloured front door should suit both your house and the surrounding plants of the front garden. These features will not only welcome you home but also act as a guide for visitors unfamiliar with how to find your home. 'It's the house with the crab apple in blossom'

Roses ('Zéphirine Droubin', 'Super Star', 'Peace'), oxalis and iberis offer a burst of colour to be enjoyed by the occupants of this modern house and passers-by alike.

can be a useful instruction. Framing the door removes any ambiguity if there is more than one door on that side of the house. It will benefit everyone if a weatherproof porch can be added to cover the step or landing. Train climbing plants or wall shrubs around a doorway for a natural framework.

The 'landing' offered to visitors arriving at a front door on foot should be spacious, and the route to the front door should be clear. Go with the flow of 'desire' lines in terms of establishing an efficient route for all users. Ignoring where it feels natural to walk towards the house will result in bare patches being worn in lawns and holes carved through areas of planting. This does not mean that strictly efficient straight lines are the rule. Paths can be diverted by strategic placement and shaping of planting areas, and changes in surface texture. They should be of the right dimensions and not form an obstacle course around intruding planting, containers and bins.

For many small-garden owners, the prospect of doing without a front lawn that has no recreational value will be very attractive. It can liberate you from having to haul the mower through the house and back again for the chore of mowing isolated areas of grass. However, avoid overlarge areas of paving, which can look stark and unwelcoming. Combinations of planting and hard landscaping, carefully worked out at the design stage, will help create an illusion of space. Use pebbles – laid loose or in mortar – and gravel to add textural contrast. If your front garden includes a driveway, larger areas of paving are inevitable. Use two or three different hard landscaping materials that combine well with each other in terms of unit size, colour and texture. Create central paving focal interest in the form of patterns, or indicate different functions by changes in the way paving is laid and detailed, useful for pedestrian paths and driveways.

LITTER, DOGS AND VANDALS

Your front garden may be subject to vandalism of plants and objects. Preventive action might include planting thorny subjects on exposed boundaries and securing any movable item firmly. Security lighting will help those who have a legitimate reason to enter the house while deterring those who have not.

Hedging, fencing and walling are all boundary choices that might be considered for front garden delineation and protection, but check first that your house is not subject to the restrictions of an open-plan development. Also remember the height restrictions for boundaries adjacent to public highways – one metre before planning law applies. Without physical barriers at the boundaries, dealing with litter and dog problems is less straightforward. A good skeleton of prickly plants such as mahonias, ordinary *Berberis* and roses will form a living litter trap to catch stray pieces of paper and similar materials. Making your garden look obviously loved may deter litter louts from throwing rubbish into it. Dog deterrence where boundary structures are not an option is not easy (see pages 32-3).

CARS

Cars, garages and driveways require a great deal of space. For a car to stand in front of a garage with side hinged doors a minimum space of 4.8m is needed: more is preferable. In a small garden it is unlikely that you will be able to construct a parking and turning area, also called a hammerhead. You need to allow 3m width for the passenger doors to be opened without stepping into planting. Turning a car through 90 degrees with two movements requires a hammerhead 6.4m deep.

The front of your house should be welcoming . . .

With a small garden, you may be reluctant even to attempt to match the space requirements in terms of the amounts of hard landscaping. To get in and out of a car comfortably you will need approximately 75cm of clearance. Most drives tend to be on the narrow side, so bear this in mind when it comes to boundary planting alongside. If you decide to resurface your drive, remember to check the position of underground services. To take the weight of a car, paving slabs must be laid on a base of hardcore at least 10cm in depth; 15cm is better. Clay or concrete pavers are bedded on sand above a hardcore foundation of the same depth. They should be edged with concrete or stone kerbs set on a foundation and haunch concrete of 15cm in depth.

It is possible to minimise the impact of a drive on a front garden by growing plants that will sprawl over the drive as they grow. Obviously, ground-level plants in this situation will have to be capable of surviving rough treatment.

Heathers and thymes are good choices, as are small types of ornamental grasses. *Festuca glauca, Milium effusum* 'Aureum', and *Carex hachijoensis* 'Evergold' (formerly known as *C. morrowi* 'Evergold') are other good choices. Larger grasses with sharp leaves such as pampas grass, *Miscanthus* and *Stipa gigantea* should not be planted where they will brush your car.

The central part of the drive between paved wheel tracks is a good place for planting. Choose alpines and low-growing plants such as *Pachysandra terminalis, Pratia pedunculata* (but this requires a certain level of moisture), all of which should survive happily.

Widening a drive without creating acres of hard landscaping is possible. This can be done in a variety of ways, from installing a simple mowing strip to give extra protection to the lawn edges, to using grass-grid paving slabs. The latter are hollow cells of concrete paving which can be filled with soil and sown with a tough but slow-growing grass seed mix. Once the grass is established, it can be driven over without causing undue damage and is suitable for mowing with both rotary and hover types. It is frequently seen as a surface treatment for emergency vehicle areas and in the car parks of large publicly owned properties where occasional parking on grass in heavy rainfall causes great damage. It is not a low-

Boulders, gravel and small paving blocks combine well in a confined area, and plants can be grown in containers.

A semi-formal chequerboard of plants and paving is a very simple design that would suit the front of many houses.

For a very informal look, mix paving slabs of different sizes and colours, leaving gaps for plants with contrasting shapes.

A symmetrical but open paving pattern gives good access to all plants.

budget option, but one worth considering where anything else will present too great an expanse of hard surface as a proportion of your front garden.

OPEN-PLAN FRONT GARDENS

Litter and dogs can be real problems on open-plan estates. Many of these have covenants governing the permitted height of hedges, walls and fencing in front gardens. It is sometimes possible to divide one garden from another but you may not be allowed to put up anything between your garden and the pavement. In some cases, landscape architects may have specified certain plantings as part of the master plan for the development. Such restrictions should be outlined at the time of purchase and enforcement will depend on the local authority. Inhibit short cuts across your front lawn by placing flower beds to indicate the correct path. If this doesn't work, put a boulder or physical object on the corner to stop this happening. A great advantage of an open-plan policy is that it can make your house appear more welcoming. It will be open to the road, and good visibility can be an added form of security. Your range of shrubs and flowers can be admired from the road, while interrupting the view from outside and so providing privacy.

A scree garden with scattered rocky outcrops helps define the bold outlines of specimen plants.

A few strategically placed paving stones will create an illusion of space among a backbone planting scheme of groundcover evergreens.

Edge a path with groundcover plants, which will soon spread around other groups.

TIPS

● Try to deal with your front garden over a short timescale.

● Check for restricting covenants concerning the treatment of boundaries – also consider listed building or Conservation Area restrictions.

● Assess the approach to your own house from all directions, both on foot and by car, as if it were the first time you had done these things.

● It is usually a good idea to create a low-maintenance scheme, dispensing with grass and choosing plants that will thrive without much attention on your part.

● A curving path to your front door may look more interesting than a straight one, but make sure people are not tempted into taking a short cut through areas of planting because the path feels 'wrong'.

This small front garden with its containers and fine lawn needs a lot of attention over spring and summer.

PLANTING

It is important to choose an appropriate tree and plant it in the right spot in a front garden. The size of tree at maturity should be small, 3.5m maximum so that it will not dwarf the house and site, or pose a threat to the foundations. It is usually a good idea in the average small front garden to plant any new trees close to the front (road) boundary. You will also need to bear in mind the position of both underground and overhead services at the time of planting tall plants. An extremely tall hedge on the front boundary is not necessary to provide privacy – one at eye level will work just as well. Choose slow-growing forms of hedging to cut down on maintenance.

If you plan to get rid of a front lawn, substitute other low-growing evergreen plants as an easy-care alternative with the appeal of a green 'surface'. Plant in a stylish monoculture block or create eye-catching ground patterns out of a variety of low-growing plants. For year-round interest, choose plants that produce long-lasting displays. Some good examples are *Cotoneaster dammeri* (prostrate habit; white flowers followed by red berries), *Ajuga reptans* (this takes a while to form covered spikes of blue flowers; different foliage colours available) and the blue-grey *Hebe pinguifolia* 'Pagei'.

A wide, colourful border is a cheery sight to accompany your short journey from road to front door. Avoid roses and bedding plants, though, if you do not have much time for maintenance, or be content with a slightly wild look, as here.

LONG, THIN GARDENS

Gardens that are very long in relation to their width are regarded as a problem because they are frequently little more than dull-looking corridors, with nothing to entice the visitor to their furthest reaches. The result is lost potential and an underused space.

In fact, the long, narrow garden is ideal material for dividing up into a series of compartments or rooms. You can control the proportions of these rooms and use dividing methods to turn these spatial constraints to your advantage. Creating a series of compartments can be a great opportunity to lay out each one in a different style. The result is a garden setting with a variety of moods to suit the particular function of each area. It becomes easier to combine the range of expectations of all garden users.

THE TERRACED HOUSE GARDEN
The *Gardening Which?* garden for a terraced house at Capel Manor illustrates perfectly the uses to which a long, thin garden can be put. Being slightly longer on one side, the plot has the added drawback of tapering to a very

Above: aerial view of lawn 'room'.

Right: view of terraced house garden before planting has had time to develop and features such as front trellis and arch have been added. When this is compared with the views on the following pages, it is easier to appreciate how well the design utilises the narrow space.

narrow pointed corner. These kinds of spaces in a garden can easily become completely dead areas.

Here, the garden has been divided up into three sections of roughly equal weight or proportion – a patio and lawn 'room', a woodland 'room' and a fruit garden 'room'.

The patio is a rectangular shape and paved with brick pavers laid in a variation of basketweave bond that gives a restful feel. It has been given an edge of low trellis to divide it from the lawn and enhance a feeling of enclosure, especially from a seated position. The lawn of the first section of this garden naturally extends the width of borders. Setting everything on the

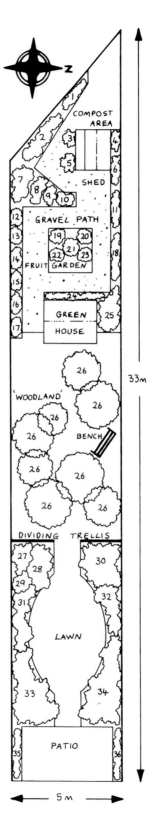

Planting list

Fruit garden
 1 Blackberry
 2 'Bramley' (apple)
 3 Sunberry
 4 Tayberry
 5 Gooseberry
 6 'Shorty Mac' (plum)
 7 'Old Pearmain' (apple)
 8 'James Grieve' (apple)
 9 'Worcester Pearmain' (apple)
10 'Blenheim Orange' (apple)
11 'Brandy Gage' (plum)
12 'Jupiter' (apple)
13 'Spartan' (apple)
14 'Ellison's Orange' (apple)
15 'Goldilock' (apple)
16 'Cox's Orange Pippin' (apple)
17 'Sunset' (apple)
18 Golden gage (plum)
19 Crab apple 'Maypole'
20 'Polka' (Ballerina apple)
21 'Ballerina' (Ballerina apple)
22 'Bolero' (Ballerina apple)
23 'Waltz' (Ballerina apple)
24 Strawberry
25 Rhubarb

Woodland
26 Silver birch (Betula jacquemontii) x 8 underplanted with dicentras, ferns, hostas and spring bulbs

Borders
27 Jasminum nudiflorum
28 Viburnum tinus
29 Clematis
30 Viburnum tinus
31 Choisya 'Sundance'
32 Skimmia japonica
33 Viburnum x bodnantense 'Dawn'
34 Mahonia 'Charity'
35 Honeysuckle
36 Ceanothus

Above: upstairs view in autumn.

Right: the same view in summer.

diagonal also provides much greater planting space. Planting taller plants at the widest point of these borders gives greater depth and direction to the layout of the garden. Take care to include a path through wide borders so that you have access to the plants to water, weed, hoe and replant.

The lawn has been formed into a regular curved shape – a design effect worth using in any garden. Its ovular shape, rather than a rectangle, broadens out the view: circular shapes have the effect of becoming foreshortened when viewed in perspective. This increases the apparent width of the garden. Another method of achieving this in such gardens is to set lawns, borders and paving on the diagonal, which draws the eye across the garden from one side to the other, creating greater width visually. In long gardens where the space is being divided, it is a way of encouraging movement from one room to another. The visitor to the Capel Manor

terraced house garden is encouraged to discover the rest of the 'rooms' by the view through the 'doorway' from the first lawn section through to the next section – an area of woodland. The view through the garden is framed by an archway through the dividing trelliswork.

There is no formal path defined by paving of any type: the route is indicated solely by the straight section of lawn going through the trelliswork. The woodland part of this garden is very informal, the 'path' meanders through the trees and planting with no structures or built features other than a rustic seat from which to enjoy the dappled shaded view. The atmosphere of a woodland glade or spinney has been achieved simply by a plantation of a group of silver birches. These can be planted three in one hole to produce a multi-stemmed specimen, producing a woodland feel in limited space. Choose *Betula jacquemontii* for its ultra white bark.

Above: the fruit garden 'room'.

ROOTSTOCKS

Use the following list of principal apple rootstocks as a guide when buying a tree.

M9 A dwarfing rootstock which will produce a bush tree about 1.8-3m tall. Usually starts to fruit in second or third year. Good for a dwarf pyramid, cordon fan or espalier, but a bush tree may need a permanent stake.

M25 Allows strong growth yet induces early fruiting. Good for half standards, but not normally used for small gardens.

M26 A dwarfing rootstock that produces trees about 2.4m high, which will often crop in the second or third year. Unlikely to need staking. Can be used for cordon, bush, pyramid and fan training. Good on very fertile soil.

M27 The one to choose for a 'miniature'. Very dwarfing and suitable for trees in pots and step-overs. Trees grafted on to this rootstock are unlikely to grow more than about 1.8m tall. Need good growing conditions to thrive.

M106 A semi-dwarfing rootstock widely used for bush apples. The trees may eventually grow to about 4.5m. Sometimes used for fans, espaliers and cordons, which are pruned to a limited height.

The greenhouse provides a physical dividing barrier at the start of the final section of the long garden, which is paved with gravel to provide a way through to the fruit trees and functional features – sheds and compost bins. Invariably, it makes sense to position sheds, greenhouses and compost bins close to fruit and vegetable planting. The beds have been edged with pressure-treated timber to stop the gravel and soil from merging. This far room is a good spot for catching the maximum amount of sun in this garden too, essential for good crop production from both the greenhouse and the fruit garden.

An orchard is impossible in a small garden, but dwarf rootstocks and trained fruit trees allow you to grow fruit in a limited space. Trained fruit trees can look very attractive but be prepared to spend time pruning. Consider buying partially trained specimens which give the basic shape. In the terraced house garden at Capel Manor, fruit trees have been included in two forms: as narrow-growing, Ballerina-type, standard trees and low-growing, step-over trained apple trees which form an edging to the kitchen garden plot.

The size of an apple tree depends on many things, but most important is the type of rootstock (see box). Some rootstocks produce dwarf trees (M27, M9 and M26) and some will produce 6m giants, too large for a small garden (M111). If you are buying a new tree, be sure to buy one grafted on to a rootstock that will produce a plant with appropriate vigour for the training method – pruning alone cannot reduce overall size. Do not buy the plant unless you know the number of the rootstock as well as the variety.

You can grow exotic fruits such as Asian pears, apricots, cherries, peaches and nectarines on sunny walls or south-facing slopes. Citrus fruits can be grown in pots and placed outside for the summer (kumquats are very hardy). Soft fruits can also be considered where space is limited or where ornamental effect is important. Gooseberries can be grown as standards to about 1m in height and along with both red and white currants can be trained as a cordon or fan. Raspberry can either be grown over a wigwam of supports or trained to give a diamond trellis effect. You can train blackberries, loganberries and the other varieties of berries up walls and fences in a similar way to a large espalier. Strawberries look very ornamental when grown in containers, which makes the picking easier and gives great splashes of colour to the edge of a patio.

TRAINED SHAPES

Cordons: good where space is tight. Cordons are tied to wires stretched between posts and can be laid over at an angle of 45 degrees, which reduces vigour and produces more fruiting growth within reach. Plant M9 and M27 rootstock 50cm apart.

Double cordons: U-shape formed by training side branches at 45 degrees away from main branch and then vertically. Each of these can be split in the same way for a double U effect.

Triple cordons: leading shoot trained vertically along with two side ones.

Fan-trained: trees grown flat against a sunny wall or fence. Allow 3 to 3.5m per tree and 1.8m height.

Espalier: two horizontal branches are trained from central stem on wires stretched between posts or against walls and fences. Allow 3 to 3.5m width.

Step-overs: low-level, single-tier espaliers that you can literally step over. M27 rootstock, plant 2-year-old partially trained trees 1.5m apart.

Dense border planting in the terraced house garden – Diascia to the left of Jasminum nudiflorum, *and in front of* Sisyrinchum *and yellow* Genista lydia.

LOW-MAINTENANCE GARDENS

Many people prefer to relax rather than work in their garden, but they still want it to look good. Cutting down on the amount of maintenance work necessary in the garden is something that appeals particularly to those who have full-time jobs or who frequently travel away from home, or who no longer have the energy or stamina for the heavier work. It is entirely possible to design a small garden with this in mind and create a beautiful outdoor area that needs only a couple of hours' attention each month, if that.

There are several key design points to follow for a low-maintenance garden. Grass requires great investments of time to look good, so a low-maintenance garden will preferably have paving rather than lawn. If having a lawn is important to you, however, or you cannot afford to pave the entire area, use a type of grass that does not contain ryegrass. (For alternatives to grass see the suggestions in the box on page 201.) You may also wish to create a mowing strip at the edges of the lawn so the blades of the lawnmower can go right over the edge, and consider leaving patches of it to grow longer than the rest, perhaps planted with bulbs. Boundaries should be constructed from durable materials rather than hedging which can be very laborious to trim each year.

It is important to create a planting scheme that focuses on easy-care shrubs rather than high-maintenance herbaceous plants or any other kind of planting such as fruit or alpines. Evergreens are excellent, whereas the fallen leaves from deciduous trees need to be cleared in the autumn. Choose hardy plants that suit both your soil and microclimate conditions so that you do not need to nurture them with special feeds. Avoid plants that need a lot of water to flourish, because you will be seeking to cut out the need to use a hose or watering can during the summer months. Mulches, for example, both suppress weeds and retain moisture and are essential elements of the low-maintenance garden.

Ground-cover plants are ideal for filling gaps between shrubs and will also keep down the weeds once established.

THE GARDENING WHICH? LOW-MAINTENANCE GARDEN

The *Gardening Which?* theme gardens at Capel Manor include a plot which requires barely any attention at all throughout the year. No maintenance of dividing structures and no pruning of climbing plants trained against them is required. Both a patio and a lawn have been included; the lawn being a semi-circular shape that echoes the boundary line and is an easier shape to mow. A brick mowing strip has been installed, eliminating the extra task of cutting the grass overhanging borders. To ensure weed-free paved areas, polypropylene sheeting (which lets through water but not weeds) has been laid beneath the hardcore foundation. Used with cobbles, this has the added benefit of stopping the material from being worn into the ground beneath. Black polythene can be used as a substitute, but this must be punctured all over to allow moisture through. Old newspapers can also be used but these will decompose after a relatively short space of time.

The entrance to this low-maintenance garden is where a house would be, leading on to the paved seating area. York flagstone reproduction slabs in varying sizes have been laid in a random style. To add interest, a raised border has been built to form an edge to the patio. The wall is 65cm high with 30cm-wide coping stone. Weep holes are set at 75cm intervals, and the inside of the wall is painted with a bituminous covering to damp-proof it. Within the raised pool is a butyl liner, the top edge of which is sandwiched between the last course of bricks and the coping stone. The pool has an overflow pipe in the corner. All the raised walls are laid on a solid concrete foundation.

As a general rule, use no more than three different surfaces for harmonious results. Here, slabs, brick and cobbles are the choices. All of the borders close to the patio have been given a pebble mulch, which, as well as suppressing weeds and retaining moisture, provides a good textural contrast, making an excellent foil for plants. The paving slabs have been extended from the patio through the widest border in the garden. This allows the garden to be maintained

Pebble mulch – attractive, moisture-retaining and helping to keep the weeds down.

Do not be put off by the number of plants in this garden – shrubs require little maintenance.

easily and for the planting in that area to be enjoyed from close quarters. The slabs sit happily with the surrounding pebbles.

The low-maintenance planting scheme aims to make good use of shrubs that require little or no pruning in order to produce flowers and fruits in sufficient quantity. A good proportion of evergreen plants is important, to provide year-round backdrop and structure. This garden includes two trees. *Crataegus* x *lavallei* (73 on the plan on the right) planted close to where a house might be helps to balance the mass of the building and paved area. The crab apple (*Malus floribunda*) (72 on the plan) near to the far boundary would make a good view in its own

garden, the lime-green inflorescences of *Euphorbia characias* ssp. *wulfenii* contrast strikingly with the purple sword-like leaves of *Phormium tenax* 'Purpureum', both of them set off by the smooth grey pebbles of the border mulch.

Planting list
1 Viburnum bodnantense 'Dawn'
2 Garrya elliptica
3 Gaultheria shallon
4 Nandina domestica
5 Acanthus spinosus
6 Senecio 'Sunshine'
7 Daphne x burkwoodii
8 Elaeagnus pungens 'Maculata'

Above right: A brick mowing strip helps to ensure that lawn maintenance is kept to a minimum.

Above left: Euphorbia wulfenii *can look stunning.*

right when in blossom and fruit – early spring and autumn – and might help to frame an attractive view beyond. Both of these trees are excellent choices for the small garden, having two periods of interest. A good proportion of the planting close to the patio of this garden is evergreen and has been chosen to provide textural contrast. For example, the bed to the front of the raised border combines *Fatsia japonica*, with its glossy green leaves, the strikingly gold-splashed *Elaeagnus pungens* 'Maculata', the grey-green-leaved *Acca sellowiana* with its white, downy undersides, all of them evergreen.

Marrying hard and soft landscaping harmoniously is as important as creating the right associations between different plants. In this

9 Arundinaria murieliae
10 Acca sellowiana
11 Cotinus rubrifolius
12 Rosmarinus 'Miss Jessopp's Upright'
13 Fatsia japonica
14 Mahonia japonica 'Charity'
15 Phormium tenax 'Purpureum'
16 Pennisetum alopecuroïdes
17 Juniperus squamata 'Blue Carpet'
18 Pinus mugo
19 Genista lydia
20 Vinca major
21 Choisya ternata
22 Fatsia japonica
23 Genista lydia
24 Pachyphragma macrophyllum
25 Prunus lusitanica
26 Acca sellowiana

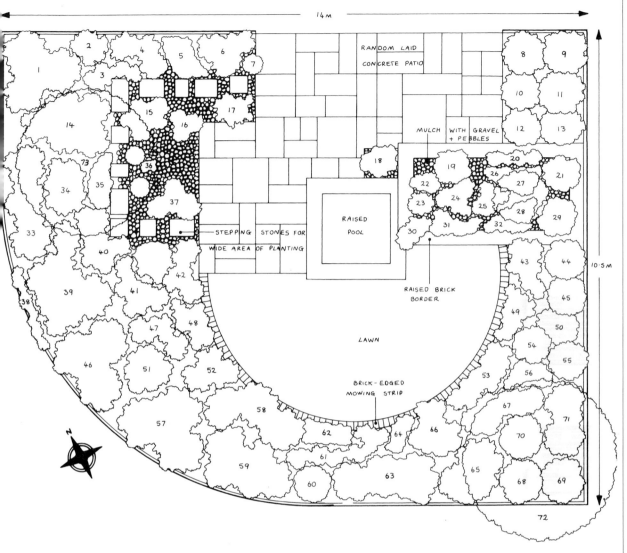

27 Amelanchier 'Ballerina'
28 Geranium macrorrhizum
29 Phlomis fruticosa
30 Pinus mugo pumilio
31 Thymus 'Doone Valley'
32 Geranium macrorrhizum
33 Viburnum tinus 'Eve Price'
34 Hypericum inodorum 'Elstead'
35 Hosta 'Aureomarginata'
36 Euphorbia characias ssp. wulfenii
37 Stipa gigantea
38 Garrya elliptica 'James Roof'
39 Cornus alba 'Elegantissima'
40 Viburnum davidii
41 Potentilla 'Abbotswood Silver'
42 Senecio 'Sunshine'
43 Lavandula 'Munstead'
44 Ceanothus impressus

45 Lonicera nitida 'Baggesen's Gold'
46 Elaeagnus x ebbingei
47 Syringa microphylla 'Superba'
48 Euonymus fortunei 'Emerald 'n' Gold'
49 Hebe pinguifolia 'Pagei'
50 Spiraea x vanhouttei
51 Escallonia 'Apple Blossom'
52 Viburnum plicatum
53 Stephanandra incisa 'Crispa'
54 Cornus alba 'Spaethii'
55 Escallonia 'Iveyi'
56 Anemone japonica
57 Berberis x ottawensis 'Superba'
58 Choysia ternata
59 Stephanandra tanakae
60 Ilex 'Silver Queen'
61 Skimmia 'Rubella'
62 Bergenia 'Abendglut'

63 Photinia 'Red Robin'
64 Prunus lusitanica
65 Ligustrum ovalifolium 'Aureum'
66 Berberis 'Rose Glow'
67 Hydrangea serrata 'Grayswood'
68 Prunus lusitanica
69 Ligusticum lucidum
70 Aucuba japonica
71 Pyracantha coccinea 'Lalandei'
72 Malus floribunda
73 Crataegus x lavallei

NOISY GARDENS

Right: Euonymus japonicus *will withstand the pollution from a main road.*

The problem of noise has become a fact of life for many garden owners. It is not only an urban problem of traffic-laden roads, railways and low-flying aircraft; noise can shatter the idyll even in rural gardens – from increasingly busy trunk roads and surface coal extraction, to the noise of neighbours using power garden tools. The problem of noise from motorways close to areas

with security and sight screening. Acoustic barriers can be planted with suitable subjects as with any other fence or construction.

Simply planting a substantial number of shrubs around noisy perimeters of a garden will muffle road noise, though best results will be through the combined use of fencing and dense shrub

Above: this front garden is less noisy because of the high fence and shrub planting. The fountain will also help divert attention from the road. However, the conifers won't stand up well to traffic pollution.

Bottom right: Fatsia japonica *will help to muffle noise.*

of housing has increased, with installations of acoustic fencing a common sight. Noise impact above a certain level from road construction work must be minimised by law, but the permitted decibels may still be too much to bear.

If you are faced with a garden that never loses the drone of nearby traffic, walls provide one of the best sound insulators, and, if you can find the money for it, it is probably worth building as high a solid wall as legally possible for your boundary. Walls deaden the worst effects of traffic noise without taking up valuable space and they require little maintenance. An alternative is to install acoustic fencing, which may prove to be the only feasible way to baffle external noise. Acoustic fencing works by either absorbing or reflecting sound, and is available in concrete panels, aluminium, plastic and timber. Many forms combine noise and safety features

planting. Plant a good selection of tough evergreens as living noise barriers – those that are used for hedging are good.

With traffic comes pollution as well. However, there are a number of plants that are tough and resistant to fumes. Avoid planting asters and petunias near heavy traffic. Conifers can suffer badly too. It may be wise to get plants that are tolerant of salt, which is often included in winter gritting of roads. The foliage may otherwise turn brown.

Particular attention to seating areas is needed in a garden open to outside noise. Additional sound insulation can be created around a patio or terrace in the form of wooden screens. The drawback of having lots of layers of screening, however, is that the light from early morning or evening sun is often cut off, a time when noise

POLLUTION-RESISTANT PLANTS

e = evergreens
p = poisonous

Acer negundo (box maple)
Arundinaria (e; bamboo)
Aucuba japonica
(e; Japanese laurel)
Berberis (some e; barberry)
Ceanothus (some e;
California lilac)
Chaenomeles superba
(japonica)
Cotinus coggygria
(smoke bush)
Cotoneaster horizontalis
Elaeagnus commutata
(e; silver berry)
Erica carnea (e; heather)
Euonymus japonicus (e)
Fatsia japonica (e)
Forsythia
Griselinia littoralis
(e; castor oil plant)
Hebe (e)
Hydrangea
Ilex aquifolium (e; holly)
Hedera (e; ivies)
Ligustrum japonicum (e)
Magnolia stellata (star-
flowered magnolia)
Mahonia (e)
Philadelphus
Prunus laurocerasus
(e, p; mock orange)
Prunus lusitanica
(e, p; Portuguese laurel)
Pyracantha (e; fire thorn)
Roses
Viburnum tinus
(e; laurustinus)
Vinca (e; periwinkle)

from traffic is actually usually reduced. One good solution is to purchase or make movable screens from large rectangular wooden or plastic planters which have trellis panel backs and castors beneath. Climbers such as honeysuckle and ivies can be grown up through the trellis. For noise shelter without shade, try polycarbonate (light, clear plastic as used in conservatory roofs), which is also useful where prevailing winds are a problem in exposed gardens. Positioning a pouring type of water feature (see pages 168-75) close to your main seating area will ensure that the sound of running water is heard over and above anything less relaxing.

Other ways to ensure that your garden provides a peaceful oasis are to eliminate features that require potentially noisy maintenance. For example, avoid or remove hedging that requires more than one cut per season with power trimmers to keep it under control. Use shears where possible. Similarly with lawns: either do away with completely, or reduce to a size that can be coped with by a traditional push-type mower (for good exercise too).

PATIO GARDENS

Patios provide the perfect space and firm ground for garden furniture and containers for plants. Dispensing with a lawn altogether and installing a large area of patio may cost a lot of money initially in comparison with laying turf and planting borders, but there will be no annoyingly tiny areas of grass to cut in the small garden, and among the wide range of materials for hard landscaping are many patio surfaces that rival the beauty of the most ornamental of lawns. Moreover, shade from walls and trees in the small garden often means that any grass is likely to take second place to moss in a lawn.

Gardening Which? designed this patio garden.

THE PATIO GARDEN AT CAPEL MANOR

This garden is a good demonstration of how design ideas can be liberated by getting rid of a lawn. Had one been included here, it would barely have been more than the size of a pocket handkerchief, and of little practical use. This kind of patio can be kept looking spruce by sweeping with a good stiff broom, backed up with a pressure hose as required.

Getting the ground plan right is even more important in so small a garden, there being, literally, no room for error. Here, it has been possible to create a sheltered seating area to the side of the main route through the garden. Setting the paving on the diagonal gives an illusion of greater space and increases the sense of movement across the garden, from the entrance to the 'exit'. In other gardens one of these might accommodate a suitable focal point.

Simple square concrete slabs, pale in colour to lighten the area and with a riven finish for texture, have been edged with brick. Brick helps to lift areas surfaced with cheaper slabs and will tie paving to the house and other features in the garden – here the boundary walls and walls of the raised water feature. The brick paving has been extended to form the entrance and exit 'landings', herringbone laid to match the diagonal flow of the garden.

A timber pergola forms a cover over one entrance providing extra vertical interest and a support for plants. Vertical height and space-saving can be combined by using the house or garden walls to support pergola structures.

All-around planting to clothe boundaries helps to create a courtyard feel. *Acer palmatum* 'Senkaki', the coral-barked maple, is classed by some as a large shrub. It has beautiful foliage for summer, excellent autumn tints, followed by shoot tips that are coral-pink in winter. Its graceful habit is shown to best effect when planted as a specimen, as here, and the pebble mulch beneath sets it off perfectly and conserves moisture around its roots. Take care with plants such as this which can be subject to leaf scorch when heat and sunlight are reflected off an adjacent paved surface. Here, the northerly aspect of the planting, coupled with the pebble mulch means this should not be a problem.

An alternative layout idea for a patio or courtyard would be one where the boundaries are completely obscured by planting, with the paving hugging the boundary, leaving the central part of the garden planted as an island. Imagine the garden in the plan with the areas reversed – paving where the planting is and planting where the paving is. With a minor adjustment to allow enough space to sit out, this would still work.

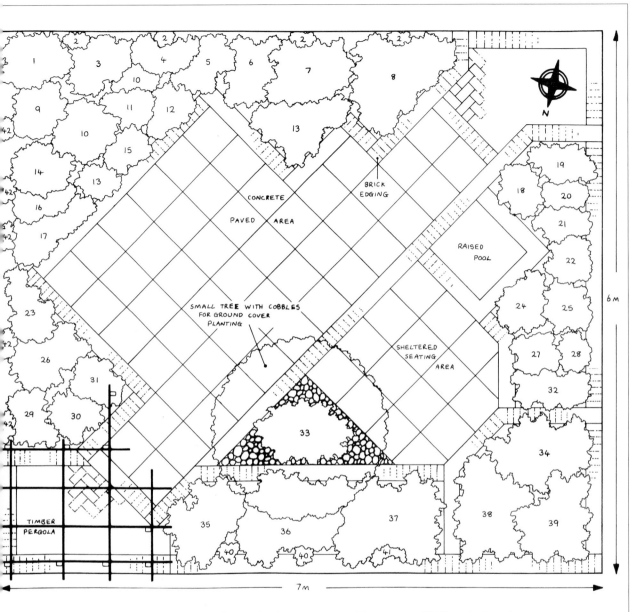

Planting list

1 Sambucus nigra 'Aurea'
2 Hedera helix 'Goldheart'
3 Phormium tenax
4 Potentilla fruticosa
5 Jasminum nudiflorum
6 Caragana arborescens 'Pendula'
7 Cytisus battandieri
8 Viburnum tinus
9 Bergenia cordifolia
10 Euphorbia robbaie
11 Ilex 'Golden King'
12 Carex
13 Euonymus fortunei 'Emerald
    n' Gold'

14 Carex hachijoenis 'Evergold'
15 Senecio greyi
16 Thuja orientalis 'Aurea Nana'
17 Nepeta x faassenii
18 Ophiopogon 'Nigrescens'
19 Festuca glauca
20 Eucalyptus gunnii
21 Hosta 'Hadspen Blue'
22 Ajuga reptans 'Burgundy Glow'
23 Berberis 'Atropurpurea Nana'
24 Heuchera 'Palace Purple'
25 Scabiosa 'Blue Mist'
26 Carpenteria californica
27 Sedum 'Ruby Glow'
28 Hebe pinguifolia 'Pagei'

29 Wisteria sinensis
30 Taxus baccata 'Fastigiata'
31 Nandina domestica
32 Sedum 'Herbstfreude'
33 Acer palmatum 'Senkaki'
34 Viburnum plicatum
35 Athyrium niponicum pictum
36 Bergenia cordifolia
37 Azalea 'Orange Beauty'
38 Euonymus fortunei 'Emerald Gaiety'
39 Photinia 'Red Robin'
40 Lonicera periclymenum 'Serotina'
41 Chaenomeles x superba 'Crimson
    and Gold'
42 Rosa 'Golden Shower'

PLANT-LOVERS' GARDENS

Most gardeners are interested in, and appreciate, plants, though their main concerns about garden design will revolve around utilising the outside space for many things other than plants. For a few plant-loving gardeners, however (often referred to as plantspersons), there is only one thing to do with a small garden – pack in as many plants as possible, to the exclusion of almost everything else. Patios and lawns are often the first features to be reduced in size in the plantsperson's garden, though a paved area might be used to display a collection of plants in containers.

A garden with predominantly one type of planting may lack depth of interest for good portions of the year. One with a great number of different plants can look 'spotty' because everything has been crammed into the plot without much regard paid to the overall picture. But it is possible to plan a plant-lover's garden to produce a harmonious composition that combines a wealth of detail in a pleasing framework. Arranging tiers of planting is a good solution.

Although keen plant-lovers often shy away from any notions of garden 'design', the challenge posed by creating a plantsperson's garden in a

Right: plants need to earn their space in a small garden, like Viburnum x burkwoodii *with spring flowers and autumn colour.*

Far right: the Japanese maple shows off its autumn colour in the Gardening Which? *'crammed' garden.*

Some plant-lovers want to specialise in collecting every variety of one particular genus of plant, while others are generalists who will take delight in growing as large a number as possible of different types of plants in whatever conditions they require. Specialists may want to arrange their plant collections in quite a formal way, similar to the systematic beds found in many botanic gardens. Generalists may prefer to create many different types of habitats and microclimates as their plant knowledge and acquisition rates increase.

The major problem of plant-lovers' gardens is that they can tend to look bitty, for different reasons.

small space still requires careful planning from the outset. How do you fit into a few square metres everything from vertical features to support climbers; paths to tend the borders; pools of the right type for growing favourite aquatic plants; somewhere to position a treasured collection of containers and their associated plants; and useful working areas of a productive garden such as compost heaps and greenhouse?

THE 'CRAMMED' GARDEN

The *Gardening Which?* 'crammed' garden at Capel Manor shows how the essential features for a plant-lover's garden can be fitted into a

The plant-enthusiasts' garden at Capel Manor is crammed with different plants and gives contrast and year-round colour.

small plot and still leave plenty of room for a choice collection of plants. The philosophy of keeping things simple definitely applies in the garden shown here: the layout is based on a rectangle turned on its side (the gravel path around the garden) with a smaller rectangle in the middle (a central border housing both a pool and a dry-stone wall that provide ideal habitats for certain types of plants).

It is not just the spatial constraints of a small plot that will make a plant-enthusiast eschew

the idea of growing grass for a lawn. The borders of lawns are edged, or the gravel retained, by timber, and neither this nor paving material can compete with plants for visual attention. In this crammed garden small maintenance paths have been left to access the back of borders and the compost bin. These would be undetectable to anyone other than the regular user, being hidden by plant growth for most of the year. There is space to tuck in a small seat for the gardener to rest and enjoy the fruits of his or her labours.

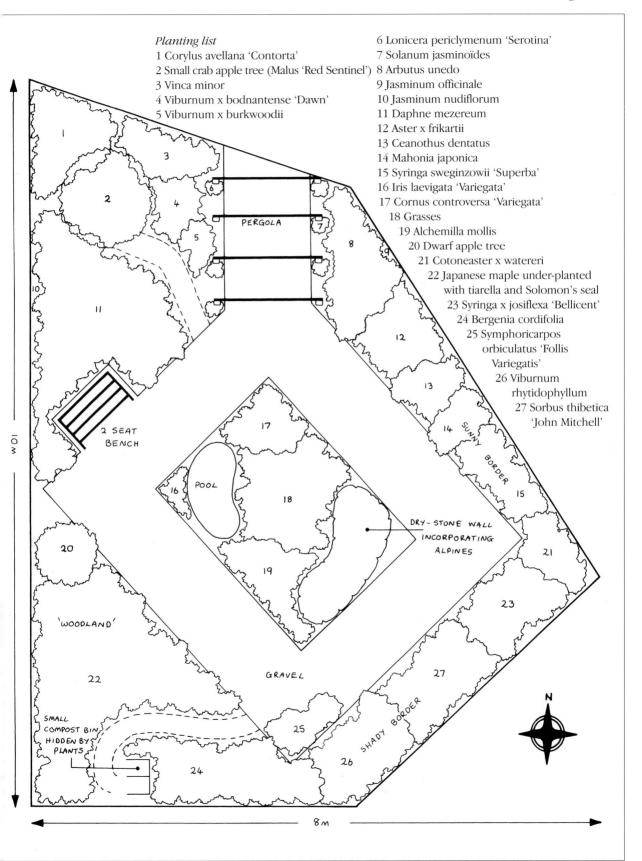

Planting list
1 Corylus avellana 'Contorta'
2 Small crab apple tree (Malus 'Red Sentinel')
3 Vinca minor
4 Viburnum x bodnantense 'Dawn'
5 Viburnum x burkwoodii
6 Lonicera periclymenum 'Serotina'
7 Solanum jasminoïdes
8 Arbutus unedo
9 Jasminum officinale
10 Jasminum nudiflorum
11 Daphne mezereum
12 Aster x frikartii
13 Ceanothus dentatus
14 Mahonia japonica
15 Syringa sweginzowii 'Superba'
16 Iris laevigata 'Variegata'
17 Cornus controversa 'Variegata'
18 Grasses
19 Alchemilla mollis
20 Dwarf apple tree
21 Cotoneaster x watereri
22 Japanese maple under-planted with tiarella and Solomon's seal
23 Syringa x josiflexa 'Bellicent'
24 Bergenia cordifolia
25 Symphoricarpos orbiculatus 'Follis Variegatis'
26 Viburnum rhytidophyllum
27 Sorbus thibetica 'John Mitchell'

PERGOLA

2 SEAT BENCH

10M

POOL

DRY-STONE WALL INCORPORATING ALPINES

SUNNY BORDER

'WOODLAND'

GRAVEL

SMALL COMPOST BIN HIDDEN BY PLANTS

SHADY BORDER

N

8M

Below: yellow flowers of Jasminum nudiflorum echo the yellow veining on the large-leaved ivy Hedera colchica *Sulphur Heart'.*

Right: striking combination of Rheum palmatum *in flower and variegated* Aralia *set against* Ceanothus *flowers.*

The planted pergola spanning the entrance to the garden creates a tunnel-like quality and provides functional support for a range of climbing plants. The construction material of the boundaries is almost an irrelevance, as the aim is eventually to obscure them by the planting. The raised area in the centre provides structural interest and habitats for different plants that like to live by pools and stone walls. Building a simple unmortared stone wall is an excellent way to provide an interesting surface and home for a broader range of plants. For example, the dry-stone wall here provides an excellent free-draining environment for alpines to thrive between the crevices and joints. The same structure at a lower level facing north, will provide ideal conditions for growing a range of shade- and moisture-loving plants such as ferns, ramondas, some of the primulas and the dwarf form of gunnera, *G. magellanica*.

A classic planting scheme for a small garden belonging to a plant-lover will be an emulation of nature's 'plan', that is definite layers, or tiers. Each of the borders in the crammed garden offers a different microclimate and each has a specific season of interest. For example, the sunny border is planted with subjects that will be at their most attractive from summer through to late autumn. The area around the specimen tree – *Malus* 'Red Sentinel' – is one of winter interest, with hellebores, snowdrops, and winter-flowering shrubs such as *Viburnum bodnantense* 'Dawn'. Grouping plants that 'perform' at similar times is one way to plan your planting. The end result being that, rather than having dots of colour about the garden throughout the year, certain areas will actually take centre stage as the seasons progress, with different groups of plants starting to flower, showing their coloured bark, displaying colourful fruits or whatever.

One of the star performers in this garden is *Cornus controversa* 'Variegata' or the wedding cake tree (17 on the plan on page 91). The horizontal habit of this plant with its tiered branch growth makes it a natural choice for a focal point. The striking foliage of creamy white margined leaves gives way to scarlet autumn colours. This is an excellent choice of plant for a small garden as the light shade it casts makes it ideal for underplanting. The only drawback is that it may be hard to find and is usually expensive.

Many of the other plants here are prize specimens. The whitebeam (*Sorbus thibetica* 'John Mitchell' is a fine example, with extra large, silver-grey leaves, downy white on the underside. These mellow to autumnal yellow shades. It is not a small tree (it can grow to 12m) but can be cut back and trained. Most plant-lovers will not be deterred by the ultimate size of a plant if they are determined to grow a

particular specimen. The Canadian lilac (*Syringa x josiflexa* 'Bellicent') is a medium to large shrub. The flowers are very large, clear rose-pink lilac type and highly scented. The plant shape is slightly arching when in flower. This is a fine plant, particularly if you have the space to let it grow unrestricted. The variegated Indian currant (*Symphoricarpos orbiculatus* 'Follis Variegatis') has lovely irregularly yellow margined leaves. It is one of the most graceful variegated shrubs and in common with others, it grows to about two-thirds the size of the plain-leaved form.

Above: the Crammed Garden showing the small raised bed for alpines in the foreground.

ROOF GARDENS

Opposite: plan of imaginary roof garden.

Right: essentially, roof gardens should be regarded as patio and container gardens, but you will have to be careful with weight and over-exposure to sun.

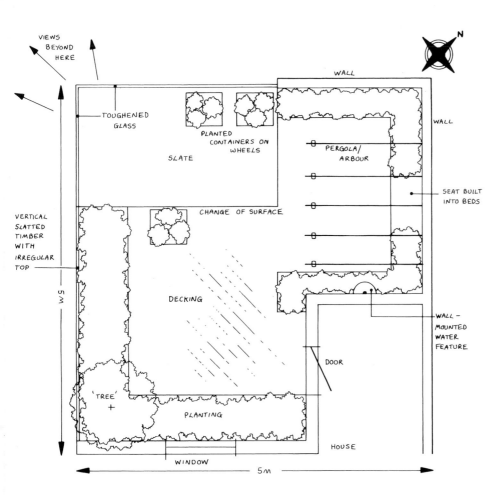

VIEWS
BEYOND
HERE

N

WALL

TOUGHENED
GLASS

WALL

PLANTED
CONTAINERS ON
WHEELS

SLATE

PERGOLA/
ARBOUR

SEAT BUILT
INTO BEDS

VERTICAL
SLATTED
TIMBER
WITH
IRREGULAR
TOP

CHANGE OF SURFACE

5M

DECKING

WALL –
MOUNTED
WATER
FEATURE

DOOR

'TREE'

PLANTING

HOUSE

WINDOW

5M

Important constraints apply to the design and construction of roof gardens. It is one type of garden where specialist advice really needs to be sought before work commences. Check planning or conservation area restrictions that apply to structures visible from the ground or those that alter the line of a roof. The structural strength of the roof must be checked – it has to be capable of supporting the additional weight not only of plants, compost and structures but also people. You may find that you need to build higher parapets for safety.

You may need to have the roof area reinforced with a steel joist (RSJ), which will greatly add to the expense. The bulk of extra weight will tend to be concentrated around the sides of the garden. The main planting can be done in specially constructed troughs supported by cross beams or strong metal brackets to load-bearing walls.

Access to roof gardens is usually situated in the middle, resulting in an L-shaped space. Care has to be taken not to breech the waterproof membrane of the supporting roof, so dealing with rainwater is a key concern. Roof gardens typically present wide views that you may want to frame or restrict a little to add interest and focus. Creating shade and shelter will be priorities as temperatures and wind will be more extreme at roof height.

All fixtures and features must be very securely and safely fitted. The weight of hard landscaping materials to be used will be of prime importance. Decking can be a good choice for the ground surface, though it is expensive. Artificial rocks made from fibreglass look realistic and are much lighter alternatives for creating natural-looking features. Water features incorporating spouts and fountains should be placed in sheltered spots, away from winds.

Right: in this roof garden, vertical height has been created with trellis-style panels.

Above: maintenance of your roof will be more difficult if you train climbing plants over it.

LAYOUT AND HARD LANDSCAPING

In the plan on the previous page two sides of the roof garden are formed by load-bearing walls. These are ideal for supporting raised beds – troughs 60cm wide and 45cm deep constructed from exterior grade plywood suspended just off the floor on strong metal brackets. Treat inside of containers with bitumen paint or line them to extend their life. To provide shelter and support for climbing plants, vertical slatted panels have been bolted to the top of the walls (these can be made in the same way as trellis panels – see pages 160-3). In the plan, the entrance is via the door from the building which intrudes into the available space. One window of the house enjoys a view to the garden and the skyline beyond. This view has been retained by using toughened glass as part of the boundary treatment, ensuring views out of the garden from here and also the main seating area. An arbour provides shade for the built-in seat between two planting beds, the bulk of the weight being taken by the wall. Lightweight wood substitutes such as Timbron (made from recycled polystyrene and plastics) can be used to reduce weight.

IMPORTANT CONSIDERATIONS FOR ROOF GARDENS

- Planning or legal constraints often apply.
- Get a surveyor to check the load-bearing capacity of the roof. Remember to take into account the weight of people as well as what's in the garden.
- Check drainage across whole area.
- Ensure all walls and railings are secure.
- Use Astroturf rather than trying to create a real lawn.
- Choose plants that withstand wind and sun.

The ground has been surfaced with timber decking and lightweight slate tiles. Decking is ideal for roof gardens because the weight is spread by supporting beams, and water can drain freely underneath. If you prefer paving, use only special lightweight tiles and provide channels for water to drain away into downpipes. There are three large containers, sitting on frames with wheels for ease of movement. Choose lightweight fibreglass or recycled plastic containers.

PLANTING

To keep down the weight, mix your own compost using equal volumes of peat (or substitute) and perlite with a base fertiliser added. As the mixture is very light, it pays to secure larger plants in their containers using support wires until they get established. Use Astroturf for the effect of a lush green sward. Roof garden plants should be tolerant of high levels of sun and wind and occasional drought. Providing shelter will prolong the growing season.

In the garden shown on the plan, much of the planting height has been achieved by clothing the walls and fencing with climbing plants, which can also be trained to cover the cross-beams of the arbour. A 'tree' has been included in the form of a large specimen of *Genista aetnensis*, the Mount Etna broom. It has almost no leaf but will be covered with golden, scented flowers in July. The thin wiry branches can withstand the wind at this level. You can plant trees on roof gardens but start them off as young specimens so they become securely rooted.

Architecturally interesting planting has been included in the form of *Yucca filamentosa* which will produce masses of creamy white bell shaped flowers from a young age, and *Pinus mugo* 'Gnom', a form of the mountain pine which will grow into a compact small tree or large shrub. Other appropriate plants included to provide structure for the whole of the planting scheme include *Mahonia pinnata*, *Berberis thunbergii*, and *Elaeagnus* x *ebbingei*. Many plants that will survive drought conditions have also been used here, again to keep maintenance levels down.

Mediterranean plants provide a good source of choices, and grey-leaved plants will be of particular interest. Here, *Teucrium fruticans* is

Above: a wonderfully lush effect has been created here with 'tree-like' plants and a surface of wooden decking.

growing against the wall. This vigorous grey leaved shrub thrives against warm walls and produces blue flowers over a long period. The foliage is aromatic, too. *Senecio viravira* is another good silver-leaved choice for this hot dry site and will thrive in gravelly soils equally well. Both rosemary and the sage family will also provide good planting selections, some of which will have the added benefit of being useful for culinary purposes too. Avoid herbaceous plants that require staking to survive stronger winds, even after filtering has been achieved. In a small enclosed space such as this, the sight of canes and other staking methods would intrude into the effect of the garden. Some sample choices for this garden are *Epilobium angustifolium* 'Album', which produces white fluffy seed heads after its long-held flowers, *Anthemis tinctoria* 'E C Buxton' and *Kniphofia* 'Little Maid'. This is a later-flowering, shorter yellow form of red hot poker.

SHADY GARDENS

Predominant shade is common in the small garden. Town houses frequently have narrow passages between back and front; the whole of the garden may face due north; or a large mature tree may be casting shade over a sizeable area. There is a world of difference, however, between shade beneath trees – which is often dry because the tree prevents much

Below: even at midday, this corner receives little sunlight, but the fern at the centre relishes the damp conditions.

Opposite page: rhododendrons and candelabra primulas are natural woodland plants and so are happy in shade.

rain from reaching the ground and then takes up most of the available water in the soil, and damp shade in sunken areas. Both conditions are overcome by careful planting.

The predominantly shady garden will rarely suffer from water shortages, so shade is one of the easiest 'problems' to deal with in terms of planting. In town gardens shady areas can still offer sheltered spots created by heat radiated from walls and because wind chill can be cut out by nearby buildings.

A north-facing wall provides reliably constant conditions. *Hydrangea petiolaris*, which grows well on north-facing walls, is deciduous, though the flower heads look attractive when held

throughout winter. *Tropaeolum speciosum* (Scottish flame flower) is a Chilean plant that thrives particularly well in the cool, moist soil in the north of the British Isles, or against a north-facing wall in the south. Its long-lasting red nasturtium-shaped flowers are followed by dark berries.

Ivy is useful in dry shade for both climbing and ground cover. *Rubus tricolor* provides vigorous ground cover – try *R.t.* 'Betty Ashburner' for slower growth. *Lamium galeobdolon* (archangel) is a good perennial for dry shade, though it can become invasive. Do not be put off by the common names of *Euphorbia amygdaloïdes* var. *robbiae*, *Lamium maculatum*, and *Iris foetidissima* – wood spurge, dead nettle and stinking gladdon, respectively – they are all excellent plants for the base of large trees or mini 'woodland' areas of the garden.

Shady gardens should be appealing and inviting. Aim for a good range of textural contrast in the foliage of the plants that you choose. Silver-leaved plants are off limits; they generally turn green if they don't get the sun. But by choosing a small number of shade-loving subjects with variegated foliage, planting can still highlight areas. Avoid packing shady borders with dark-leaved plants. *Ilex aquifolium* is very hardy and comes in variegated forms, and *Brunnera macrophylla* 'Hadspen Cream' has particularly good variegated foliage. Choose shade-lovers with pale flowers, for example the pale forms of *Digitalis purpurea*, as another way to brighten dark borders. The white form of *Anemone japonica* 'Honorine Jobert' is appropriate, as are the white flowers of *Vinca minor* 'Alba'.

Seasonal planting in the form of bulbs and bedding can also heighten the impact of relatively sun-free areas but involve a little more maintenance.

Good annuals for shady gardens include busy lizzies (*Impatiens*) and honesty (*Lunaria annua*). Try variegated and white-flowered forms of the latter. Bulbs that do well in shady gardens include grape hyacinths, crown

SHADE-LOVERS

DRY SHADE

Shrubs
Berberis x *stenophylla*
(barberry)
Hedera helix (ivy)
Lonicera pileata
(privet honeysuckle)
Mahonia aquifolium
(oregon grape)
Ruscus aculeatus
Symphoricarpos
(snowberry)

Perennials
Euphorbia amygdaloïdes
(wood spurge)
Iris foetidissima
(stinking gladdon)
Lamium (dead nettle)
Liriope muscari
(lily turf)
Vinca major, V. minor
(periwinkles)

MOIST SHADE

Shrubs
Buxus suffruticosa
(dwarf box)
Fuchsia 'Versicolor'
Ilex aquifolium
Sarcococca humilis
Viburnum davidii

Perennials
Anemone japonica
Aquilegia vulgaris
(columbine)
Bergenia
Brunnera macrophylla
(forget-me-not)
Corydalis flexuosa
Dicentra (bleeding heart)
Digitalis purpurea
Epimedium
Ferns
Gentiana asclepiadea
(willow gentian)
Heuchera (alum root)
Omphalodes cappadocica
(blue-eyed Mary)
Pulmonaria officinalis
(lungwort)
Saxifraga
Tiarella cordifolia
(foam flower)
Tellima grandiflora
(fringe cups)

imperials and lilies. For bedding, alyssum and impatiens are hard to beat, but begonias, lobelias and fuchsias should also do well.

Many of the most spectacular shade plants need an acid soil. These include azaleas, camellias, pieris and rhododendrons. Fortunately, all these shrubs have quite a shallow root system and they do very well in tubs containing a peat-based compost if you don't have the right soil. Add leaf mould to *Smilacina racemosa*, and plenty of humus to *Tellima grandiflora*.

One way to avoid dark, dank looks is to use pale-coloured slabs for an area of paving that receives little sunlight. Because shady paths and paving build up moss and algae quickly, choose materials that can easily be kept clean and slime-free. A textured surface will also help. Dark walls can be painted a pale colour to reflect more light. Similarly, light-coloured mulches such as white gravel can help brighten up the darkest corner and look very effective with the right plants. The disadvantage is that they will attract algae, but can easily be hosed down.

If the shady area includes utility items such as bins, disguise them with trellis and incorporate them into planting schemes by using them as shelves and supports for a range of plants. Choose pale-coloured containers and decorative objects to continue the theme.

SLOPING GARDENS

Most gardens benefit from simple changes in level such as one step up or down from the patio into the main area. Gardens with steeper slopes have many positive aspects to them. They may present you with superlative views – the land falling dramatically away from the house – or feelings of enclosure – the ground sloping towards the house. Simple slopes can be taken up by shallow banks, the soil 'retained' by low-growing planting. Choosing plants with root structures that bind the soil of a bank is the cheapest method of dealing with the problem. They can be given more 'weight' by incorporating them into a system of stones and wooden battens that act as low walls or soil dams.

Very steep sites can pose genuine difficulties, however, in terms of designing a garden that is functional. There is no doubt that coping with a steep slope will add to the complexity and cost of building a garden if the design involves excavation, wall building and regrading of soil. But to increase the area of usable space and for ease of maintenance, you will have no choice but to stabilise the slope with some form of terracing. If several large 'steps' or terraces are created based on the same shape they will give the impression of 'hanging gardens' when viewed from the bottom of the slope. Repeating the same shape will produce a harmonious result. The terraces do not have to be straight, they can be curved to fit with the rest of your

Planting up a steep bank is one of the easiest options in the sloping garden.

design and style of garden. Creating even a small terrace can involve moving tonnes of soil. Plan to use the soil that you remove from a slope to fill in behind a retaining wall lower down. It is expensive to dispose of soil, and with terraced houses all soil may have to be brought through the house – a tiresome d-i-y chore and an expensive element of hiring a contractor.

Low walls are cheaper to build than high walls. Because their design is less critical, it is usually a sound policy to step a series of lower walls down a hill than to build one very high wall. Walls can be indented to create sheltered areas and landings around linking steps.

Each level area can be given a different function. Ponds and water features involving standing water will require some levelling of the ground, as water does not slope. Having said this, the

LAYOUT AND HARD LANDSCAPING

Retaining structures can be made from a variety of materials in different styles and at different prices and should be chosen for strength to suit the steepness of the ground. Building a timber deck can be a very cost-effective solution and it will sit easily an informal garden. To save time and money, position patios and decks to fit the existing levels. Decking can be supported on legs to save having to create a terrace.

The solution shown in the plan overleaf uses flowing shapes. The ground slopes up from the house, so, in order to create a level patio for seating, the ground has been pushed back from the building and is retained by a low wall which does not obscure the view up towards the higher parts of the plot. Its shape reflects the second wall in that it is a looser, 'unwound' version.

A retaining wall is often necessary if you want to create a level area within sloping ground.

Cross-section of terraced garden (see plan on page 103).

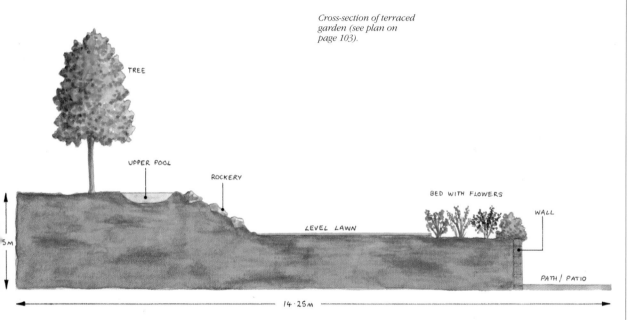

TREE

UPPER POOL

ROCKERY

BED WITH FLOWERS

WALL

LEVEL LAWN

5 M

PATH / PATIO

14·25 M

sloping garden offers more planting area in the same lateral space as a flat garden, and slopes can create microclimates that enable a wider variety of plants to be grown. They allow convincing rock and scree gardens to be incorporated because the slope ensures that a retaining or backing wall will not be required. Ramps, steps and interesting water features, including water steps, streams, falls and cascades, all become design possibilities in the sloping garden.

Because of the informality of the rest of the garden and its location, all walling is of local stone, facing concrete blocks to keep costs down. Planting holes have been incorporated into the wall, to be filled with suitable alpines. The stone matches the surface treatment of the paved area, and a gravel margin has been included between both paving and house, and the patio and retaining wall, for maximum drainage of both surfaces. It will also encourage the self-seeding and spreading of low-growing plants.

At the widest point of the patio, a colonnade of posts has been placed to give a feeling of enclosure and to allow interesting glimpses through the rope swags that hang between the posts to the rest of the garden. At the far end of the wall, a pool forms the lowest point and bottom reservoir of the water feature. A short flight of steps gives access to the main part of the garden – the first level. Steps in the garden should be less steep than indoor stairs and

Below: a small, natural-looking waterfall would be an exciting feature for a sloping garden.

should be as wide as the path leading to them. The width of the treads should provide a comfortable foothold.

The level lawn here forms the middle terrace of this garden. Mowing problems can arise where lawns abut walls – here this has been solved by including a small bed at the top of the first wall, and by providing a mowing margin or strip against the top wall. The top wall has an interesting serpentine shape that extends the area of lawn into the highest part of the garden and provides a playing area for outdoor games.

Beyond the pool on the right of the garden, the wall disappears into the slope and emerges as a rockery. To look convincing, rockeries should use as large pieces of stone as possible,

Opposite: design solution for a sloping garden. For cross-section see previous page.

arranged so that they sit into the slope, appearing to emerge from it. Through the middle of the rockery, the water course winds its way down a small cascade from the top pool, emulating a natural series of small falls. Constructing such a water feature with a header pool and bottom reservoir will entail getting the capacity of the pump just right.

A less formal flight of steps leads up to the highest part of the garden, to a shady vantage point that enjoys a view back to the water feature on the opposite side of the garden.

PLANTING

For the plant enthusiast, slopes present more planting space in the same horticultural area than a flat garden of the same size. Planting can be used as a method of preventing soil erosion on simple slopes; planting through a layer of weed-suppressing fabric mulch pegged to the ground will also help to stabilise the top layer of soil. Sloping lawns are fine, provided the gradient of the ground does not fall below one metre in every five of horizontal space. On steeper slopes mowing becomes dangerous, so use groundcover plants instead. In the plan, the lawn has been levelled for maximum recreational use.

If you are regrading soil around existing trees and large shrubs, build walls or wells around their roots to avoid damaging them. Covering the trunk around the base of a tree can kill it. For sloping garden schemes that do not require retaining structures, let beds follow the contours of the slope for a harmonious look.

Use the direction of sloping areas of planting to extend the growing season. Slopes will create microclimates as they present more soil surface to the sun or shade. So south-facing slopes will warm earlier in the spring, giving more shelter to planting and so producing earlier flowers. But beware of the damage that late frosts can inflict in such situations.

North-facing slopes will present cooler conditions. In the plan, the rockery faces south so plants there reflect these conditions, allowing a good choice of sun-loving alpines. On a north-facing slope ferns and primulas should do well. In contrast, the marginals around the lower pool face north – choose from plant varieties which thrive in such cool conditions.

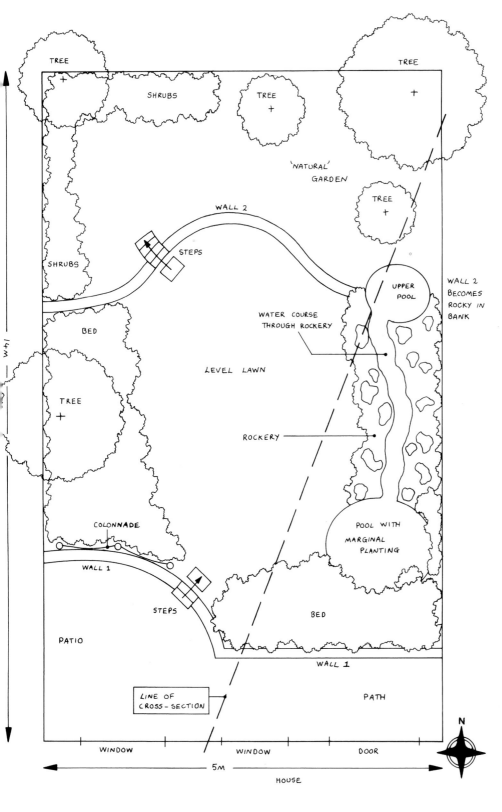

TREE

SHRUBS

TREE
+

TREE

TREE
+

'NATURAL'
GARDEN

WALL 2

TREE
+

SHRUBS

STEPS

WALL 2
BECOMES
ROCKY IN
BANK

UPPER
POOL

WATER COURSE
THROUGH ROCKERY

BED

LEVEL LAWN

TREE
+

ROCKERY

COLONNADE

POOL WITH
MARGINAL
PLANTING

WALL 1

STEPS

BED

PATIO

WALL 1

LINE OF
CROSS - SECTION

PATH

N

WINDOW

WINDOW

DOOR

5M

HOUSE

PLANTS FOR SLOPES

Cotoneaster microphyllus
(herringbone branches
bearing bright red autumn
fruit; copes with full sun)
Cotoneaster dammeri
(slightly arching habit with
glossy evergreen leaves,
good for trailing over
walls and covering slopes)
*Epimedium
perralderianum*
ivies
Lamium galeobdolon
(archangel)
Pachysandra terminalis
(leaves may yellow in full
sun; needs acid soil)
Vinca major
Vinca minor
(periwinkle)
Waldsteinia ternata
(small yellow early season
flowers)

TINY GARDENS

If your garden is very small, utilising the space efficiently should be the major priority. Taking hours, even days, to plan the position of every element will be time well spent. There will, literally, be no room for correcting such errors as getting dimensions and the scale of things wrong. Balanced proportions will be vital if you are to be successful in distracting attention from the smallness of the plot. If proportions are unbalanced it is all too easy to turn an already tiny garden into something resembling an oppressive pit. Lack of light is a common problem in tiny gardens, because they are often overshadowed by nearby buildings and trees.

A tiny garden will not have the space for division into different smaller rooms. Creating an outdoor room that maximises uncluttered floor space will be the chief consideration. The essential element of mystery will come from creating an illusion of the very small garden being much larger than it really is, and this is a key aspect of most design solutions for tiny gardens. You will have an advantage over larger garden owners, as pacing and measuring your plot will be a much faster operation. Moreover, it often works out that the more minuscule the plot, the more creative gardeners become.

HIDING BOUNDARIES

The tiny garden in our plan enjoys uniform boundary walls. Having one style of boundary treatment is a good starting point in creating a spacious feel in a small area. Views out of tiny gardens will not be of prime importance; creating plenty of interest within is. Because the house and seating area are so close to the boundaries, the scale of the boundary treatment should not be obtrusive. For example, small-gauge trellis panels will look better in the tiny garden than in other situations and can be used as a base for most of the wall surface. If you are considering fencing, small, vertical slatted panels will work better in an extremely shallow space than will larger, horizontal ones.

Your boundaries should not intrude into the rest of the space, so avoid rampant hedging. Textural contrast between the foliage of climbing plants and trellis looks good and will not compound the problem of closeness. This kind of framework to the garden will provide a harmonious backcloth to the other features and planting.

In terms of colour and style, co-ordinating your tiny garden with the room of the house that leads to it should be considered from the outset. The boundary planting in our imaginary tiny garden would include a good mix of evergreens and deciduous plants. The golden hop (*Humulus lupulus* 'Aureus') is good despite its reputation as a very vigorous grower. Its golden foliage, which will appear more lime green in shade, provides a wonderful contrast for brightening a small garden. The evergreen *Pileostegia viburnoides* could be chosen for its self-clinging qualities, keeping it close to the wall, and creamy flower heads late in the season.

Pyracantha rogersiana and Humulus lupulus *'Aureus' could both be at home in a tiny garden.*

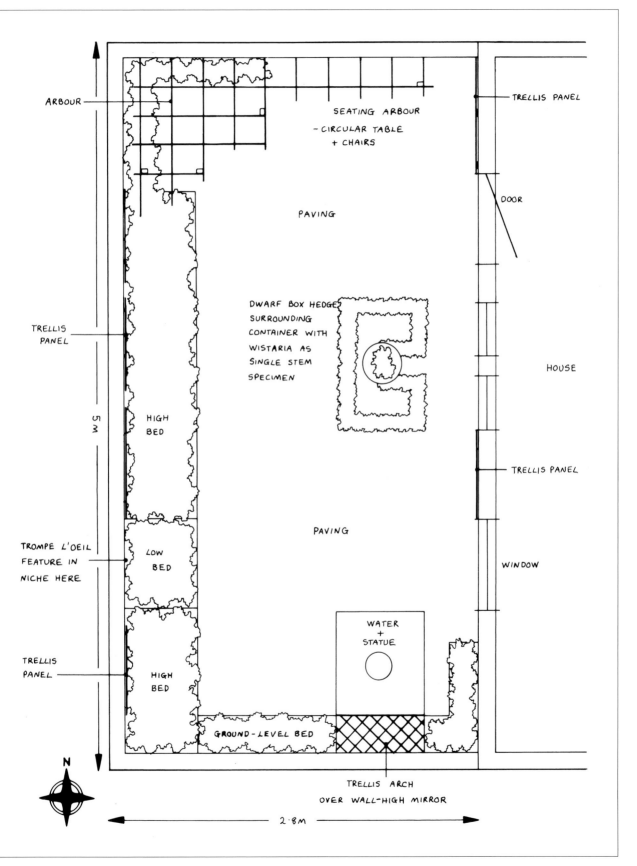

ARBOUR

SEATING ARBOUR
– CIRCULAR TABLE
+ CHAIRS

TRELLIS PANEL

DOOR

PAVING

TRELLIS
PANEL

DWARF BOX HEDGE
SURROUNDING
CONTAINER WITH
WISTARIA AS
SINGLE STEM
SPECIMEN

HOUSE

5 M

HIGH
BED

TRELLIS PANEL

TROMPE L'OEIL
FEATURE IN
NICHE HERE

LOW
BED

PAVING

WINDOW

TRELLIS
PANEL

HIGH
BED

WATER
+
STATUE

GROUND-LEVEL BED

N

TRELLIS ARCH
OVER WALL-HIGH MIRROR

2.8M

These would appear at the same time as the red berries on *Pyracantha rogersiana* for good autumn colours. A pyracantha could be trained flat against a wall in the same manner as an espaliered fruit tree. Good evergreen texture could be provided by *Hedera helix* 'Parsley Crested' with crimped edges to its leaves. Restricting the number of different plants will lead to a more harmonious composition. One or two points of incidental interest might be included on the boundary in the form of flowering climbers such as clematis – choose varieties that flower at different times of the year.

PAVING versus LAWN

A very small lawn serves no recreational purpose, and if you have problems such as overhanging trees and shade from surrounding

If you plan to use a tiny garden for eating out and already have a table, make sure you have enough space to pull chairs out around the table in comfort before deciding where to include beds for planting.

RAISED BEDS AND DIFFERENT LEVELS

To achieve maximum use from a tiny space, exclude large borders. For the same reason, avoid cluttering up the seating and eating area with containers. But maintaining coherence need not mean flat-looking planting effects. Making use of raised beds, even in a limited way, creates an interesting tiered effect and brings impact to every part of the available space.

If your tiny plot has a change in level requiring steps, make these wide enough for the edges to

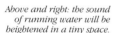

Above and right: the sound of running water will be heightened in a tiny space.

walls, there is even less point in persisting with a swathe of grass. For our plan, the decision has been made to pave the whole area on the basis that using just one surface treatment will help to maximise the feeling of space. If space and the arrangement of the garden allow, you could vary the texture of the paving by the way in which it is laid. For example, reconstituted stone slabs in honey tones could be random-laid and edged with creamy yellow bricks. Courses of the same bricks could also be laid to give detail to different areas of paving.

be used as a home for large containers with eye-catching plants, or include tiered flat sills to the side of steps wide enough to take large containers. Having a tiny garden does not mean that all the planting should be scaled down. Maintain the impact of plants by using containers large enough to grow plants to mature specimens, as you will invariably need to increase growing opportunity space.

Raised beds need not be restricted to gardens with changes in level. Used correctly in the tiny

USING MIRRORS AND TROMPE L'OEIL

garden, they can add tremendously to planting space and help to create different levels of surfaces and plants. In the imaginary garden, extra height is achieved through raised beds of varying levels along one wall. If possible, design raised beds to provide a seat – dual-purpose items are very valuable in small gardens. A height of 45cm with a seat of about the same depth will provide a useful place to rest and enjoy a different view of the garden. Similarly, raised water features can be included in the tiny garden.

Enhancing light and space in the tiny garden can be achieved by making use of mirrors and *trompe-l'oeil* effects. Mirrors can be used to reflect light and internal views giving an illusion of space. In our plan of a tiny garden a mirror has been included in a trellis arch that is the same height as the boundary wall behind. The mirror rests on the ground and immediately in front of it is the water feature, a rectangular pool sunk into the ground with a statue on a plinth in the middle. Small jets of

Look very carefully at this garden to find a plant that takes up no space at all!

water spurt from the sides, bringing the relaxing sound of running water to the tiny courtyard. The pool is the same width as the trellis archway behind.

Placing the mirror directly behind the pool increases the pool's apparent size and creates the illusion that the garden continues through to the other side of the arch. Such effects will be enjoyed from inside the house if the mirror is placed opposite a ground-floor window. From the viewpoint shown on the plan, people will enjoy the effect from the seating and eating area at the other end of the garden. Mirrors used in

MAKING THE MOST OF VERTICAL HEIGHT

Some of the problems with creating height in a tiny space have already been hinted at with regard to boundaries. In addition, it is not advisable to plant a tree closer to a building than the distance of the tree's ultimate height at maturity. Use the walls of the house or boundary as a place to grow climbers. If window locations do not make this a viable option, you could try attaching trellis to the wall and leaving it unplanted. In our plan of a tiny garden, planting against the long side of the house wall is not feasible, so trellis panels have been used. Climbers planted elsewhere can be encouraged

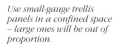

Use small-gauge trellis panels in a confined space – large ones will be out of proportion.

the garden must be heavy-duty and suitable for outdoor use. This can be achieved by coating the back of a standard mirror with several layers of red oxide bitumastic paint. For extra protection and hard wearing, the edges should be covered with waterproof tape, especially where they are close to water.

Trompe l'oeil features are designed deliberately to deceive the eye. In our tiny garden, a niche in the wall opposite a window has been framed with trellis painted with taller plants and trees, to give the effect of a garden beyond a hole in the wall extending into the distance. Trellis panels of the same size have been repeated along the wall, each one creating a false perspective. These panels are intended to be left almost completely visible and not obscured by plants. Simple *trompe l'oeil* effects can also be created, should you be artistically inclined, by painting shadows of plants on pale walls to give the illusion of perpetual sunshine and dappled shade.

to cross to an adjacent wall via wires stretched between vine eyes.

Raised beds will also go some way to creating vertical interest. In the imaginary garden, a seating alcove has been created by making an arbour that is supported by a boundary wall. This widens out as it approaches the corner to give a shady corner, support for climbing plants, and vertical interest. The timber structure is painted the same colour as the trelliswork, a grey-blue colour that harmonises well with plants and contrasts with the yellow brick details.

Extend planting in a tiny garden with hanging baskets, wall-mounted containers and window boxes beneath first-floor windows, all of which add to the effect of planting tiers and heights. Maintenance will increase as more containers are added, but an opportunity to utilise every available growing space should not be passed up in the tiny garden, and you won't have far to walk with the watering can.

Opposite: use mirrors in a tiny garden to lighten shady corners and create the illusion of space.

WILDLIFE GARDENS

Above: red admiral feeding on Sedum spectabile.

Right: wildflower garden.

The key features of a wildlife garden are lack of geometric shapes (invisible edges), longer grass than normal and a mix of planting that reflects the natural habitat of wildlife: it is not a style for the fastidious gardener to adopt. This is not to say that wildlife gardens are not carefully planned – they are, but the aim is to make the garden look as 'natural' as possible, rather than like a series of defined borders and areas. Establishing an ecological balance is a major part of wildlife gardening, and organic methods of weed and pest control will form a part of this approach.

Use a discreet controlling hand in the initial layout and aftercare of a wildlife garden to ensure that it is pleasing to the eye and not just a patch of rampant weeds. A simple, informal layout, coupled with a structure to the planting may seem stark on plan, but once the garden is planted up it will feel natural. The underlying structure will be heavily blurred by planting. Essentials for a wildlife garden are a pond, native plants and varieties that produce nectar, seeds and berries, and nooks and crannies for wildlife.

HARD LANDSCAPING

Suitable boundary treatments for a wildlife garden include natural organic materials such as wattle fencing, reed panels and willow or hazel hurdles. Space permitting, heavy planting of tallish trees and shrubs that can be 'coppiced' or left as a wild hedgerow are a good choice. Plants such as blackthorn, buckthorn, crab apple, dog rose, field maple, guelder rose, hawthorn, hazel, wayfaring tree and wild privet all provide homes and food for birds and a wide range of insects.

For paved areas and paths, use natural stone, or natural-coloured reconstituted slabs. Lay with open unmortared joints and sow the space with grass or low-growing wild plants that tolerate being walked on. Create paths through areas of long grass by mowing them as often as short grass is mown and use log rounds as stepping stones set flush with the ground for extra definition. Timber decking can bridge the gap between a wildlife pond and a bog garden.

If you want to include arches and pergolas, use treated timber with a natural rustic finish and

TREES FOR SMALL WILDLIFE GARDENS

● Silver birches grow quickly – try *Betula tristis* for a slim form, *Betula jacquemontii* for extra white peeling bark. Cut trees back to around 45cm from ground level every three or four years to achieve the look of a coppiced woodland and stop them getting too big.

● Willows are useful for damp soil, but use *dwarf* varieties only.

● Alder is good for damp soil.

● The mature height of limes is very tall but they can be cut back or pollarded each spring.

● Rowan can be kept pruned as a bush.

no added colour. More temporary supports for plants can be made from offcuts and prunings of larger shrubs and trees, bound together with neutral-coloured twine.

ABODES FOR WILDLIFE

Every surface in your garden can provide a habitat, either existing or potential, for different forms of wildlife. House and boundary walls, for example, will be used by birds, small mammals and insects if you let them. As the age of the structure increases, so

do the crevices and cracks and the diversity of animals. You can give nature a helping hand, though – particularly if the thought of so much wildlife in the very walls of your house is alarming and potentially ruinous. Bats and birds, in particular, can be provided with proper nesting boxes away from the eaves of the roof and out of the reach of natural predators such as cats. Place the box on any wall other than a south-facing one, as these often become too hot. Hedgehogs will be attracted to log piles and debris.

PLANTING

Generally, native plants support more forms of wildlife than introduced plants, even compared with some that have been here for a long time. You may want to include plants native to your area of the country as an aid to their conservation, but remember that digging up plants in the wild is against the law, so grow from seed or buy plants.

There are two ways to propagate a wildflower meadow, depending on whether you are starting from scratch or on an existing lawn. To sow a meadow, you first need to create a weed-free seedbed. On no account apply fertilisers – many native plants are adapted to a particular type of soil and so will not thrive with additives. Buy a mixture of wildflower and grass seeds. Include about 20 species of wildflowers, concentrating on either spring or summer flowers to maximise the effect. Grasses can be either fine lawn grasses (such as fescues and bents) or wild meadow grasses (such as meadow foxtail and meadow barley). Avoid perennial ryegrass as it will grow too well at the expense of the flowers. Spring meadows can be cut down in July once most of the flowers have seeded, and kept short for the rest of the year. Summer meadows should not be cut until autumn.

To let an existing lawn go wild, reduce its fertility by letting grass grow to about 8cm and cutting it short, removing all the clippings. It may take up to two years of this treatment if you have regularly fed the lawn in the past. A number of wildflowers will then grow naturally, though invasive species should be controlled by spot weeding. The best way to introduce new ones is to raise them in a seedbed and transplant into the meadow. Sowing direct into grass is unlikely to give good results.

PLANTS FOR BEES AND BUTTERFLIES

Winter/spring
Alyssum saxatile (gold dust)
Aubrieta deltoidea (rock cress)
Chaenomeles speciosa (ornamental quince)
Doronicum (leopard's bane)
Erysimum (perennial wallflower)
Hesperis matronalis (sweet rocket)
Muscari (grape hyacinth)
Myosotis (forget-me-not)
Ribes sanguineum (flowering currant)
Salix caprea (pussy willow)
Vinca minor (periwinkle)

Summer
Buddleia alternifolia (fountain buddleia)
Dianthus barbatus (sweet william)
Hebe
Iberis sempervirens (perennial candytuft)
Lobelia
Scabiosa atropurpurea (sweet scabious)
Tagetes (African, French marigold)
Thymus vulgaris (thyme – common form)
Valeriana officinalis (valerian)

Autumn
Aster (Michaelmas daisy)
Buddleia davidii (butterfly bush)
Calluna (summer/autumn heathers)
Ceratostigma wilmottianum (plumbago)
Colchicum autumnale (autumn-flowering crocus)
Crocus nudiflorus (autumn crocus)
Hyssopus officinalis (hyssop)
Lavandula angustifolia (lavender)
Lythrum (purple loosestrife)
Monarda didyma (bee balm; bergamot)
Origanum vulgare (wild marjoram)
Phuopsis stylosa
Sedum spectabile (iceplant)
Verbena bonariensis

Preserve any existing native trees if at all possible, otherwise choose small-growing varieties for new ones. Flowers, foliage and fruit will provide food for bees, birds, ladybirds and other helpful creatures. Native plants that have the added bonus of attracting birds include hawthorn, ivy, holly, alder buckthorn, spindle and guelder rose. Six good shrubs for birds are *Berberis darwinii*, *Cotoneaster cornubia*, privet, *Mahonia aquifolium*, *Pyracantha* and *Rosa glauca*. Plant shrubs and herbaceous plants to attract butterflies and bees to the

Below: frogs will always be welcome in the wildlife garden.

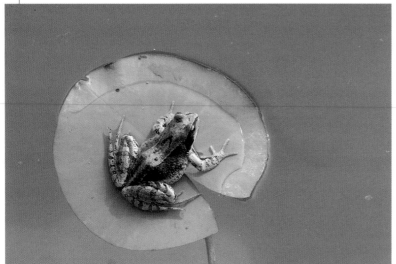

garden (see box on page 111). You could even consider planting a clump of nettles in a sunny spot to attract butterfly larvae – nettles are one of their major sources of food. Planting wall shrubs and climbing plants provides fairly instant cover for newer walls, and this in turn gives shelter; include some native plants in your wall planting.

WILDLIFE PONDS AND BOG GARDENS

It is important for the wildlife pond to provide access and hiding spaces for frogs and other amphibians – create a gently sloping edge. Without assistance, insects will soon arrive to colonise water – damselfly nymph, back-swimmer and great diving beetle, for instance. Mayflies, caddis flies, gnats and midges will spend their early lives in the water and take off later. A bog garden is an area of ground that is always moist and so supports plants that demand moisture the whole time. For details on how to make these water features, see pages 170-72.

Above: little owls like this one might visit a natural-looking garden.

Left: this woodland garden planted with ferns and perennials is teeming with tiny creatures.

MAPPING OUT YOUR PLANS

For any major garden work, and particularly if hard landscaping is involved, you will need to make a plan, which involves measuring and drawing a map of your garden. It is easy to move features around on paper, re-positioning greenhouses, sheds and pergolas at will. Doing so is an essential part of the design process, and having a scale drawing will enable you to order the correct amount of materials when you or your contractor are ready to start work.

MEASURING UP

If you have a newly built house, there may be a site plan or scale drawing of your house and its plot, a copy of which will be a suitable base for drawing your design. Similarly, if an extension to your house has been carried out recently, a copy of the plan submitted for local authority approval may exist. If you have plans, check them for accuracy by taking a few measurements on the ground and comparing them. If you do not have a plan, create one of your own using the tried and tested methods described in this chapter.

Start by making a rough sketch of your garden and house so you can record measurements as you take them (see opposite). You need to include on your sketch any immovable objects such as buildings, trees, and the locations of overhead and underground utilities. Use the longest tape measure you can buy. Check the aspect of your plot with a compass and mark magnetic north clearly.

Many gardens are irregular in shape, so it is often best to start by measuring the outside walls of the house to use as a baseline and locating the boundaries from this. Lay the tape along the walls and note on your sketch the running measurements of windows, doors, drains, ventilation points and other permanent features. Taking running measurements is more accurate than re-measuring from point to point. Note the level of the damp-proof course if you are thinking of changing the level of the ground near the house, as this must not be bridged. If your house is detached you need to locate it within the boundaries by 'sighting off', as described. Push in pegs, canes or skewers to establish corners where necessary – for instance beneath a hedge where you judge the corner of a boundary to be or if you are intending to take out a fence – and measure from marker to marker. Where boundaries are curved or irregular in any way, use the methods described to plot them accurately.

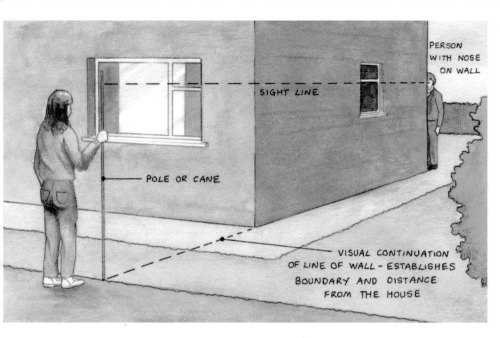

Left: sighting off.

SIGHT LINE

PERSON WITH NOSE ON WALL

POLE OR CANE

VISUAL CONTINUATION OF LINE OF WALL - ESTABLISHES BOUNDARY AND DISTANCE FROM THE HOUSE

If you intend to use an existing plan as your base, check the accuracy of any topographical detail. You need to measure the height of walls, fences, steps, slopes and so on. For mature trees, measure the girth of the trunk at ground level and also from the trunk to the extent of the canopy of its branches. Estimate the height of the tree and name it on your sketch; if it is a young tree you should find out how much more it will grow. When you come to draw up your scale plan you will want to indicate the extent of the shade cast by trees and other permanent features on the surrounding ground throughout the day. Inspect any area of the garden with a drainage problem, which at the least may affect the positioning of a water feature, and estimate the extent of the problem by digging a trial hole.

SIGHTING OFF

If your house is detached and therefore one or more of the boundaries do not connect with it, you need to establish a straight baseline from which to plot boundaries and other points in the garden. Stand behind a corner of the back wall of your house and look down the length of it so that the edge of the wall is only just visible as a fine line. You will need to press your nose right against the wall to do this! Looking down the wall to the boundary beyond, ask your helper to mark that point. This should be perpendicular to the house and you can take measurements from any point along this line to the far boundary and other points.

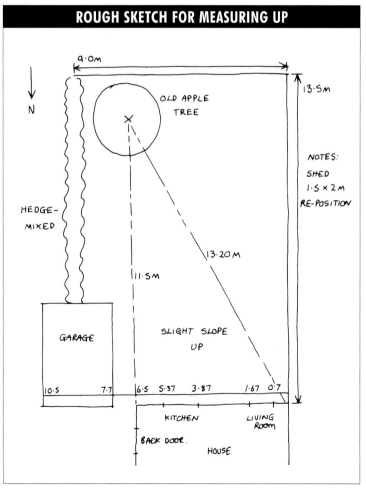

ROUGH SKETCH FOR MEASURING UP

9·0M

13·5M

N

OLD APPLE TREE

NOTES:
SHED
1·5 × 2M
RE-POSITION

HEDGE-MIXED

13·20M

11·5M

GARAGE

SLIGHT SLOPE UP

10·5   7·7   6·5 5·37   3·87   1·67 0·7

KITCHEN   LIVING ROOM

BACK DOOR.

HOUSE

Near right: triangulation.

Far right: measuring a curve.

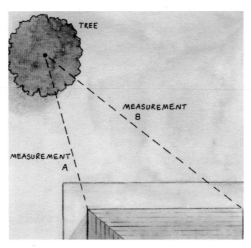

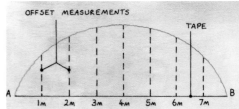

the edge of the curve at right angles, taking the measurements at regular intervals – say one metre or less. These are known as offset measurements. When you draw up to scale, these offset measurements can be easily plotted and joined to form the shape of a curve. The process is reversed when it comes to marking out curves on the ground for a new garden layout.

TRIANGULATION

Use triangulation for plotting features within the boundaries of the garden such as trees. Measure from two known points – two corners of your house, for instance – to the tree. Draw in the lines you have measured, mark in the measurements and the tree itself. When you draw up to scale, use geometry compasses. Set them to the first measurement, put the point on the relevant corner of the house in the drawing and draw a short arc. Repeat with the second measurement. Plot the correct position of the tree by marking with an 'x' where the two arcs intersect.

MEASURING CURVES

Use the following method for ponds, curved beds and walls or boundaries that will not be changing. Plot the two ends of the curve using triangulation methods. Mark on your rough drawing and take two pegs or canes and peg the tape along the straight line between these two points. Using a long metal rule or a cane with metres marked, measure from the tape to

MEASURING SLOPES

Note on your sketch any noticeable changes of level. To measure a slope you will need a stake or peg, a board (one marked in centimetres will help) and a spirit level. Put a peg in the ground at the top of the slope. Butt the board against it horizontally, checking with the spirit level, and measure the distance from the bottom of the board vertically down to the slope. Note the two measurements A – the point on the board (horizontal) – and B – the height above ground. Work down the slope noting both measurements in two columns. Add all the A figures together and then all the B figures to give the overall slope (for example, 1:5 would be one metre vertical drop to five metres horizontal distance. Very steep gardens or difficult slopes may require either a professional surveyor or the hiring of surveying equipment.

Right: measuring a slope.

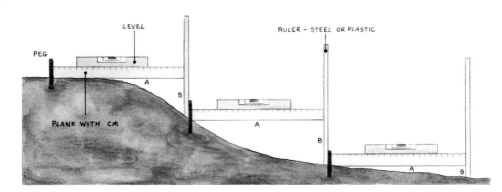

WORKING TO SCALE

DRAWING A SURVEY PLAN

Tape a large sheet of graph paper to a flat surface such as a tray. Looking at your measurements of the overall dimensions of the plot, choose an appropriate scale that allows you to fit the whole of the garden on to the sheet. Work to as large a scale as possible – 1:50cm is generally most suitable for small gardens. Using a scale ruler (from special stationers) will save you having to do calculations and count squares on the graph paper. Draw in the outline of the house at the bottom of the sheet and then mark in the boundaries at the correct angle. Mark north by drawing an arrow at the top of the sheet. Plot all the other measured points and immovable features on to the graph paper, using compasses if necessary. Do not include anything that can be changed or moved at this stage.

Gradients can be depicted on the plan if you refer to the vertical and horizontal figures that you measured with the spirit level and plank in the garden and plot these as contour lines. You can make the measurements more meaningful by relating them to a known fixed point close to the house, such as a manhole cover or a paving slab. This point is properly referred to as 'datum' and marked on plans with the figure 0.00 alongside. Vertical measurements can then be marked with a plus or minus sign on the plan to indicate a slope going up or down relative to datum.

To complete your survey plan, mark in your garden's good and bad points. These include prevailing winds, lovely views out, areas you will want to screen for privacy, eyesores, noisy places, patches of weeds, frost pockets, access points, early evening sun, condition of soil – everything relevant to creating your ideal garden. Looking at the north point, draw in areas shaded at a certain time of the day by tall structures – walls, trees, buildings. Shade is an important factor for making decisions about plants and seating areas. Although the height of the sun varies with the seasons, and it may be difficult to work out the changing patterns of light and shade for the whole year, marking it up for a particular time of day will still be useful when it comes to positioning various features. Hatch in the areas with closely drawn pencil lines.

All factors – both the positive and the negative – will have to be considered during the planning of a new design. In particular, microclimates (see pages 40-2) may affect your siting of a patio and will definitely influence your planting choices. Neither your plants nor you will flourish in a wind tunnel, for example, and you would not want to waste time and effort siting a herb or Mediterranean garden in a frost pocket.

When you have finished this basic plan you can ink over the pencil with a fine felt-tip pen. It is then worth making a few copies so you can use them to try out different ideas.

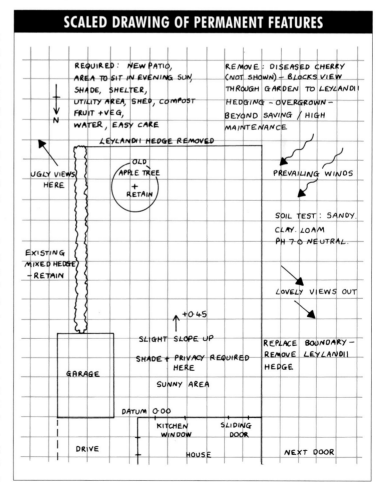

SCALED DRAWING OF PERMANENT FEATURES

REQUIRED : NEW PATIO, AREA TO SIT IN EVENING SUN, SHADE, SHELTER, UTILITY AREA, SHED, COMPOST FRUIT +VEG, WATER, EASY CARE

REMOVE : DISEASED CHERRY (NOT SHOWN) – BLOCKS VIEW THROUGH GARDEN TO LEYLANDII HEDGING – OVERGROWN – BEYOND SAVING / HIGH MAINTENANCE

LEYLANDII HEDGE REMOVED

N

UGLY VIEWS HERE

OLD APPLE TREE + RETAIN

PREVAILING WINDS

SOIL TEST : SANDY. CLAY. LOAM PH 7·0 NEUTRAL.

EXISTING MIXED HEDGE – RETAIN

LOVELY VIEWS OUT

+0·45

SLIGHT SLOPE UP

SHADE + PRIVACY REQUIRED HERE

SUNNY AREA

REPLACE BOUNDARY – REMOVE LEYLANDII HEDGE

GARAGE

DATUM 0·00

KITCHEN WINDOW

SLIDING DOOR

DRIVE

HOUSE

NEXT DOOR

FITTING IN FEATURES

You can now begin to experiment with new features on plan. Tape some tracing paper over the scale drawing of the permanent parts of your garden. Look at the list of all the things you want in your garden. If you have lots of features that you want to include experiment with them in order of priority so you can make fast decisions if you realise that you do not have enough space to fit them all in. Draw freehand circles or 'bubbles' (see diagram below) on the tracing paper and mark them with names indicating what you might do in those spaces. Fill the whole garden by making the bubbles almost touch and do not think in too much detail at this stage. Work out different ideas and designs on individual sheets of tracing paper and modify them until you arrive at what you want. You may want to colour code your bubbles according to type – red for functional, green for recreational, yellow for access, for example.

Right: use colouring pencils and coloured card to make small images of the features you want to fit into your garden.

As you progress and start to refine your bubbles, cut shapes out of thick coloured paper to represent areas with a specific function – lawns, patios, sheds – and realistic dimensions, which can be moved around the plan. Use double-sided tape for keeping them in position, or double-over masking tape which can be peeled off easily.

Identify areas of planting on your drawings in terms of function – structural, backbone, screens of whatever height, specimen or focal point. Label them simply as such without going into the detail of type and variety at this stage. Use the squares of the underlying graph paper as a quick reference for comparing relative sizes and spaces. Getting the scale of things right is a critical factor of the design process. Sizing lawns and borders correctly will save time and effort later on.

You may see shapes emerging on your drawing as you try to link different areas together. Sketch the position of paths that might take a person from area to area but do not think about the exact lines of paths at this stage. Think instead about the shapes that features make together and design out any awkward corners at this stage of the process. By keeping shapes on the ground simple you are more likely to get pleasing results. Keep areas in proportion to each other – the aim is to arrive at a harmonious design that looks balanced. As you work up to a more detailed design you may find inspiration coming from many different sources – other gardens or parts of them, paintings, forms found in nature. For example, you may already have some paving with a particular

BUBBLE EXPERIMENTS ON TOP OF SCALED DRAWING

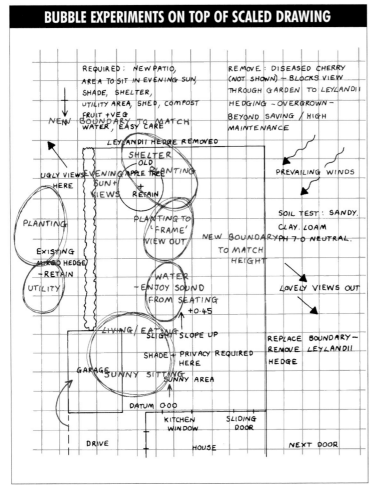

motif, or the shape of your plot and its contours may suggest using one shape over another.

THINKING IN THREE DIMENSIONS

A useful way to visualise how your plans will look is to enlarge some photographs of particular areas of your garden, lay tracing paper over them and sketch on your ideas. This is particularly useful if you are contemplating removing large trees, building tall structures or making other significant alterations. Include people in your photographs to relate your plans to a human scale. You may want to do this with alternative designs before making your final decision. If photographs are not to hand, you can draw simple elevations of parts of the garden, to scale if possible.

Cross-section details through parts of your garden where there are changes of level – ponds, retaining walls, the whole length of the garden if it slopes – will give you an insight not possible with photographs. If you draw all the vertical objects beyond the line of the cut through a section the result will be a realistic 'slice' of terrain. On pages 101 and 120 are examples of cross-sections.

A simple scale model of your garden can be one of the best design tools. There is no need for this to be elaborate. For instance, use a cutaway cardboard box to imitate the walls of the house and boundary heights on three sides. Try drawing patios and lawns at ground level on to the box and use small cardboard shapes to give an accurate indication of relative heights of structures and the space that is shaped by them. If children's toy models of trees and so on are to hand, use them, or perhaps adapt the techniques used by paper models of the theatre, cutting out pictures of plants and trellises to scale and sliding them around. Two model-making ideas are illustrated on pages 121-2.

A three-dimensional model allows you to view the results of your plans in a way not possible with a flat scale drawing. For instance, consider how much time you spend looking out over the garden from the inside of your house – possibly far more time than is spent actually being in the garden. By working with some kind of three-dimensional model of your garden, you should be able to simulate the viewing points from the windows of your house (see page 121). This is especially useful if you are trying to hide an

SOME USEFUL MEASUREMENTS

● Patio – an average-size table and four chairs for sitting and eating will need a minimum area of 3.6x3.6m.

● Sunlounger – takes up 2x1.2m, plus 1m access to front and 40cm clearance behind.

● Paths – main paths should be 1m minimum width; 1.5m allows two people to walk abreast between planted areas. Other paths can be 60cm.

● Steps – risers should be of uniform height, about 15cm each for an easy climb. Treads should be 30cm minimum, 45cm for a generous width. Provide a landing/resting space every sixth step if flights are steep.

● Built-in seats – 45cm high will be comfortable for most people.

● Barbecues and worktops – 75-85cm high is a good average.

● Pergolas and arches – minimum height 2m, more if planting large plants such as wistaria. Keep posts 45cm from edge of path.

eyesore and are not sure if some shrub planting, say, will eventually be tall enough to obscure the eyesore from your living-room window.

Return to the garden and pace out the changes you are planning, sit where the patio will be and envisage the finished scene. If you are planning on planting trees, this is a good opportunity to gauge their growth and how your garden will look in 5, 10 or perhaps even 25 years from now. Mark out your designs on the ground by measuring off areas exactly as they are on your plan. Circular shapes can be formed by using a peg as the central point of a circle. String attached to this and another peg describe the radius of partial or complete circles. Using canes and hosepipes you can indicate the edges of patios, mark the heights of fences, retaining walls and planting. Hook binliners over sticks and stuff them with newspaper to simulate the bulk of planting after a few years of growth. Paths and lawns can be marked out with sand, and border shapes lined with canes joined with coloured string or wool so they can be seen at a distance. Walk around your new 'virtual' garden and view it from the house, including from upstairs windows. You will feel better prepared to make decisions after visualising your plans in such a way.

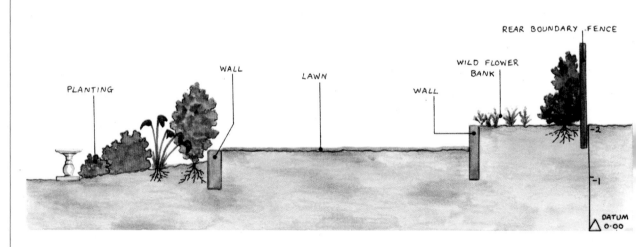

Simple cross-sections of different parts of your garden will give you a clear idea of the relative heights of different features. Include areas of hard landscaping and planting.

If you have a sloping garden, measure gradients from a known, fixed point and mark this on your plan as 'datum' (see page 117). This will help you to map out your plans accurately.

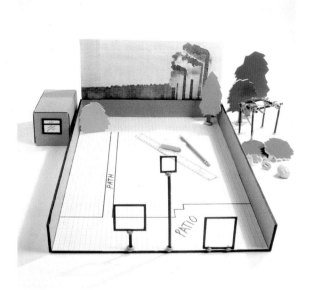

In this model, the three frames in the foreground represent the views from (left to right) the kitchen window, bedroom window and patio doors.

The utilitarian wall of a neighbour's garage can be seen from the kitchen window. Look through the model window while you experiment with different features.

In this position, the tree blots out the view of the garage.

Here, a pergola has been sited in front of the patio doors, effectively framing the view to the end of the garden, where a tree has been positioned to obscure the sight of factory chimneys in the distance.

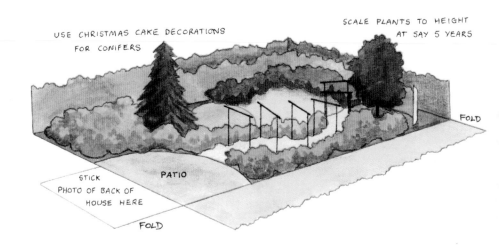

USE CHRISTMAS CAKE DECORATIONS
FOR CONIFERS

SCALE PLANTS TO HEIGHT
AT SAY 5 YEARS

FOLD

STICK
PHOTO OF BACK OF
HOUSE HERE

PATIO

FOLD

The more attractive your model is, the more inspired you will be to put the plan into practice. An excellent scale model of your garden can be made if you take a copy of your plan and stick it to a piece of large card. Draw in the boundaries on the card, score along the sides and fold up. Then experiment with features using small toys, coloured cotton wool for planting, cocktail sticks for timber structures etc. A touch of realism can be added if you stick a photograph of the back of your house on the rear wall of the model.

HIRING A DESIGNER

There are three types: landscape architects, garden designers and landscape contractors. Mail-order services are also available.

Landscape architects usually work on large private and public schemes but some deal with private garden owners. Garden designers usually specialise in private gardens and so are a more obvious choice for the small garden owner. Some work on a referral basis in conjunction with large garden centres and landscaping companies. Many have a consultation service too. A fee is usually charged for consultation, but you will be able to look through a portfolio and gain an idea of a designer's style, methods of working and scale of charges.

Both landscape architects and garden designers will undertake a survey of your garden and draw up a design, working from a list of your needs and wishes. They can also draw up planting plans for all or part of the garden and advise on local contractors for the work.

For garden design by mail, you will have to take measurements of your garden, listing the permanent items and submitting these with photographs. A final design and planting plans are returned to you within a given timespan. This is cheaper than hiring a designer because there are no site visits.

Landscape contractors normally concentrate on the actual building work in the garden, but some also offer a design service costs being waived if you go ahead with the work. Good contractors will discuss materials and provide samples for your inspection. Sometimes they have portfolios of completed work and lists of satisfied customers to consult. Beware the contractor who makes drawings on the back of an envelope.

Ask friends for recommendations if you are thinking of hiring a professional. If you have a particularly difficult, sloping site, doing so should save time and money and ensure safe and sound results.

AVOIDING COSTLY MISTAKES

Failing to make a scaled plan of your garden when you want to alter it can result in a lot of extra hard work, heartache and added expense if you discover after the event that you have not allowed enough space for a path or have bought the wrong size of shed, and so on. Throughout the design process you should, of course, remember the budget you have set aside to realise the project (see 'How Much Money?', pages 8-17). It can be argued that gardening or landscaping are evolutionary, and a garden never really gets finished, but, even so, common mistakes include over-ambition in relation to available time and money and starting work on features here and there without a clear vision of the whole. Nothing is more demoralising than an unfinished garden project. If your list of features to fit in is too long, and the design looks cluttered on the plan, chances are that it will not transfer successfully into your garden. Keeping things simple is more likely to produce pleasing results.

Utility features should be placed for ease of use. If you want electricity in a shed, plan for it to be near a mains supply to keep installation costs down. A greenhouse should not be over-shadowed by trees or buildings. Site a compost bin in a dry, sheltered, partially shaded spot. For your own convenience, make sure there is sufficient room alongside to park a wheelbarrow. Position a barbecue – either a built-in one or space for a movable gas type – near to the kitchen, to avoid lengthy treks with trays and dishes. Again, with limited space, it makes sense to put all utility features – compost bin, shed or greenhouse, clothes-drying equipment, coal or log store – in one place, making them easier to screen.

Consider the lifespan of materials that you plan to utilise in the garden. A well-constructed patio or path will last a lifetime, if need be. Assess the effects of weathering on different materials in five, ten years and beyond. Think about future needs, including the saleability of a scheme. It can detract from the value of your house if too much garden space is occupied by features such as conservatories or sheds in town gardens.

Before finalising your plan, test it out on the ground – for instance, wheeling a barrow along a main access path – and weigh up the reactions of everyone who is going to use your garden. Double-check critical measurements, particularly of permanent features.

THE FINAL PLAN

Having condensed and rejected ideas as you progressed with sketching or making models of different designs and checked that your ideas are feasible in terms of cost, construction and maintenance, you will eventually be in the position to draw up a final detailed master plan.

Working with the scale drawing of your garden as it is now, tape a fresh piece of tracing paper over the top and draw your preferred design to scale and in detail. Check the dimensions of key elements with the suggested minimums in the box. Some refinement and fine-tuning of shapes inevitably occur at this stage. Your design may look very stark on plan – curves will look sharper and flatter than they will on the ground. The visualisation tips given earlier should reassure you, but remember that once your design is planted up many of the hard edges will be softened.

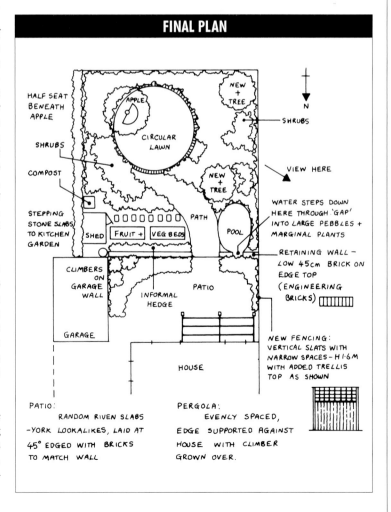

FINAL PLAN

HALF SEAT BENEATH APPLE

APPLE

CIRCULAR LAWN

SHRUBS

COMPOST

STEPPING STONE SLABS TO KITCHEN GARDEN

SHED

FRUIT + VEG BEDS

PATH

CLIMBERS ON GARAGE WALL

INFORMAL HEDGE

PATIO

GARAGE

NEW + TREE

SHRUBS

VIEW HERE

NEW + TREE

POOL

WATER STEPS DOWN HERE THROUGH 'GAP' INTO LARGE PEBBLES + MARGINAL PLANTS

RETAINING WALL – LOW 45cm BRICK ON EDGE TOP (ENGINEERING BRICKS)

HOUSE

NEW FENCING: VERTICAL SLATS WITH NARROW SPACES – H 1·6M WITH ADDED TRELLIS TOP AS SHOWN

PATIO: RANDOM RIVEN SLABS –YORK LOOKALIKES, LAID AT 45° EDGED WITH BRICKS TO MATCH WALL

PERGOLA: EVENLY SPACED, EDGE SUPPORTED AGAINST HOUSE WITH CLIMBER GROWN OVER.

N

GETTING STARTED

Armed with your final plan, you are in a position to start the work. Decide on a feasible timescale for your project, and arrange suppliers and contractors according to it. You need to transfer the outline of your plan on to the ground and prepare the site thoroughly before you start installing individual features. If you are intending to move large quantities of earth, you will need to hire specialist equipment.

MAKING A SCHEDULE

COSTING THE FINAL PLAN

You will be able to work out detailed costings for the project once you have completed your final plan (for a general guide to costs, see pages 8-17). If you intend to hire landscape contractors, it is a good idea to give them a copy of your plan so you can get an itemised quote. Make sure that you include labour costs, hire charges and prices of all materials with your own calculations.

If you need to cut costs and the plan involves considerable labour charges, you may be tempted to do the work yourself. Remember that some work may be beyond your capabilities and should be undertaken by a professional contractor for safety reasons. Installation of an outdoor electricity supply and building retaining walls to hold back steep slopes are two items where money savings could jeopardise safety. Identifying what can be done, and when, may be a better approach.

For instance, work such as excavation is more cost-effective when tackled in one go, rather than having the expense of hiring equipment and/or labour several times. Having the same features but buying cheaper materials will obviously help matters. It can pay to shop around for materials, too.

TIMESCALE

An appropriate timescale for work could be expressed in weeks, weekends, months, years or growing seasons, depending on the scale of the works and what you are doing yourself. Our 'typical' work schedule is set out intensively over three weeks (see overleaf).

If the project is to be a long-term one it makes sense to devise a 'waiting' list. For this, identify the features that the garden users need now to get maximum enjoyment and use from the garden, and what can be put on hold until circumstances change. A natural priority may establish itself in some circumstances. For example, space for children to play and a level seating area might be most important. A front garden may need to be sorted out first if it causes access problems.

If you plan to do most of the work yourself, perhaps concentrate on one area at a time and let the enjoyment of finishing each area spur you on to complete the project. It may make sense to start on the area closest to the house because this is seen the most, but remember work further into the garden may require heavy machinery.

The time of year may also help you decide on a schedule of works. Major planting is best carried out in early spring or autumn. Construction can be done at any time, but major excavation will be better carried out in reasonable weather conditions. Heavy machinery will compact any soil during frosty spells in winter and can create problems on clay soils in extreme wet weather.

CONTRACTORS AND SUPPLIERS

If you plan to use a contractor for all or part of the project, establish exactly what work the quote covers and whether it is a fixed price or an estimate of costs. If the work is to be divided between yourself and a contractor, decide who is responsible for each part of the work at the outset. Contractors vary in how they present bills, periods of credit and payment stages, so these should be established before the work starts. It is standard practice for a percentage of the total bill to be held back until the satisfactory completion of the work – that is, to your satisfaction. This may include ground being made good and prepared for planting, all structures being built and all excess materials removed from site. Having a basic specification for the work, which can be drawn up from your plan, may be helpful.

If you are responsible for ordering materials you will need to establish delivery dates and methods of payment. These should become part of your scheduling notes, as delays in the arrival of materials can prove expensive. Materials should be delivered to the site according to when they are required. Storing large quantities of hard landscaping materials for weeks at a stretch is to be avoided at all costs.

Apart from taking up valuable space, they will also cause compaction of the soil, so checking availability and delivery dates is important. You should agree with any contractor where materials and machinery are to be stored while work is in progress. Topsoil is another material that you will want to store carefully if excavation work will require its removal. If you need to import supplies of topsoil to make up new ground levels, make sure you specify carefully the quality and amount, and check the load before accepting.

ACCESS

Small gardens often have limited access points for machinery and bulky materials. Check the dimensions of access routes to both back and front gardens – even if you are working only on the back. Be careful when hiring a skip to choose one that is large enough for the waste you want to dispose of and make sure that it will be with you for as long as you need. Overestimate rather than underestimate the amount of waste you will have – hired skips rarely prove to be too large for the job. Opting for a small skip may be a false economy. Choose a large skip with a gated end for ease of getting spoil packed in.

Periods of hire vary, and there are often restrictions as to where a skip can be placed and for how long it can remain there. It may need to be illuminated at night for safety. If a skip can be placed on your own land, this is far less complicated than it standing on a highway.

Similar conditions apply to loose construction materials such as sand and gravel. Many building suppliers deliver these in bags, so the load is self-contained but still takes up space. Suppliers of materials, machinery or equipment frequently ask about site access problems. Awkward roads and drives may necessitate using smaller vehicles for delivery. If you have access problems that can be foreseen at the outset, mention these when you arrange delivery of goods or machinery. If access for particular work involves going through jointly owned boundaries you will have to seek permission from your neighbour. As a matter of common courtesy, it makes sense to inform anyone affected by the work.

Town-houses and terraced houses in particular present problems because all garden waste, new materials and machinery have to be taken through the building.

Substantial dust sheets should be laid over carpets, and delicate or precious items removed from the passageways. You may have to settle for smaller machines or tools if doorways are too narrow. The whole job will take longer because skip-loading and delivery of bulky materials are necessarily slow. The level of upheaval and perhaps the additional expense of labour spread over several stages of work means that, where possible, a back garden project in a terraced house is best carried out in one go.

WORKING OUT A SCHEDULE

- List tasks in order of completion

- Estimate time and people requirements

  e.g.   site clearance   1 day   self+2

          marking out and

          digging foundations   1 day   self+1

          laying foundations   1 day   self+1

          laying patio/paths   3 days self

- Arrange quotes from contractors if required

- If doing the work yourself, work out machinery requirements and check hire companies for price, delivery and site access

  e.g.   skip

          concrete mixer

          plate vibrator

          roller

          rotovator

          posthole borer

          strong wheelbarrow

- Calculate quantities of materials – check suppliers for price, delivery and site access

  e.g.   sand

          paving slabs

          bricks

          topsoil

          timber

- Place orders for materials and equipment

- If access involves pathway through house, find temporary homes for movable items and lay down large, tough dust sheets

- Ask neighbours to leave enough parking space for lorries on delivery days

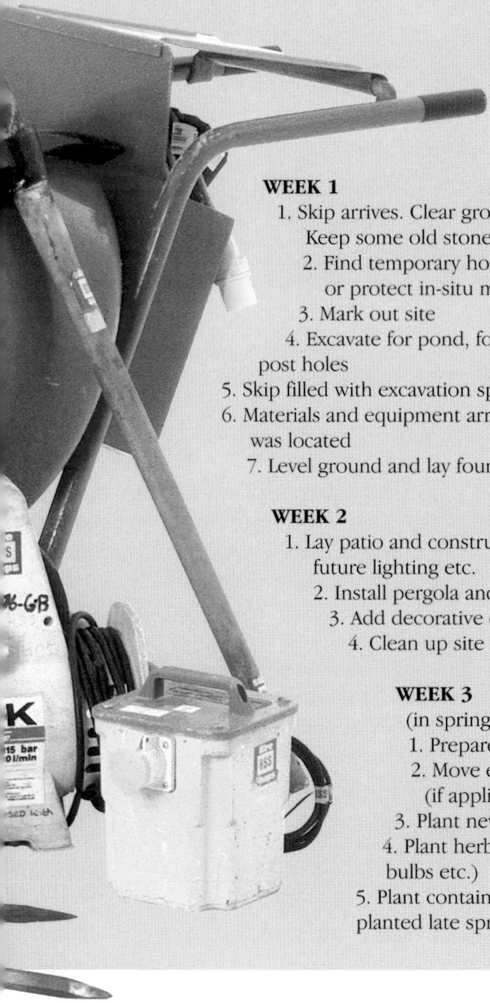

3-WEEK SCHEDULE

A 'typical' d-i-y schedule for design including new patio, raised beds, pond, pergola and new planting. Weeds would have been treated 2-3 weeks ahead of starting work

WEEK 1

1. Skip arrives. Clear ground of everything that cannot be used. Keep some old stones and smashed paving as hardcore
2. Find temporary home for existing plants that are to be kept, or protect in-situ mature trees and large shrubs
3. Mark out site
4. Excavate for pond, foundations of patio and raised beds; dig pergola post holes
5. Skip filled with excavation spoil and removed from site
6. Materials and equipment arrive for hard landscaping: put where skip was located
7. Level ground and lay foundations for new features

WEEK 2

1. Lay patio and construct raised beds. Include cable runs for any future lighting etc.
2. Install pergola and pond
3. Add decorative details
4. Clean up site

WEEK 3

(in spring or autumn)

1. Prepare ground for planting
2. Move existing backbone planting to new sites (if applicable)
3. Plant new climbers, trees and shrubs
4. Plant herbaceous plants and season fillers (eg. bedding, bulbs etc.)
5. Plant containers, ponds and water features (ponds are best planted late spring or early summer)

PREPARING THE SITE

Whatever type of garden you are working with, most will require some kind of preparation before you can put down the first paving slab. Prepare the whole area in one go, even if your timescale for the project is going to be spread out over months. You also need to mark out everything at this stage. Not preparing the site

Getting rid of tree stumps is generally a good idea, even if they lie in a planted border, as they can harbour and encourage disease. If a stump is in an area of lawn or paving, subsidence problems may occur when the roots eventually rot down. However, the removal of a tree stump close to a house can cause problems, and it is

Use your local tip to dispose of large items of rubbish. Be careful when burning waste not to throw old chemicals on the fire. Shred and compost organic materials.

properly at the start can lead to problems later that will be a major expense, not to mention upheaval, to rectify.

SITE CLEARANCE

You need to remove every item of plant growth that is not retained in the new scheme – trees, shrubs, tree stumps – together with any unwanted old paving, bricks and so on.

Perennial weeds should either be completely dug out or treated with a systemic weedkiller and left to die, with the ground then being dug over to remove all dead material. When grubbing out unwanted plants, take care that excess soil is not mounded around the roots of living trees and shrubs that you want to retain – this prevents air circulating around the roots and they will die. Take care also not to damage the root system of existing large plants retained in-situ while major garden works are taking place.

worth consulting a specialist. Tree surgeons can grind out stumps with specialist equipment in a fraction of the time that it takes to dig them out by hand.

If you are planning a new patio, heavy-duty path, shed or greenhouse, you will need hardcore for foundations – old paving broken up, rubble and stones can be used for this purpose, so retaining suitable material is a good idea. Similarly with ground that requires levelling, look carefully at how much soil is required for filling in hollows or cutting and filling larger areas of sloping ground. Keeping and re-using materials that are already on site could well save you time and money.

LEVELLING

To flatten off minor gradients and small undulations simply rake soil from high spots to low ones, firming in between stages to consolidate the new layer of soil. This is fine for

That depressing sea of mud will be transformed over the next few weeks.

areas that are to be planted or grassy spots where the odd bump is not critical: for instance, areas of grass that will be mown infrequently. Small hollows and hills can make mowing a bore, though, and for a formal lawn or paving greater accuracy will be required.

A more precise method is to rake and consolidate within a grid of marked stakes or pegs. If the area is next to existing level paving, use this straight edge as a starting point. Take a number of identical stakes and mark each one the same distance from the top. Put a row of stakes into the ground, so that the marks are at the height of the required level area. Continue in parallel rows until the whole area is covered with a grid. Use a spirit level to check that the stakes in each row are all at the same height. Then adjust the soil by raking exactly to the level marked on the stakes.

CREATING A GRADIENT

To create a slope you can use a grid method similar to creating an accurate level area. Longer pegs or stakes will be necessary depending on the overall change in level. Drive the stakes in so that the tops of them are level (use a spirit level), but the marks on them will differ from row to row, gradually going either down or up. In raking up soil to the level of the marks you will create an even gradient.

TERRACING

Terracing is the term given to creating level areas on sloping ground. The cut-and-fill technique described here must be used if the topsoil is shallow or the slope is steeper than one that can be dealt with simply by using the grid method for levelling outlined above. The benefit of the cut-and-fill method is that earth is relocated within the garden, minimising the amount of waste material. (Attempting to cut out and discard earth from a slope in order to create a level area, or importing vast amounts of material to add an embankment, are expensive and inconvenient methods.) Cut-and-fill can be done manually, but hiring a small excavator will make lighter work of the job.

To prepare, mark out the area of slope to be altered. Remove the topsoil and store. If the work is being carried out over a long period of time, note that the soil should stay in good condition for about six months, before nutrients break down.

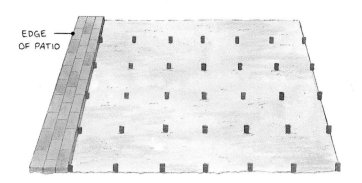

Stake out a grid for levelling.

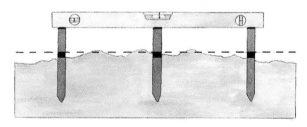

Mark pegs at same height to create a flat area.

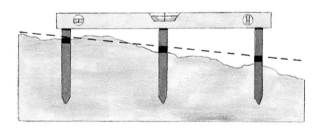

Mark pegs at progressively lower heights to create a slope.

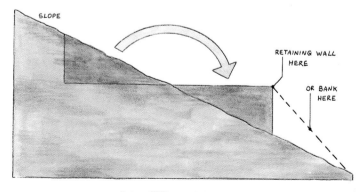

Cut-and-fill to create terraces.

Having stripped the topsoil, position a stake where the new flat level is to begin so that the top of it is at the height of the new level – this is the datum or zero for the area to be re-graded. Mark out with stakes the area between top and bottom of the slope to be filled in. Doing this on a grid basis will work best. A spacing of about 1m should be adequate, depending upon the length and width of the slope. Stretch string between the stakes and position at the required new height or level of the ground.

To determine how much fill you will need to level a slope, work out the cubic capacity of the area (height or level × width of slope × length of slope). If you do not have enough fill or excess soil on site, you will have to bring it in.

Excavate material from the slope roughly to the desired level, transferring the material down the slope to create the terrace. Consolidate the earth in layers not exceeding 15cm, replacing the topsoil last.

It is good practice to finish with the topsoil slightly above the required level, as soil will sink after such upheaval. The site should be left to settle before any further preparations.

MARKING OUT

Your plan should be a blueprint for this operation, so it may be worth having a copy laminated in clear plastic to give you a working version that will survive exposure to both weather and garden soil.

You may have already roughly plotted some parts of your design when visualising how it would look on the ground. Now you need to mark out accurate lines, many of them geometric shapes. Using pegs and string delineate the shape of all the main elements such as paved areas, the shape of the lawn and beds, the line of divisions or boundaries and the site of sheds, ponds and so on. Even if you plan to do the work in stages, still plot everything now. Locate starting points with reference to

Right: mark out corners as shown and check angles with a builder's square.

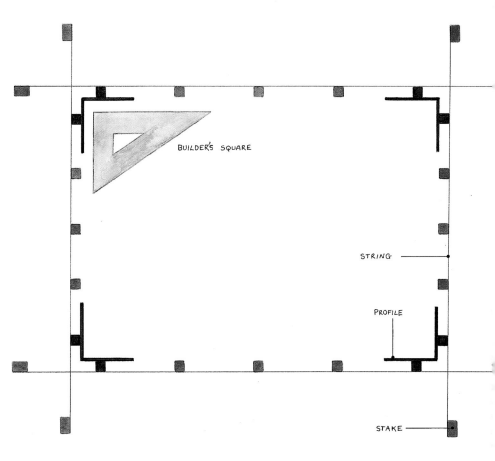

BUILDER'S SQUARE

STRING

PROFILE

STAKE

immovable features so that any error with one element does not translate into errors with others. Taking running measurements from a known point will give greater accuracy when marking out.

Though you are aiming simply to transfer the outlines of your plan on to the ground, you could still adjust some dimensions if the need arises. If you are intending to lay a path or patio and are about to order a specific material, you could plot carefully so that no cutting of slabs is required (see page 144).

Corners

On rectangular elements – perhaps a path or patio – you may need to adopt a profile system for marking out 90 degree corners accurately. Profiles can be made by nailing cross pieces to stakes. You will need two for each corner, positioned 30cm or so beyond the prospective edges. Stretch string between the boards and square them using a plumb line. Mark the location of the true corner with a peg.

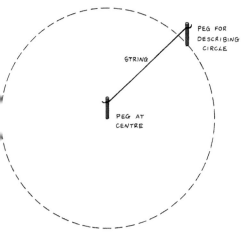

Circles

It is very difficult to achieve a convincing circle by eye alone, yet extremely easy using the method described here. Mark out circles or part-circles by using two pegs linked with string as a compass. Locate the centre of the circle from your plan and insert one of the pegs. Adjust the length of the string to the radius of the required circle or curve. Mark the circle on the ground with the other stake. Permanently mark on the ground using spray paint, or drive pegs in at 30cm intervals.

Curves

The line of a long, sweeping curve can be as difficult as a circle to plot accurately by eye alone. The process described here is the reverse of taking offset measurements to plot and draw a curve on a plan described earlier. You may want to create a grid overlay for the curve on your plan to make the process easier.

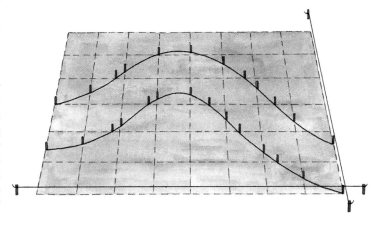

Establish the start and end of the curve by using triangulation and marking with stakes. Stretch string between the stakes to form a straight line. Measure along the stringline in intervals that match the scale of your drawing or grid – every 50cm, perhaps – and plot the curve as a series of measurements coming away at right angles from the string. Put marker stakes into the ground at each point, then join the points with string or hosepipe.

Measure across at 90 degrees to the correct width and mark the second side. If the path is to change in width as it curves, you will have to mark out each side individually.

Above: marking out a curved path.

Left: marking out a circle.

PREPARING FOR A LAWN

An ideal topsoil for a lawn is a well-drained sandy loam about 20-30cm deep, which should cover a free-draining subsoil. Grass will develop good, deep roots in these conditions. A range of other soils will be suitable, but good drainage and a sufficient layer of good-quality topsoil are always needed for success.

After clearing the site, dig or rotovate the entire area, removing large stones, and rake the ground to a fine tilth. Working the soil in this way makes subsequent levelling easier. It also remedies any compaction and helps to improve the soil structure. Beware rotovating on heavy clay soils as you could make drainage problems worse by creating a compacted layer or 'pan' below the top level.

An accurately levelled area should be created for formal lawns (see *Levelling*). In general, it is good practice to make a lawn slope away from both house and patio – it will improve the drainage of the lawn and ensure that no water runs off and pools on the patio or into the foundations. To achieve an even gradient for this purpose, use the grid method described above. Whatever the gradient you want to achieve, say 1:100, mark each row of pegs successively lower by 1/100 of the distance

between the rows. If your lawn slopes down towards your house and you do not wish to regrade it, you can install a soakaway or drain to ensure that water does not run into the foundations of your patio or house.

Final preparations for a lawn involve firming and raking. Tread the soil evenly all over the final lawn shape to firm it completely. You may have to repeat the process, but this will eliminate soft spots. Take care not to overdo it and compact the earth. Soil should never be firmed in such a way when wet.

After firming, the soil should be raked to a fine tilth with no humps, hollows or stones. The texture should be one of fine crumbs. Leave it

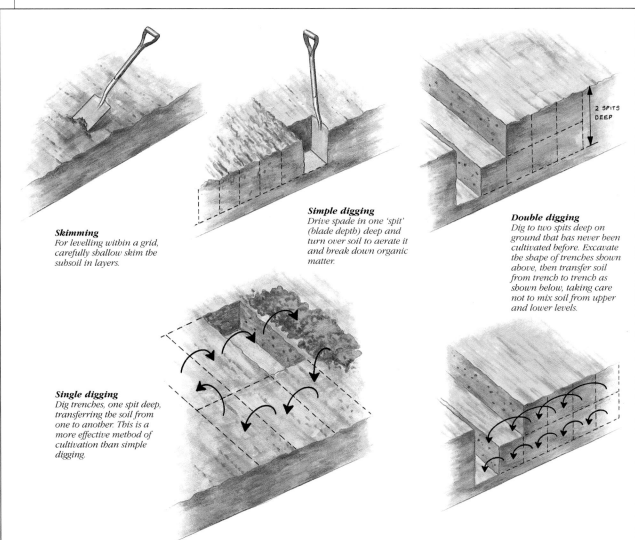

Skimming
For levelling within a grid, carefully shallow skim the subsoil in layers.

Simple digging
Drive spade in one 'spit' (blade depth) deep and turn over soil to aerate it and break down organic matter.

Double digging
Dig to two spits deep on ground that has never been cultivated before. Excavate the shape of trenches shown above, then transfer soil from trench to trench as shown below, taking care not to mix soil from upper and lower levels.

Single digging
Dig trenches, one spit deep, transferring the soil from one to another. This is a more effective method of cultivation than simple digging.

for three to four weeks to see how many weeds germinate. Hoe them off or treat with weedkiller and rake off after they have died. Take care not to disrupt all the hard work of levelling the soil. For sowing and turfing advice see pages 192-5.

PREPARING FOR PAVED AREAS

Dig away all loose topsoil from the site for the paving until firm subsoil is reached. Excess topsoil can be used to fill hollows in the garden or be incorporated into areas of planting, though take care not to kill existing plants by mounding soil over their roots. The depth of the excavation will vary depending on the function of the area and the finished surface (see pages 142-51). Once the correct level of earth has been excavated, the subsoil should be consolidated with a plate compactor. Any reduction in level can be made up with hardcore – rubble from elsewhere in the garden may come in useful for this. If you are dealing with unstable soil types such as peat or clay, or very sandy soil, lay a 15cm layer of hardcore as a sub-base, whatever type of paving finish you have chosen.

Some form of firm edge restraint should be used, either permanently or at least during construction. Make sure dimensions are not lost to this from the overall area of paving.

All paving requires proper drainage to ensure that water is shed from the surface. The gradient needed can vary according to the type of hard surface, but a fall of 1:80 should be adequate for most garden requirements. Provided the surrounding surface is well drained, it is acceptable to angle the fall into planted or grassed areas. For large expanses, however, drains linked to a soakaway or surface water drainage system will be necessary.

You can use the grid method to create a suitable gradient for paving. Alternatively, span across the edges of the formwork with a spirit level on a long plank. Place a small piece of wood known as a 'shim' underneath the end of the plank at the proposed lower side of the paving – away from the house. Adjust the depth of the formwork to ensure that the level shows horizontal. To produce a fall of 1:80, the thickness of the shim should be 1/80 of the distance across the patio.

PREPARING FOR PLANTING

Trees and shrubs can live for a long time, so the soil they grow in should be thoroughly prepared. Ideally you should prepare every part of the area to be planted, rather than selectively preparing where you know you want to plant something, but be careful not to disturb the root systems of existing trees, shrubs and plants.

Best seasons for cultivation are spring and autumn, so if you plan major planting, undertake the work at these times. Where you have marked out beds and borders, remove all weeds, paying particular attention to perennial ones. These can be killed with a systemic weedkiller, but if you are gardening organically

Avoid having untidy heaps of building materials all over the garden; stack pavers near the patio.

(without using pesticides and other chemicals) then weed control has to be done mechanically or by hand. After weeding, dig over the ground. Vegetable gardens and large new areas for planting should be double-dug (see illustration), adding organic matter to the soil. Single digging plus organic material should be adequate for existing beds. Add a general or slow-release fertiliser if necessary.

If you have prepared your site but will not be able to plant up for some time, you can cover the area with black polythene to stop the germination and regrowth of weeds. It is better to 'neglect' cleared soil in this way. Constant digging and weeding can undermine the structure of the soil and even cause weed seeds to be thrown up to the surface where they will germinate.

HARD LANDSCAPING

Once the ground structure has been created through digging, levelling, excavation and so on, you will be in a position to put in garden features such as walls, paving, ponds, bog gardens and timber structures. There is a wide range of ready-made items on the market, which need to be installed securely. Some of these, such as trelliswork, are also easy to construct from scratch.

BOUNDARIES

A physical barrier around the edge of a garden serves to keep the world out and the garden in: boundaries not only delineate the edge of your property, they can also keep pets and children safe from wandering. You can make them serve a further role of providing shelter for both plants and yourself. Boundaries can be marked by walls, fences, hedges, and – less substantially – willow hurdles and trellises.

FENCING

Timber has many advantages as a boundary material. It is easy and relatively cheap to install, and there are many different types of fencing to suit most gardens and locations. However, fences have a shorter lifespan than walls and require more maintenance. You can paint them with preservatives (non-poisonous to plants) to prolong their life. Covering fences with plants creates extra weight and wind resistance; in turn, this increases the stress on fence posts.

The two most common types of fencing are prefabricated panel and closeboarded. Panel fences are cheaper to buy and quicker to install than boarded fences but are less durable. Both require secure installation of fence posts. The posts for panel fences must be precisely spaced to fit the dimensions of the panels. This spacing is not so critical with closeboarded fences, as horizontal rails are fitted between them, and overlapping boards are then nailed to the rails to form the fence.

Mark out the line of the fence with pegs and string. For panel fences mark the sites for posts at the required intervals, remembering that accuracy is necessary if the panels are to fit. If making a boarded fence, divide the boundary measurement into a series of bays of even length along the run. Mark where each post is to go. When calculating the height of posts, take into account the height of any decorative top finish you may be adding.

PUTTING UP FENCE POSTS

One way to secure a fence post is to sink about a quarter of its length into the ground and surround the post with a collar of concrete. Make sure the post is long enough overall for a quarter of it to be below ground. Use a post-hole borer for an easier job, and excavate the hole to about 30cm square and a bit deeper than a quarter of the finished height of the post. Put some hardcore in the bottom of the hole. Prop the post in and set it perfectly vertical by checking each side with a spirit level, bracing it with two lengths of scrap wood temporarily nailed to its sides. More hardcore can be added around the post and then a fairly dry mix of concrete should be trowelled into the hole around the post. Compact it to dispel air bubbles. Shape the top of the small mound so that rainwater will run off it.

On firm, rock-free ground, metal fence spikes can be used. These are hammered into the ground. The posts, which will be shorter than those used in the first method, are then fitted into the sockets and the integral bolts tightened to fit. This second method is more expensive because of the spikes.

intervals that the spike is vertical by holding a spirit level against each side of the holder. If it is not, remove and re-drive it into the ground. Cut the post to the finished height and push it into the collar or holder. Tighten the integral bolts to secure it.

An alternative method combines both of these approaches. Excavate a hole with a post-hole borer or spade. Position the fence spike in the hole and brace it in a vertical position. Wedge with stones and check again. Trowel in concrete around the spike. This enables a fence post to be replaced easily while adding strength to the finished structure.

FITTING GRAVEL BOARDS

These are fitted to the bottom of fences to close the gap between fence and ground. They stop the fence from coming into direct contact with damp soil, thereby extending its life. Gravel boards are easy and cheap to replace. At the base of the fence, nail 150mm lengths of 35mm square timber vertically to the inner faces of the posts. Measure between these supports for the dimensions of the gravel boards required and cut lengths of 150 x 250mm of softwood or

Below left: set fence posts in concrete or use fence spikes in rock-free ground.

Middle: for a panel fence, space the posts to match the panel size and brace them upright. Nail clips to the posts and support the panels clear of the ground while you drive in the nails.

Below right: finally add gravel boards.

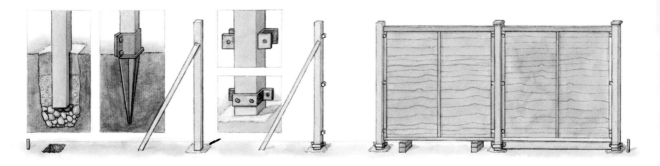

Fencing spikes come in various heights and sizes to suit different fence heights and post dimensions. For fences over 1.2m use a spike 760mm long with a 75 or 100mm square post. For fences lower than 1.2m use a spike 610mm long with a 50 or 75mm post. To install, position the spike where the post is to go and drive it into the ground using a special hammering block or a piece of offcut post as protection from the sledgehammer. Check at frequent

pressure-treated wood to fit. Treat with preservative if using the former. Position the gravel board between the posts and set it horizontal. Check with spirit level and nail to the vertical supports using galvanised nails.

PUTTING UP FENCE PANELS

To fit fence panels, install one post, then position the second post in the run. Check to ensure that the space between them matches the panel dimensions – lay the panel on the ground between the posts as a guide. Mark a centre line down the inner face of the posts to ensure the correct position for the clips. Nail the fence clips to the inner faces of the posts so that they are ready to receive the panels. Clips provide better fixing than do nails driven through the edges of a panel. Position the panel between the posts and raise it off the ground with bricks or timber offcuts. Secure it by driving nails through the clips. Remove the support.

It is unlikely that your fencing run will match an exact number of prefabricated panels, so you will have to cut one to fit the end gap. Measure the width of this or hold a full-size panel against

one at the top and one at the bottom. Secure using the brackets. Check that they are parallel with the ground and each other using a spirit level. For fences up to 1.2m high, use two rails; higher fences require three.

Nail gravel boards of 150x25mm timber to short support battens nailed to the inner face of the posts. Recess the battens so that the gravel boards are flush with the posts.

Nail and stretch string guidelines to the tops of the posts to enable levelling of the boards. Place the first feather-edged board on the gravel board support, thicker edge butted against the post and top aligned with the guideline. Drive

Below: with a closeboarded fence, precise positioning of posts is not so critical. Add the arris rails and nail on the boards so the thick edge of each one overlaps the thin edge of its predecessor by about 12mm. Reverse the last board in each section so its thick edge abuts the post.

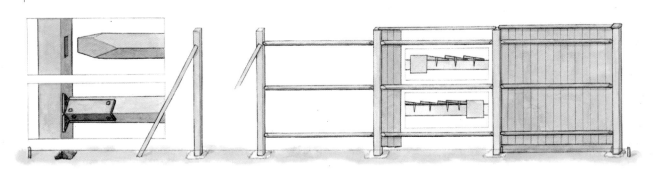

the final posts. Mark with a large felt-tip pen or pencil the edge against the last post to show the overlap. Prise the edging battens off the panel and reposition to line up with the mark. Nail the batten into the new position with the panel lying flat on a hard surface. Supporting the panel firmly, cut though the protruding framing battens (top and bottom) and saw off the surplus slats, cutting as closely as possible to the repositioned side batten. Fit the pared-down panel as normal. Add gravel boards to the bottom of the fence and post caps as required.

PUTTING UP CLOSEBOARDED FENCES

Closeboarded fences can be bought ready-made but this type of fencing is normally erected on site from separate parts. Posts may be ready-mortised to take the horizontal arris rails, or you can cut these yourself. A far easier option is to fit the arris rails using special galvanised arris rail-fixing brackets. Using this method, all the posts can be installed first.

Install the fence posts along the boundary. Cut the arris rails to fit between each of the posts,

two nails through the board into the top arris rail, check level of the board, then repeat for the lower arris rail. Add the next and subsequent boards so that each overlaps the edge of the previous one by about 12mm – you can make a spacing gauge to get this spacing consistent from an offcut of timber. Use one nail per rail only.

Check with a spirit level to ensure the boards are vertical and either secure with a second nail or adjust. Complete the fence and reverse the last board so that its thick edge is against the final post. Weatherproof the fence and finish it off by fitting a coping strip to the top of the boards. The coping strip will prevent rainwater from seeping through the end grain of the feather-edged boards – a vulnerable spot. Cut lengths of bevelled coping strip and fit these at regular intervals to the top of the boards. Weatherproof the top of each fence post by nailing preformed chamfered post caps to them. These are slightly wider than the post dimensions and will shed rainwater, which will help to extend the life of the posts.

ADDING DECORATIVE FINISHES

Fences do not have to be brown. Timber stains and paints that are suitable for outdoor use and safe near plants are available in a wide range of colours. These can be chosen to match or contrast with the rest of the features in your garden. Ready-made shapes or finials can be bought in a variety of shapes to add to fence caps – it is worth using these as a good method of weatherproofing the post beneath. You may want to make your own to ensure that the structure matches the rest of your garden.

Extra height can be given to a fence by including low trellis panels on the top. These can be

straight-topped or curving, again to reflect the other elements of the garden. It is worth considering the effect they have on any views beyond, as they might be used to frame them. Take account of the overall height of the structure when choosing and installing fence posts. Other finishing options include using taller fence posts and putting a simple timber cross beam between them, or using a 'swagged' rope in a similar way. Boarded fences can be created with spaced slats to baffle winds effectively, and random tops for decorative effect. To make the appearance of closeboarded fences more attractive, add trellis panels, which can be either painted to match or given a contrasting finish.

MAKING PALISADE OR PICKET FENCING

Ready-made picket and palisade fencing can be bought, but you may prefer to produce them from scratch. This type of fencing is more decorative than substantial. Many kinds of decorative tops are appropriate. The fence top can also be curved or staggered in a zig-zagging line for an alternative effect.

Posts are installed at a height to suit the site. Cut the arris rails to size – on middle posts the rail should finish halfway across with another length butt-jointed to it. On end posts the end of the rail fits flush with the outer edge of the post. Mark the positions of the rails on the posts. For fences about 1.2m high, the lower rail

should be about 30cm above ground level and the upper one about 15cm down from the top of the pales or palisades. Measure this distance and lay the same spacing apart on a hard flat surface with the ends aligned.

Cut the pales as required and lay out on the rails. Space them as required, using a spacer for uniformity, and align them with a spare length of timber placed along the tops. Secure with galvanised nails, two per fixing, and place nails diagonally, angling them inwards for a more secure fixing. Leave a small amount of rail at each end of a panel to fix to the posts. Fix the panels to the front of posts, checking with a spirit level that rails are horizontal and pales vertical.

Above left: hurdle fencing.

Above right: rustic pole fencing.

LOW BRICK WALLS

Boundary walls up to a height of one metre need planning permission. Naturally, any garden wall you build yourself must be soundly constructed for safety. Choice of material will be governed by availability and cost – man-made materials such as brick or blocks of some sort are common choices. Bricks should be suitable

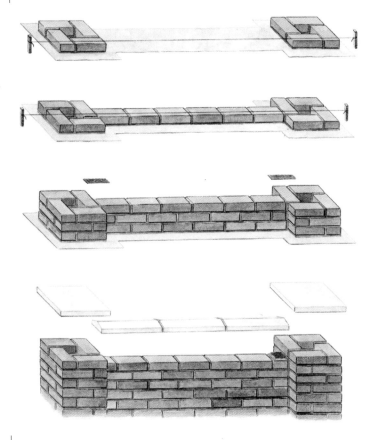

Above: build up a brick wall course by course, setting out the piers first, then adding the first course between the piers. After the third course, bed strips of metal mesh in alternate courses to help bond the wall and piers together. Complete the wall with coping stones and pier caps.

for outdoor use to withstand exposure to severe conditions. Known by a number of different names, they are available in a variety of colours to match or harmonise with other bricks in your house and garden. It is worth paying more for engineering bricks that do not absorb water and remain durable even below ground level.

Any garden wall requires a proper concrete foundation, and the width and depth of this depends on the dimensions of the wall. Bricks are laid in overlapping bonds to create rigid structures. Half-brick walls are single thickness with the bricks laid in stretcher bond – long face outermost and alternate rows staggered by half

WALLING DETAILS

BRICKS
● Facing bricks – also known as stocks.
● Common bricks – used where appearance is not vital.
● Engineering bricks – fired to a higher heat to produce greater density and durability, available in different colours but commonly seen as blue brick.

FOUNDATIONS
● Allow 15cm depth of concrete strip for walls up to 75cm and twice as wide as the wall thickness.
● For taller walls increase the foundation width to three times the thickness of the wall.
● Foundation strip usually finishes at least two courses (15cm) below the ground, to allow soil or turf to be laid right up to the wall.
● On sloping ground foundations should be laid as a series of overlapping steps.

PIERS FOR STRENGTHENING AND EXPANSION JOINTS
● Piers are constructed on the centre line at each end of the wall as an aid to stability.
● For walls longer than 3m include intermediate piers.
● 675mm is the maximum height a half-brick 102mm wall should be built with single-brick piers.
● Expansion joints – 1cm joint – allows structure to expand, vertical, spaced every 6m along the length of a wall and filled with flexible mastic.

DAMP-PROOF COURSE
DPC can be included 15cm or two courses above ground level. Membrane types should not be used, as they do not provide adhesion across the joint. Use two courses of engineering bricks or two courses of 5mm slates fully half-lapped and bedded in mortar.

the length of the brick. Single-brick walls are double thickness with parallel pairs of half-brick walls laid as a course of 'headers' – bricks laid across the width of the wall leaving end faces visible. It is this type of wall that would normally be constructed on a boundary because it results in a stronger structure.

BUILDING BRICK AND SOLID BLOCK WALLS

The foundations must be accurately marked out, and the wall must be laid level and square with the correct depth of foundation. Low walls built in stretcher bond should have a pier one brick square at each end for strength. If you plan a wall that is more than 3m in length, intermediate piers should be included.

Having laid the foundation, set up wooden profile boards as guides at each end of the trench, with string stretched between them. Lay the first course of bricks at each terminal pier position. A pier one brick square is made by placing two bricks side by side. For a brick and a half pier, lay four bricks at 90 degrees to each other (34cm).

on walls 225mm thick, finish with a course of bricks laid on edge or tile coping.

BUILDING SCREEN BLOCK WALLS

Pierced screen block walls are constructed in a stack bond with no overlaps between courses. Strength is provided by piers, and walls in excess of 3m in length will require intermediate

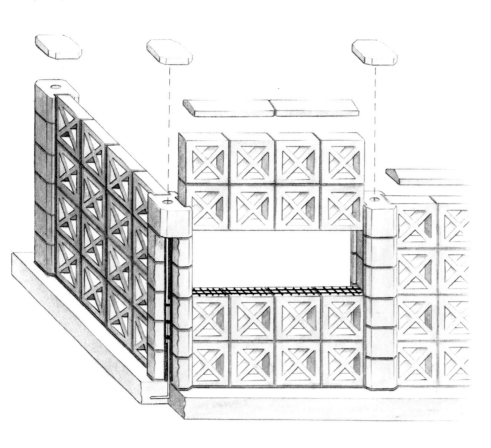

Left: when building with screen blocks, set the hollow pier blocks over reinforcing rods and fill them with mortar, then lay the wall blocks between them. Use a strip of metal mesh on top of every second course of blocks to bond the wall to the piers.

Lay the first course of bricks between the piers. Build up the wall by adding a course to each pier and adding another between them. The last stretcher in the wall on alternate courses will overlap the pier, which is completed with a header and a half brick. For one-and-a-half brick piers, reverse the brick alignment in alternate courses, and bond the wall to its piers using strips of expanded metal mesh. Or bond alternate courses of the wall into the piers, completing the course with two whole bricks and two three-quarter bats as shown here.

When you have raised the wall to the required height, end with a course of bricks laid frog down. Finish with coping stones as shown, or

piers. The maximum safe height for a screen block wall is 1.8m or six courses.

The foundations are laid in the same way. For walls higher than two courses, include steel reinforcing rods in the foundations at each pier position as high as the wall is planned.

Put the first pier block in place on a bed of mortar, or on to the reinforcing rods if one is being used. Check that the indent in one face lines up with the direction of the wall, and fill the centre of the block with mortar.

Raise the pier to a height of three blocks, checking that it is vertical. Set the first walling

Moss-covered limestone wall.

WALLING TERMINOLOGY

Batter Mostly applicable to retaining walls, where the sides of the wall are not perpendicular, the wall being thicker at the bottom. It is expressed as a degree – the usual graduation is that for every 300mm of wall an additional 25mm of batter from the perpendicular is required. The wall's centre of gravity is lowered, thus making it more stable.

Bond Two meanings: first, the traditional arrangements and patterns of materials in a wall; second, the way in which vertical and horizontal joints are arranged to give strength to the wall – bonding.

Capping or coping The top finishing layer of a wall. Capping usually is flush with the wall; coping extends beyond the wall's main body and may be of a different material.

Course Horizontal row of bricks or stones.

Damp-proof course (DPC) Impermeable membrane included in wall to prevent water penetration.

Frog The indented top of a brick.

Header The short side of a brick.

Jointing Treatment of mortar used to bond bricks, stones etc.

Pier or column Extra-thick section of wall incorporated at regular intervals to increase strength and/or improve appearance. The height of a pier/column should not exceed 18 times its own thickness.

Stretcher The long side of a brick.

Wall face Outward, visible side of a wall.

● The thickness of brick walls is referred to in terms of 'half-bricks'.

● The dimensions of a common brick are 100x215x65mm.

● Different bonds are achieved through different arrangements of bricks. Stretcher bond, for instance, refers to walls where each brick has been laid simply with its stretcher side showing, the courses staggered evenly.

block in place on a mortar bed. Mortar one edge beforehand and fit this edge into the groove of the pier block. Add a second block on top of the first and check that the top is level with the top of the pier.

Lay the rest of the first course of blocks, then build up the other end pier to the same height as the first – three blocks. Complete the second course of blocks.

If the finished height of the wall is higher than two blocks, the wall is tied to the piers by inserting a strip of expanded metal mesh in the bed of mortar every second course. Then add three more pier blocks to either end of the wall and lay two more courses of blockwork between. Each horizontal course is reinforced by bedding a continuous strip of mesh in the bedding mortar.

Complete the wall by bedding square capping stones on top of the piers and chamfered coping pieces along the top of the screen block wall. These not only look more attractive than the edges of the blocks but shed rainwater quicker. To give the joints a neat appearance, they need to be smoothed (pointed). Point the joints neatly by running a small piece of hosepipe along the setting mortar to give a rounded profile.

BUILDING STONE WALLS

Natural stone walls suit country gardens. They can be built as a free-standing structure without mortar (dry-stone) or as a retaining wall, supporting a bank of earth. Their informal look can be increased by packing soil into the joints or planting. Stone can be bought from larger garden centres or local stone quarries. Use local stone if possible (for the wall to fit in with the vernacular architecture), preferably of a hard and impervious type.

Mark out and create a foundation of compacted earth, then set batter frames at the end of the wall run. Lay one layer of large foundation stones. Interlock edges for strength. Build up the ends by several courses of edging blocks and alternate through stones. Stretch a piece of string between batter frames as a guide to wall shape.

Fill cavity between front and back with small infill stones and ram them down firmly. Tie outer surfaces of the wall with through stones laid across at random intervals. Continue to raise the wall with squarer edging blocks. Fit a row of coverband stones along the top of the wall to close the top. Ideally, the row should slope slightly to shed water. Finish the wall with a row of coping stones (style to suit) placed along the coverband.

DRY-STONE WALLS

Dry-stone walls appear random in construction but must be made to a strict formula to produce strong stable structures.

Foundations Well compacted and stable subsoil with large flat foundation stones on top.

Batter and batter frames Unmortared walls must be built with a broad base narrowing towards the top – the batter. This gives rigidity and spreads the loading to the foundation stones. A typical batter is 915mm wide at the base narrowing to 300mm at the top. Batter frames are used to set the angle during building. Make from 50x25mm softwood made to size.

Edging blocks Fairly uniform stones laid on foundation to from outline of the wall with a central cavity.

Infill stones Small irregular shaped, used as infill in the cavity.

Through stones Long, flat stones called random throughs, placed randomly along wall to tie outer faces together.

Coverband Row of large, flatter stones laid on the top of a wall to support the coping.

Coping stones Flatter stones for top finish. Various styles, some special to region of the country. Examples: 'Jack and Jill' – two rows upright on edge, 'Buck and Doe' – alternate flat and on edge arrangement to give turreted finish.

PATHS AND PATIOS

Curved steps can create more interest than straight ones, but you will need to take more care in marking them out.

At the planning stage, you will have sited a patio in the most appropriate place for your needs. The dimensions should have been determined by the shape of the area, the overall dimensions of your garden and what the patio will be used for. For a tiny garden, you may decide to pave the entire ground surface other than planted areas. Once the site of the patio is marked out, check again that furniture can be accommo- dated without overlapping the proposed paved area. Similarly, before excavating foundations for paths, check that they are wide enough for their function (including wheelbarrow and mower manoeuvres) and that they are logically routed to link the elements of your garden. It is worth considering installing armoured cabling at this juncture for an outdoor power supply (see pages 214-5).

Patios must be laid so that rainwater drains away from the house or other walls. They are commonly positioned near to or incorporating existing drain runs and inspection covers. These must not be paved over. If at a lower level than the proposed paving, build up the walls of a manhole to set the cover at the new surface level. Template covers, which can be inlaid with paving, or planted, are available. Alternatively, disguise mahole covers with a prostrate conifer which can be pruned back for access.

Use prime datum peg to mark the finished height of the new patio or path, which must be at least 15cm or two brick courses beneath the damp-proof course of your house. If you plan steps or retaining walls that fall within this area allow for their foundation requirements. Never build walls on top of paving.

LAYING FOUNDATIONS FOR PAVING

All paving materials must be laid on a flat, firm and stable base. The type and depth of the foundations will depend on what the area is going to be used for and the type of soil in your garden. For example, maintenance and other minor paths receiving little wear may be laid on compacted soil. The finished surface level of your patio or path will be achieved by excavating to a depth that includes space for a layer of well-compacted hardcore, a laying course into which the slabs are set, and the slabs themselves.

Patio foundations
Having marked out the area of your patio, dig out the top soil. Skim the surface in shallow layers to avoid disturbing levelling stakes or prime datum pegs: these should be kept in position throughout. Either re-use the soil in another part of the garden or dispose of it via a skip. Every 10 square metres excavated to a depth of 10 centimetres produces about 2 cubic metres (2.5 tonnes) of loose soil, so laying patio foundations represents major earth movement and disposal. Once the subsoil is reached, compact it. Lay a 100mm layer of hardcore as a firm base. Firm well by using a tamper or, better still, a vibrating plate compactor (both of which can be rented).

Then add a 50mm layer of sand to the area; spread and compact it. Divide the area into bays for ease of spreading. Levelling pegs should protrude above the layer of sand to the depth of the paving you have chosen: for example, for bricks this would be 76mm.

To stop outer edges of patio foundations creeping once the slabs are laid, set edge restraints in place. House walls may form one edge. For others, edging treatments include bricks, precast concrete or timber, which must be pressure-treated. Make sure that the thickness of the edging treatment does not encroach on the patio dimensions.

Path foundations
As with patios, the ideal depth of foundations for paths will vary according to the use they will get. On firm ground, paths that will not be used heavily may be laid on compacted subsoil with a sand base. But for major paths a minimum 75mm layer of hardcore base should be used. For a path that runs around a house into a patio, use the same amount of hardcore base so that the area is excavated to one level. Where paths join a lawn, set the paving about 20mm below the level of the lawn so that lawnmowers can run over the edge without damaging the blades.

Mark out the path by setting string guidelines 50mm wider than the finished path width. Concrete or gravel paths require an edging: for example, pressure-treated timber boards. Narrow paths of other materials are usually safe from creeping. Dig out turves and the topsoil within the string guidelines. Re-use or compost turves. Compact the subsoil base with a roller or compactor, then add the hardcore to the required depth. Compact well and finish to the correct depth. Finish with a layer of sand 50mm deep, filling in hollows in the hardcore as you spread it.

LAYING CONCRETE

Concrete can be poured into virtually any shape and can be textured and coloured, and embedded with other materials such as stones and pebbles. For large expanses, however, divide into sections with breaks or expansion joints to prevent the concrete from cracking. Laying concrete is a two- or three-person job. Furthermore, once concrete is in place, repair and replacement are expensive and difficult.

Mark out your site and dig out about 20cm by skimming the earth in shallow layers so as not to disturb the levelling stakes and string reference lines. Fill any low areas with small stones or gravel, tamped down or compacted. Create the drainage gradient. Drive wooden levelling pegs into the ground around the edge

If you build a straight path, the eye will be drawn to whatever is down it.

of the area at intervals of one metre along the string lines, ensuring that the thickness of the formwork does not intrude on the finished shape. Remove the string lines and nail wooden planks to the pegs, butt-jointed at the corners. This wooden structure is the formwork which will hold the concrete in place until it has hardened.

Divide large areas into smaller sections no more than four metres long using timber formwork. Spread the area with hardcore 100mm deep, and firm with a tamper or plate compactor.

Mix the concrete to the desired ratio or use ready-mixed. Starting with the first section, tip the concrete mix in and spread from the barrow. It should be just above the level of the formwork and worked well into the edges.

Compact the concrete with a timber beam or screed that spans the width of the sections. Get a second person to help with this. Use a chopping motion with the beam to get rid of air, and slide the timber from side to side to give a level finish to the surface. Fill in any hollows that may appear after the levelling process using fresh concrete – a third person might do this task. Level again.

The surface can now be 'floated' or smoothed down with long-handled or hand-held concrete floats, according to the size of the project. This smooths out any high spots and hollows left after screeding. At this point, decorative finishes and textures should be applied.

When laying paving slabs on sand, slide each one into place off its neighbour to avoid disturbing the sand bed.

Right: a cross-section through typical paving.

Cover the area with plastic sheeting and leave to dry. Remove the formwork when the concrete has set hard, and fill expansion joints with a proprietary filler. The surface will set in a few days, but for maximum rigidity leave to harden for about a week.

LAYING PAVING SLABS

Laying a slab patio or path is a relatively simple d-i-y task. Cutting slabs, however, is not easy, so you could choose your paving unit to fit the patio or path exactly or adjust the dimensions to fit. Estimate how many slabs you will need and add some extra for breakages and other emergencies. Work out how much sand you require as a laying base: with a depth of 50mm multiply the square metres of the area by 0.05 to produce the answer in cubic metres.

When using slabs, once you have laid the foundations, treat the area with a total weedkiller, which will help suppress weeds from regrowing through the joints in the paving. You could also include a geo-textile membrane beneath the hardcore sub-base. As with all forms of hard surface, check that you have created the correct drainage fall if the patio or path adjoins the house, and that the finished surface will not breach the house damp-proof course. Paving should finish at least 150mm, or two brick courses, below this.

Create an even bed of sand by dividing the area into sections about 1.2m wide with lengths of 50mm-wide timber. Barrow and shovel the sand into the formation and level roughly with a

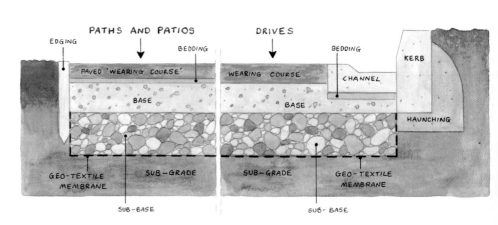

rake. Level each section with a timber beam or screed which can be pushed up and down along the timber edges. Spread your own weight as you do this job by kneeling on a board. Lift the dividers out and fill the gaps with sand.

If you plan to edge the area of paving, this is the time to do so. With a patio or path adjoining the house, lay the first row of slabs against it. Work by kneeling on a board to preserve the level surface of the sand. Slide each slab off the neighbouring one into position. As each slab is laid, tamp it down with the handle of a club hammer. This ensures that slabs sit level with neighbours. Check with a spirit level, and repeat the process until the area is completed.

If you have to cut slabs to fit, mark or score along the line on the slab face. Cut along this with a sharp brick bolster and a club hammer. Alternatively, you can hire an angle grinder to cope with cutting – make sure that you are provided with the appropriate safety gear at time of rental. Angle grinders are the best method of cutting awkward shapes such as

around down-pipes, inspection chambers and other likely obstacles.

Finish the job off by brushing sand into all the joints. Tidy up the edges by replacing turf alongside the newly paved area.

Laying slabs with mortar
Prepare the area and lay the hardcore to the correct height excluding the paving slab. Make a bedding mortar mix.

Trowel five dobs of mortar, one at each corner where the slab will be laid, and one in the centre. Position the slab and tamp down with a club hammer handle. Check with a spirit level. Repeat using spacer of 10mm from wood offcuts for uniform mortar joints between slabs.

Remove spacers and leave slabs for a few days to let the mortar set. Fill joints with a stiff mortar; point using a spoon handle. Alternatively, a dry mortar mix of 1:3 cement and sand can be used. Brush it into the joints, and water in with clean water – use a watering can fitted with a fine rose.

Rectangular paving slabs can be laid for a 'random' effect.

LAYING CONCRETE BLOCK PAVING

Concrete blocks (also known as block pavers or paviors) are described as flexible paving because the units are laid dry on sand without mortar and can be lifted if required. Small units

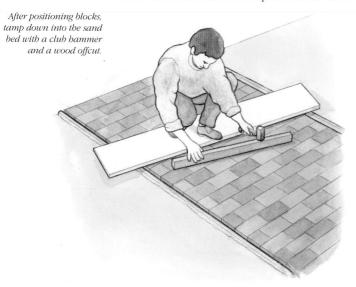

After positioning blocks, tamp down into the sand bed with a club hammer and a wood offcut.

Above: finishing the edge of a patio with a brick edging makes more of a feature of it.

of paving can be laid in a variety of patterns or bonds for patios and paths. Concrete block paving is a good choice for drives because it is strong enough to take the load of heavy vehicles. Herringbone pattern is perfect, because the interlocking of units gives great strength. But avoid creating over-large expanses of uninterrupted block pavers – break up the area with other materials.

First of all, estimate how many blocks you will need. As a rule of thumb, most measure 200x100mm, which works out as 50 blocks per square metre. Calculate the volume of sand required. A form of edge restraint will be needed. For drives, set concrete kerbs in a haunch of mortar. Other treatments to consider include treated timber and rows of blocks set on edge in concrete.

Excavate the area to the required depth. For drives, add an extra 100mm of hardcore and compacted aggregate. As with paving slabs, treat the area with total weedkiller and lay geo-textile fabric as required.

Place the edge restraints in position around the area to be paved. Nail boards to stout pegs and bed kerbstones or rows of blocks in concrete (drives). Finish the concrete at least 75mm

below the top of the edge restraints on the inside. This allows the sand to cover it.

With large areas, work in sections as described for laying slabs. Barrow and shovel the sand into the formation. Roughly level with a rake and smooth with a timber straight edge. The top should be about 50mm below the top of the edge restraint. This allows the blocks to be laid a fraction above the top of the restraint to be levelled when compacted with a plate vibrator.

Check the position of obstructions relative to the finished level of the blocks. Begin laying the blocks from one corner in an appropriate pattern. Work systematically across and down the area. Kneel on a board to spread your weight. Butt the blocks against the edge restraints and against each other. Leave spaces where blocks require cutting to fit until the end of the job.

Areas of light wear can be tamped down with a club hammer and a protective wooden block. For heavy-duty areas, hire a plate vibrator to settle the blocks until they are level with the edge restraints. It is probably best to use one of these for a really firm professional finish.

Some patterns such as herringbone will require blocks to be cut. This can be done with a brick bolster and club hammer but is hard work. With lots to cut, hire a hydraulic block splitter. When all blocks have been laid, brush sand into the joints. Finally, run over the surface with a plate vibrator again.

LAYING BRICKS

Using bricks to build patios and paths next to a house is a perfect way of providing a visual link between the house and garden. As with block pavers, because they are small units they offer greater design flexibility than slabs. Not only can they be laid in a variety of patterns, they also make good edging for other materials and can be easily laid to form curved shapes. If you need large quantities, contact a brick company to see if they will deliver to you. Otherwise, builders' merchants will supply bricks in any quantities. Make sure that the ones you choose are suitable for outdoor paving and can withstand rain and frost. Clay pavers are similar to bricks but have a thinner profile than either bricks or concrete block pavers. They are usually available in warm reddish shades.

Create a suitable sub-base for the area you plan to lay. Bricks should ideally be laid on mortar. Lay edging strips or bricks and bed them on a concrete footing. Prepare the bedding mortar and lay in the formation to a depth of 25mm. Bed the bricks in the mortar, in the pattern of your choice. Tamp them using the handle of a club hammer and a piece of wood to spread the weight exerted on to the bricks. Space the bricks with thin strips of hardboard or wood to give uniform joints. Check the levels in all directions at regular intervals.

Once the area is completed, spread a thin layer of dry mortar mix over it, using a soft broom. To remove air gaps, press into the joints with a narrow piece of wood. Use a fine spray from a hose or watering can to moisten the surface with water and set the mortar mix.

LAYING GRAVEL

Gravel is easy to lay and can give either formal or informal results according to the type of edging used. Creating curves is simple. Gravel can also be formed to create features – Japanese gardens often have areas of gravel deep enough to be raked into patterns that emulate water flowing around large rocks and stones. The variety of shapes and colours of gravel depends on the original stone – from sharp particle chippings to smooth pea-shingle. Match the type of gravel you use with any natural stone or reconstituted slabs for harmony.

Unless gravel is well laid and contained it will migrate into adjoining surfaces. It can be uncomfortable to walk on, too – getting the depth right is essential if walking across it is not to resemble wading through a shingle beach. Some maintenance will be required to keep it weed-free and looking good. In its favour, the noise of someone approaching on a gravel path can be a burglar deterrent. (For more on garden security see page 217.)

Having marked out the site, construct the foundations by digging down to a depth of about 180mm, or 200mm if the path borders a lawn. The area must be below the level of the turf. Set the edges to be used in place. If using timber, this should be pressure-treated. Drive pegs into the ground at one-metre intervals to hold the edging restraints. Apply a total weedkiller and include a layer of geo-textile membrane if you want to suppress weeds

permanently. Lay a sub-base of hardcore 100mm deep and roll to compact thoroughly.

Next, spread a mixture of sand and coarse gravel, 50mm deep, over the hardcore and roll to compact it. Finally, spread a layer of gravel with particles of 10-20mm to a depth of 25mm. Pea-shingle gives a fine-textured finish. Apply the gravel in stages and damp down between rolling to compact each layer. If laying a gravel drive, give extra depth to the sub-base. The gravel must be contained across the apron or entrance into the drive. The depth of gravel can also be increased, as it will be subject to greater weights and movements of vehicles.

Gravel is a suitable material for a path unless a person with restricted mobility is using the garden. Also think twice about laying it if you have young children, as they may try to throw it around or hurt themselves falling on it. You will need to contain gravel to stop it slipping into lawns, beds and ponds.

CREATING CURVES AND PATTERNS

The majority of paving materials are square or rectangular and, when laid without cutting, form angular, geometric-shaped areas. Cutting is time-consuming. If your design includes curving areas of paving, think carefully about choice of materials. Smaller units (the smaller the better) will form curves far more readily and can be laid without widening joints. Some slab types are available ready-formed in circular shapes of varying radii, which will create circular and curved features when laid. It may be possible to give a rectangular patio laid with slabs a 'bay' end either by laying a brick-on-edge detail in a semi-circle and cutting the slabs to fit at the edge, or by using a different smaller unit of paving. Otherwise, choose an appropriate material such as one of those listed below to realise curved and circular forms.

A sweeping curve adds a sense of movement to a garden.

MATERIALS THAT FORM CURVES EASILY

● In-situ concrete.

● Bricks and pavers.

● Gravel – use bricks or setts for edging and creating features in larger expanses.

● Cobbles and setts – both natural stone and concrete, some of which have wedge stones to form the centre and which create good concentric circles.

To create curved areas of paving

Mark out curved areas (see pages 130-1) and hammer stakes into the ground close together. Prepare the sub-base according to your choice of materials. Soak lengths of softwood in water to make them pliable, and bend and nail them to the stakes to give a timber formwork to the shape. Scoring through the back of the wood with a saw is another method of achieving curved forms. Thin hardboard is easy to bend and can be used in several thicknesses to build this up. Pave the area to match your design.

To create patterns

Paving materials can be laid in a variety of patterns, known as bonds. This is particularly true of bricks and block pavers, and the results can create a feeling of texture. Another way to create interest is to treat joints between slabs. It is usual to lay natural stone and concrete slabs butt-jointed – that is, with no mortar showing between them. Leave wide joints between natural stone slabs and fill with gravel and low-growing plants for an informal, textural path.

Also consider juxtaposing materials in an area to give textural contrast, and avoid the monotony of a single treatment in a large area. Work out on squared paper exactly how to achieve such patterns on the ground: it will save much time when it comes to laying the paving. In addition, take into account the varying thicknesses of the different materials you will be using.

BUILDING STEPS

If you have a sloping garden or one that is on several different levels, steps make it easier and safer to get from one area to another.

Outdoor steps should be much lower than indoor stairs. The overall width is up to you, but width, treads and risers should be uniform throughout the flight. Treads should be at least 300mm from front to back to give a secure foothold. If the steps form part of a pathway, they should be the same width, otherwise a minimum width of 600mm allows one person to use them at a time. Risers should be about 200mm high, which is the equivalent of two bricks and a paving slab in height – it is not a good idea to design steps with a riser less than 10cm high as this will tend to cause users to trip and miss the step. Include a landing on long flights, every six steps, made as wide as you can.

The front edges of the treads (the nosing) should overhang the risers by about 25mm, which helps to make the edge of each step more visible. Each tread should slope very slightly from back to front to ensure that surface water drains from the step.

Both built-in (i.e. on slopes) and free-standing steps are commonly constructed from brick risers and paving slab treads. Your material should match other hard materials or existing masonry if you are not renewing patios and paths.

Built-in steps

Mark out the flight by pegging out two parallel string lines the width of the steps from the top of the slope to the bottom. Work out how many steps you will need by measuring the vertical height of the slope. Use string attached to a peg at the top of the slope and hold it horizontal at the bottom of the step by tying it to a can or post. Check with a spirit level and measure the height of the string on the cane from the ground and the length of the flight. Divide the height of the slope by 200mm to give the number of steps you will need. Next, divide the number of steps into the length of the slope to give the tread

At the base of the slope, create a concrete footing by digging beneath the bottom riser a hole about twice the depth of the tread, 10cm wider than the steps, and about 10cm deep. Create a strip foundation with hardcore and concrete, and leave to harden for 48 hours.

Create the first riser by laying two courses of bricks on the concrete strip and back-filling behind it with fine-grade (i.e. small) hardcore and stones. Compact well and top with sand to fill any hollows.

Spread mortar around the perimeter of the slab position and bed the first tread on this mortar base. Align the nosings with the string guidelines stretched across the flight. Tamp down with the handle of a club hammer. Check the treads are level across from side to side and have a slight slope from back to front. A shim can be used to keep this consistent.

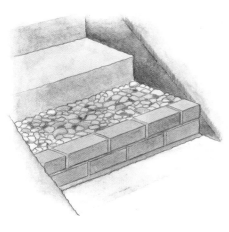 

Built-in steps: cut step shapes in a slope, then build the first riser on a concrete foundation strip. Backfill behind it, bed the first tread slabs in place and add further risers and treads to complete the flight.

depth. If this works out at under 30cm, reduce the number of risers by increasing their height slightly. This will increase the depth of the tread to the safe minimum.

Mark the position of the tread nosings by driving pegs into the ground along the sides of the flight at correct intervals and stretching the string across. Start digging out the rough step shapes from the top of the flight down to the bottom. Work downwards to ensure that the edges of the steps are not broken down. Compact the earth with a large timber post, again avoiding crumbling the cut-out shapes.

Build the second riser on the back edge of the first tread and repeat the process described above. Continue adding risers and treads until you have reached the top of the flight. Finish by tidying up the pointing between the risers.

The cut into sides of the slope may be unstable and crumble on to the steps. Contain this soil by building dwarf retaining walls at the sides of the treads to slope with the steps. On slopes steeper than 30 degrees, fit a post-and-rail handrail at the side of the steps.

Free-standing steps

Work out how many steps you will need, as with built-in steps. Tread depth can be any figure above 30cm – work out multiples of the paving slab you are using to avoid unnecessary cutting to fit. Lay out the lower level of the flight with bricks. If it is part of a patio, do this as you prepare the foundations of that. Mark out with pegs and string.

Free-standing steps require firm foundations. Lay a concrete foundation 100mm larger than the outline of the steps and about 100mm thick. Leave to harden for 48 hours.

Free-standing steps: build on a concrete foundation slab for stability. Build up each riser and the perimeter walls to the required height and backfill each section before bedding the slabs in place.

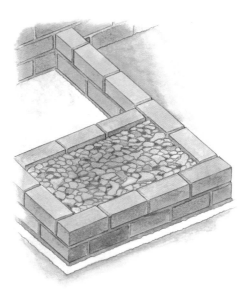

Tie string lines across the concrete as a guide for the first riser. Lay the bricks in two courses of stretcher bond, aligning the outer top edge with the guidelines. Tooth the risers into the terrace wall against which you are building by chopping out the brickwork at alternate courses. This bonds the new brickwork with the old.

Raise the brickwork from the foundation slab within the perimeter wall to form the other risers. Check that the brickwork is horizontal and that the sides are not bowing. Tip hardcore into the plinth and compact it thoroughly. Spread sand over, smooth with a straight edge of wood and finish with a layer of fine concrete.

Bed the slabs to form the treads on the mortar and tamp them down. Make sure that the

nosings overlap the risers by 25mm, and check that the slabs are level across their surface but slope slightly from back to front.

LAYING STEPPING STONES AND LOGS

If you are aiming for an informal look, stepping stones and log paths can be an appropriate choice. Stepping stones can be laid in an area of gravel to define a path or in a lawn to give extra surface strength and durability to a grass path through the garden. Log sections are available from garden centres and can be laid either in a similar way to slabs, so that most of the surface of the path is 'paved' by them, or they can be

laid as stepping stones. Alternatively, log edging – either vertical in roll form or as horizontal timber pieces – can form the edge of paths. The surface of the path can be made from gravel or bark flakes.

Slab stepping stones

If the stepping stones are to cross an area of gravel, lay the foundation for the area and position the slabs. These should be spaced an average stride-length apart. Position the slabs on beds of sand 50mm deep. Tamp down with the handle of a club hammer, and fill the surrounding area with gravel.

Give a stepping-stone path an edging of timber. If you want to alternate between having pairs of stones set side by side with singles every

For a stepping-stone log path lay as for slabs. A good filling could be bark chippings.

alternate stride, make sure the path is wide enough for this. Dig out to a depth of 100mm and compact the soil. Place the slabs in position, again matching them to a stride's length and bedding them on sand 50mm deep. Tamp each slab down. Fill between the stones with a pebble mulch. Consider using a geo-textile membrane beneath loose material to keep the materials from wearing into the soil beneath. Less topping up will be needed to maintain the finished level.

For stepping-stone slabs cut into a lawn, position the stones or slabs in the line required and test the stride-length. Mark the shape of each stone with a trowel or sand and remove the turf from the spaces. Lay the paving 15mm below the surface of the lawn on a 25mm bed of sand. This ensures that a mower can be taken across the surface without damage. Fill any gap around the stones with fine soil.

Log paths

The wood must be pressure-treated. If the log rounds are deep, make sure that they are all the same height to give an even surface. For a 'paved' path, prepare as for a gravel path. If the path runs through a woodland area, the edges need not be contained so long as the surrounding grass is not regularly mown lawn. Lay the log rounds close together, almost touching on a base of sand and gravel. Fill the gaps between the logs with a mixture of sand and gravel, brushed in with a stiff broom. Log stepping stones should be placed at stride-lengths apart.

RAISED BEDS

Well-designed raised beds add interest to flat gardens. In sloping gardens raised beds can help to provide a smooth transition between different levels in the garden. You can use them to create 'sunken' gardens without having to excavate large amounts of soil. They are also useful if you want to grow plants that you might otherwise struggle to cultivate – azaleas and rhododendrons in alkaline soil, for instance – and are of great benefit to gardeners with limited mobility and sight (see pages 26-8). Raised beds can be designed to any shape and height you require – you can even create them with an edge that provides seating space.

Part of, if not all of, the outline of a raised bed will take the form of a retaining wall so the materials you can consider using will be the same as for any other retaining wall – wood, brick, concrete blocks and stone. However, raised beds rarely have to withstand the pressure exerted on ordinary retaining walls, so construction is relatively simple. Most d-i-y raised beds will come in the height range of 30 to 60cm. For higher walls or for walls of a length exceeding 6m, greater levels of expertise will be required for their design and construction. This is due to the force of soil in such larger volume constructions. It would be best to seek advice from an architect, engineer or builder if your plans involve this scale of work.

Drainage of a raised bed is very important. If the bed is open at the base any excess water should drain out. If it is totally contained, you will have to include weep holes about 5 to 7cm above the

The colours and texture of this low raised bed blend well with the path next to it.

ground, spaced 60 to 90cm apart. An 80-cm layer of crushed rock should be placed in the bed before it is filled with soil.

Link beds together to form interlocking shapes. This will give interesting ground patterns and also corners to enjoy them from. Moreover, you can fill raised beds with things other than planting – water, barbecues, large stones, and sandpits for children, perhaps. A raised bed might be appropriate if you need to make a significant change in level around a mature tree. The bed would contain the soil around the roots of the tree. If the ground level is to be raised, build the wall around the tree before levelling. Soil can be piled up against the wall as if it were the outside of a well. These types of raised bed should be built around a tree in line with the outermost part of its canopy, which mirrors the extent of the root structure.

USING BRICKS AND BLOCKS

It is easy to build a rectangular brick or block bed, but the results can look a little dull. Creating a series of raised beds of different heights and sizes will provide much more visual interest.

Excavate and prepare a strip foundation suitable for the size of the wall. If you are building a raised bed at the edge of a new patio, incorporate the footing as part of this work. Mark out the dimensions of the raised bed, using timber profiles to establish corners, and stretch string between to give guidelines as you build up the walls.

The first course of bricks should be below ground level. Leave drainage holes (i.e., small unmortared gaps between every three or four bricks) in larger beds after one course of bricks above ground level, or include a plastic drainage pipe just above ground level, particularly in areas with heavy soils. Include a damp-proof course by using two courses of engineering bricks just above ground level. With single-brick walls, finish the top with a coping stone – if using paving slabs, use these cut to width or in the correct size. Make sure that the front edge of the coping stone overhangs the top of the wall. Another finish would be a single row of bricks on edge. Alternatively, you could use chamfered coping bricks, which eliminate sharp edges. These can be the same colour as the wall or in a contrasting one.

For low-budget raised beds, use concrete blocks. The finished wall can be rendered and painted to match the rest of your garden, or simply painted with a suitable masonry paint.

If you plan to grow ericaceous plants in brick or block raised beds, the walls must be lined to prevent the lime in the mortar from leaching into the soil. Lining a raised bed or retaining wall can also be done to stop the effects of damp – the appearance of inflorescence on the front of the wall. Use a butyl liner, heavy-duty black polythene or bitumastic paint.

USING LOG ROLLS

Pressure-treated prefabricated log rolls are available from garden centres and timber suppliers. A versatile material, they can form curves and circles easily and are available in heights ranging from 15 to 45cm. Remember that about half the height will be buried beneath the ground. A big advantage of using log rolls is that they do not require foundations.

Mark out the area where you plan to install the raised bed. Dig a shallow trench about half the height of the log roll around the edge. This will secure the log edging. Drape heavy-duty polythene over the back wall of the trench to provide damp-proofing to the back of the log roll. Although the timber is pressure-treated and guaranteed for some years, this will extend its life by reducing contact with damp soil.

Unroll the log edging and position it in the trench. You may want to use stakes or stones to hold it while you backfill the trench with soil. Dig over the rest of the soil and add more prior to planting. You may want to create a contour in this area by mounding the soil towards the middle of the bed.

USING PALISADES

Wooden stakes or palisades can be used to create beds of great variety, both in their shape and height, in fact the height can be varied within a single bed. An uneven or random finish to the top of the palisades creates interest. However, palisades are not as simple to install as log rolls.

Mark out the outline of the bed. Dig a trench 40cm wide and half the finished height of the bed in depth. Install guidelines along the length

Right: raised bed and ground-level bed.

of the bed where the palisades should form the wall. Fill the trench with 20cm of gravel and insert the palisades, packed together. Brace in position and pour a 20cm layer of concrete over the gravel to secure them in position.

Leave to set – at least 48 hours – and fit a waterproof membrane to the back of the timber for extra protection. Then backfill the soil above the concrete. Prepare the base of the bed by breaking up the soil using a fork. Fill the bottom of the bed with about 30cm of hardcore – large stones, broken bricks etc – followed by a layer of smaller grade stones. A layer of permeable material such as geo-textile membrane can be laid at this point to stop soil from sinking into the hardcore. Fill the bed with soil or the required compost.

USING RAILWAY SLEEPERS

Railway sleepers, available from sleeper merchants and salvage yards, make an excellent building material for raised beds. They are cheap and will last indefinitely. Standard size

Pansies in raised bed made of logs.

sleepers are 240cm x 25cm x 12.5cm, but some outlets also stock crossing timbers. These are longer wooden sections, used at railway junctions and points, and they can be up to 6.5m long.

Sleepers are heavy to work with and will ooze tar in hot weather for several years, ruling them out if young children are going to be playing near them.

Horizontal
When the sleepers are laid horizontally, no footing is necessary as stability comes from the length and weight of the sleeper. If in doubt,

SOIL IN RAISED BEDS

To ensure good drainage, line the bottom of the bed with a layer of coarse gravel or stones. To prevent this getting clogged, cover it with a permeable material such as Plantex (sold at garden centres). For most plants, filling the bed with topsoil should be perfectly adequate. However, if your soil is poor, mix it with mushroom compost or similar to improve. To grow alpines, you need sharp drainage. Use an equal mixture of soil and sharp grit (substitute half the soil for peat or potting compost if your soil is very heavy). For acid-loving plants, fill the bed with moss-peat mixed with a base fertiliser but no lime.

Raised bed planted with pelargoniums and Helichrysum petiolare.

Vertical

Use railway sleepers vertically for a different effect. (You will need more sleepers using this method.) Mark out the raised bed, and dig a trench around the perimeter 45cm deep. Place some gravel in the bottom, then bed the sleepers in the trench so that they form a wall. Either concrete them in or backfill with soil and compact. For a staggered top, lay the sleepers out prior to use and cut the ends to form a random turret effect when positioned vertically.

USING GRAVEL BOARDS

Use pressure-treated softwood gravel boards (from fencing suppliers) to create relatively inexpensive raised beds. They can be painted with a timber stain to match other timber features in your garden – for example, an adjacent pergola and rose arch. There is a limit to how much soil can be retained in this way, though, and the structure will have a limited lifespan. But if you have rock-free soil, this is a good way to add interest to your garden.

sink up to half the depth into the ground. Give the structure a rolled gravel base to aid drainage. Use a bow saw to cut the sleepers to length, but aim to build the walls in multiples of full or half sleeper lengths to reduce the amount of work. Lay sleepers like bricks, positioning them on their base to create a running bond. The joints are therefore staggered and the corners formed by placing two sleepers at 90 degrees to each other. Hold the sleepers together with metal joining plates and screws or lengths of thick galvanised wire secured with heavy duty staples. For walls over 75cm insert steel rods through the sleepers to make sure they are secure.

Use 150x25mm lengths of gravel board supported by 5x5x100cm stakes for an edge that has a finished height of 45cm. The boards are fixed to the stakes by galvanised nails or brass screws. The length of the stake will be determined by the type of soil that you have and the height that you want to make the timber beds. In firm ground, sink the vertical stake up to about half its length into the soil; in softer sandy soil sink them slightly deeper. Position the stakes at 1m intervals and sink the first board about 5cm into the soil for extra stability.

GARDEN BUILDINGS

Well-designed raised beds add interest to flat gardens. In sloping gardens raised beds can help to provide a smooth transition between different levels in the garden. You can use them to create 'sunken' gardens without having to excavate large amounts of soil. They are also useful if you want to grow plants that you might otherwise struggle to cultivate – azaleas and rhododendrons in alkaline soil, for instance – and are of great benefit to gardeners with limited mobility and sight (see pages 26-28). Raised beds can be designed to any shape and height you require – you can even create them with an edge that provides seating space.

Part of, if not all of, the outline of a raised bed will take the form of a retaining wall so the materials you can consider using will be the same as for any other retaining wall – wood, brick, concrete blocks and stone. However, raised beds rarely have to withstand the

pressure exerted on ordinary retaining walls, so construction is relatively simple. Most d-i-y raised beds will come in the height range of 30-60cm. For higher walls or for walls of a length exceeding 6m, greater levels of expertise will be required for their design and construction. This is due to the force of soil in such larger volume constructions. It would be best to seek advice from an architect, engineer or builder if your plans involve this scale of work.

Drainage of a raised bed is very important. If the bed is open at the base any excess water should drain out. If it is totally contained, you will have to include weep holes about 5-7cm above the ground, spaced 60-90cm apart. An 80cm layer of crushed rock should be placed in the bed before it is filled with soil.

Link beds together to form interlocking shapes. This will give interesting ground patterns and

Sections of a typical ready-to-assemble garden shed.

TIPS FOR SHEDS

● If you plan to use the shed as a workshop, the ceiling inside must provide adequate headroom for the user to stand upright. Check if it is constructed with interior cross braces.

● The floor should be firm – test by jumping up and down on it.

● Check to make sure that no gaps are visible in the cladding. A shed roof should be strong enough to resist sagging – roof panels should not flex when pushed in the centre.

also corners to enjoy them from. Moreover, you can fill raised beds with things other than planting – water, barbecues, large stones, and sandpits for children, perhaps. A raised bed might be appropriate if you need to make a significant change in level around a mature tree. The bed would contain the soil around the roots of the tree. If the ground level is to be raised, build the wall around the tree before levelling. Soil can be piled up against the wall as if it were the outside of a well. These types of raised bed should be built around a tree in line

with the outermost part of its canopy, which mirrors the extent of the root structure.

USING BRICKS AND BLOCKS

It is easy to build a rectangular brick or block bed, but the results can look a little dull. Creating a series of raised beds of different heights and sizes will provide much more visual interest.

Excavate and prepare a strip foundation suitable for the size of the wall. If you are building a raised bed at the edge of a new patio, incorporate the footing as part of this work. Mark out the dimensions of the raised bed, using timber profiles to establish corners, and stretch string between to give guidelines as you build up the walls.

The first course of bricks should be below ground level. Leave drainage holes (i.e., small unmortared gaps between every three or four bricks) in larger beds after one course of bricks above ground level, or include a plastic drainage pipe just above ground level, particularly in areas with heavy soils. Include a

Your garden shed need not be brown. Consider making a feature of it by painting it a bright colour.

damp-proof course by using two courses of engineering bricks just above ground level. With single-brick walls, finish the top with a coping stone – if using paving slabs, use these cut to width or in the correct size. Make sure that the front edge of the coping stone overhangs the top of the wall. Another finish would be a single row of bricks on edge. Alternatively, you could use chamfered coping bricks, which eliminate sharp edges. These can be the same colour as the wall or in a contrasting one.

For low-budget raised beds, use concrete blocks. The finished wall can be rendered and painted to match the rest of your garden, or simply painted with a suitable masonry paint.

If you plan to grow ericaceous plants in brick or block raised beds, the walls must be lined to prevent the lime in the mortar from leaching into the soil. Lining a raised bed or retaining wall can also be done to stop the effects of damp – the appearance of inflorescence on the front of the wall. Use a butyl liner, heavy-duty black polythene or bitumastic paint.

TIPS FOR GREENHOUSES

● To make the best use of summer light, position the longer axis of the greenhouse north–south. To get plants off to an early start in spring, and for overwintering tender plants, place the longer side along an east–west axis.

● Avoid siting your greenhouse at the bottom of a slope because there may be a frost pocket.

● Place lean-to greenhouses on a wall of the house that receives a mixture of sun and shade: avoid a south-facing wall.

● Keep some work space to the front of the greenhouse for unloading plants etc.

● Remember possible need for water and power. Electricity is useful for lighting, time switches and thermostatic controls. Water on site saves the need for trailing hosepipes and allows the installation of an automatic system.

USING LOG ROLLS

Pressure-treated prefabricated log rolls are available from garden centres and timber suppliers. A versatile material, they can form curves and circles easily and are available in heights ranging from 15- 45cm. Remember that about half the height will be buried beneath the

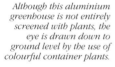

Although this aluminium greenhouse is not entirely screened with plants, the eye is drawn down to ground level by the use of colourful container plants.

ground. A big advantage of using log rolls is that they do not require foundations.

Mark out the area where you plan to install the raised bed. Dig a shallow trench about half the height of the log roll around the edge. This will secure the log edging. Drape heavy-duty polythene over the back wall of the trench to provide damp-proofing to the back of the log roll. Although the timber is pressure-treated and guaranteed for some years, this will extend its life by reducing contact with damp soil.

Unroll the log edging and position it in the trench. You may want to use stakes or stones to hold it while you backfill the trench with soil. Dig over the rest of the soil and add more prior to planting. You may want to create a contour in this area by mounding the soil towards the middle of the bed.

USING PALISADES

Wooden stakes or palisades can be used to create beds of great variety, both in their shape and height, in fact the height can be varied within a single bed. An uneven or random finish to the top of the palisades creates interest. However, palisades are not as simple to install as log rolls.

Mark out the outline of the bed. Dig a trench 40cm wide and half the finished height of the bed in depth. Install guidelines along the length of the bed where the palisades should form the wall. Fill the trench with 20cm of gravel and insert the palisades, packed together. Brace in position and pour a 20cm layer of concrete over the gravel to secure them in position.

Leave to set – at least 48 hours – and fit a waterproof membrane to the back of the timber for extra protection. Then backfill the soil above the concrete. Prepare the base of the bed by breaking up the soil using a fork. Fill the bottom of the bed with about 30cm of hardcore – large stones, broken bricks etc – followed by a layer of smaller grade stones. A layer of permeable material such as geo-textile membrane can be laid at this point to stop soil from sinking into the hardcore. Fill the bed with soil or the required compost.

USING RAILWAY SLEEPERS

Railway sleepers, available from sleeper merchants and salvage yards, make an excellent building material for raised beds. They are cheap and will last indefinitely. Standard size sleepers are 240cm x 25cm x 12.5cm, but some outlets also stock crossing timbers. These are longer wooden sections, used at railway junctions and points, and they can be up to 6.5m long.

Sleepers are heavy to work with and will ooze tar in hot weather for several years, ruling them out if young children are going to be playing near them.

Horizontal
When the sleepers are laid horizontally, no footing is necessary as stability comes from the length and weight of the sleeper. If in doubt, sink up to half the depth into the ground. Give the structure a rolled gravel base to aid drainage. Use a bow saw to cut the sleepers to length, but aim to build the walls in multiples of full or half sleeper lengths to reduce the amount of work. Lay sleepers like bricks, positioning them on their base to create a running bond. The joints are therefore staggered and the corners formed by placing two sleepers at 90 degrees to each other. Hold the sleepers together with metal joining plates and screws or lengths of thick galvanised wire secured with heavy duty staples. For walls over 75cm insert steel rods through the sleepers to make sure they are secure.

Vertical
Use railway sleepers vertically for a different effect. (You will need more sleepers using this method.) Mark out the raised bed, and dig a trench around the perimeter 45cm deep. Place some gravel in the bottom, then bed the sleepers in the trench so that they form a wall. Either concrete them in or backfill with soil and compact. For a staggered top, lay the sleepers out prior to use and cut the ends to form a

This greenhouse has been partly screened from the house by the use of a trellis and strategic planting of shrubs.

TRELLISWORK

Trellis is a popular choice for divisions and screens. Its applications are numerous: small trellis panels can be added to the top of a fence for extra height and interest, or an area of trellis can be attached to a dull wall, perhaps as a support for twining plants; trellis will make an excellent temporary screen to protect a young hedge; and a wall can be given the illusion of greater depth and space with the use of false perspective trellis panels – these look good either with or without a central *trompe l'oeil* to frame.

Timber is the most common material for trellis; it can look good even when left without a clothing of plants, particularly if it has been stained to match or harmonise with surrounding colour schemes. Timber trellis can be bought in prefabricated panels ranging from rustic-style half-log to simple squares and elaborate styles with curved edges. At the top of the range, trellis panels can be made to size from hardwoods such as oak, which will weather to a wonderful silver. You can use ready-made trellis columns or pilasters for an open but substantial-looking structure (a useful disguise for ugly downpipes). Ready-made softwood panels, which should have been treated with wood preservative, will need some maintenance every few years.

Panels made from plastic, coated steel or Timbron are also available. (Timbron is actually recycled polystyrene that looks like timber but is lighter in weight.) These can be wiped free of garden grime and are a good choice where weight is a consideration (for example, in roof gardens and balconies), and for gardens with a very modern look. Colour choice can be extended through the use of spray paints. Coated steel systems are usually supplied in a flat-pack kit and include all necessary fixtures and fittings. These should be assembled according to the manufacturer's instructions.

For something completely unique, you may want to design and build your own trellis from scratch – useful if you have unique size requirements or want to follow a particular theme through. It is not necessarily a cheaper option than buying ready-made trellis, though.

MAKING SCREENS FROM TRELLIS

The principles for installing a ready-made trellis screen are the same as for installing a panel fence. The height of the posts depends on the size of the prefabricated panels chosen and the style of the barrier you wish to create. For example, the panels do not have to be full length but might be positioned with a space beneath them. Or, using full-length posts, a low panel can be placed at the bottom of the gap with a crossbeam or rope swag above. In this way, an element of individuality can be achieved using ready-made components.

Mark out the run of the barrier and put a stake where each post is to go. Install the first post using fence spikes for flexibility. If the panel is to be clothed with climbing plants it will offer increased resistance to the wind, so it may be a good idea to fix the fence spike into concrete for extra strength. Check that the posts are the right distance apart by laying the trellis panel along the ground between them.

The panels can be nailed to the posts using galvanised nails, but for a neater look, pre-drill holes in the posts and use screws. For a really professional-looking finish – especially in tiny balcony and roof gardens where every detail is noticeable – countersink the screws, using brass ones with surface cups. Add any top detailing above the panels, as well as post caps and finials to the posts. Stain with your chosen colour prior to planting up, or touch up around screws.

FIXING TRELLIS TO WALLS AND OTHER STRUCTURES

Trellis panels can be attached to walls, fences, external doors and gates. Shadows cast by the trellis provide attractive relief to solid masonry. For wall mounting purposes, panels do not have to be as substantial in construction as free standing types. You can use the expanding diamond latticework variety available in wood or plastic. Light ready-made panels should provide continuity with free-standing structures, or you can make your own to match other features and the style of your garden.

To fix trellis panels to walls or fences, a spacer should be left between the panel and surface

behind to allow air to circulate freely and climbing plants to wind around the support. This can be done using small offcuts of wood. Old cotton reels may be ideal – stain them to match the panel before fixing. Some panels are pre-drilled; if not, drill holes for screws in the edge of the panel. Hold it against the wall in the right position. Mark through the holes where the wall is to be drilled and drill holes.

Push in the wall plugs, then secure the panel with screws that are long enough to go through the reels or spacers. The process is similar for attaching trellis panels to close-boarded fences. To fix to the back of the fence, attach the panel to the arris rails.

The need to maintain a wall or fence behind trelliswork should always be considered. One solution is to screw a batten on to the base of the wall or fence and to attach the trellis to this with hinges. Attach another batten to the wall near the trellis and screw the trellis on to this.

Use trellis to add height to walls and fences. This will increase privacy without making your garden feel like a fortress. It looks better than a solid wall or fence, too. Check whether there are any boundary height restrictions first, though, particularly in a front garden. If the boundary itself belongs to your neighbour, ask permission first.

Fence posts have to be extended to take an additional trellis panel. The options are to use ready-made metal fence extenders or pieces of exterior-quality plywood to join an extension to the original post. Trellis tops for fences and walls range from diamond latticework and basketweave, both with straight tops, to convex or concave curves. Finish the job by attaching protective post caps to the extended uprights and decorative finials.

MAKING YOUR OWN TRELLIS

When designing and making your own trellis, make sure the timber such as tiling battens or

Perspective trellis (see box).

Trompe l'oeil Create a false sense of perspective by using increasingly smaller frames linked by straight pieces of timber positioned to look like vanishing lines (see picture to left). Perspective panels are more effective if used to contrast with a real view – e.g. incorporating real doorways or windows to heighten surprise. Draw up to full size on the wall to calculate perspective. Use exterior-grade plywood (18mm) with 38x18mm battens for the frame. Arches can be pitched or semi-circular.

Drainpipe disguise (see picture to right) Use 38x18mm tiling batten to construct a three-sided box. Side battens are fixed inside, front ones on the outside. Create a base from 18mm exterior plywood and secure to the wall on to pre-placed 50x25mm battens. Latticework pilasters or columns are good.

Arches for mirrors Use ready-made trellis archways or make your own. Attach outdoor, weatherproof mirror to the wall – this should fill the arch. Fit arch to the wall to enclose the mirror.

Scroll-topped trellis panel (see picture on page 13) Create a shaped top to mimic shapes elsewhere in your garden. Build the panel using 38x18mm tiling battens or roofing laths. Draw a template of the top first and use this to mark up the outline on external-quality plywood. Cut two identical shapes using a jig-saw. Nail to both sides of the top of the trellis panel. Trim the protruding pieces of batten. For weatherproofing, use good-quality paint or stain for both top and panel.

roofing laths, has been treated with preservative. These can be coloured with outdoor paint, wood stains, or interior paint diluted in a 1:3 mix with white spirit. It is easier to paint the timber prior to assembly – using paint pads can give better results.

For a simple panel, make a rectangular frame to the required size, using 25x50mm sawn timber. For the slats, use 38x18mm tiling battens (from roofing merchants). Join the frame and slats with galvanised nails that are around 12mm longer than the joint thickness of the wood. Once you have hammered in the nails, turn the trellis over and flatten the protruding nail points, ensuring the heads are supported on a solid surface. Space the slats 75mm apart, depending on the degree of privacy required.

For a basketweave trellis panel, you can buy fence slats from fencing suppliers. Paint or stain to suit. First nail the upright slats to the frame, leaving 100mm spaces. Then weave the horizontal slats through and secure in position.

As well as traditional square and diamond trellis, you can create all sorts of designs such as herringbone, diagonal stripes or even spider-web. Curved or ornate shaped tops can be cut from exterior grade plywood using a jig-saw. Join identical pieces to either side of the panel.

When making extension panels for the tops of fences and walls, the dimensions of the framework will depend on the space between the supporting posts. Use 50x25mm timber for the frame for both extension trellis panels and hand-made wall trelliswork.

Use trellis to disguise a utilitarian drainpipe (see box).

ARCHES AND PERGOLAS

Timber pergola in corner of the Gardening Which? *family garden.*

Arches, pergolas and structures such as arbours and obelisks add instant vertical height and year-round interest. They can be positioned to frame views, define axes and mark transitions. They can also support climbing plants, adding another dimension to planting.

Arches should link with another structure or be placed in a position such as at the beginning or end of a path. Their dimensions should be in scale with the surrounding garden and the function they are to perform. Position them to mark changes in areas of the garden, such as a transition from formal to informal. They are also excellent framing devices. Placing one to span a path will encourage visitors to walk under the arch to discover the garden beyond. This will work equally well with a dead straight path, where the arch will frame a perspective view with a focal point at the end, or a path that curves intriguingly out of sight.

The term pergola has come to mean any garden structure with a series of upright columns or posts supporting crossbeams over which climbing plants are trained. In past times, it referred more strictly to a plant-covered walk. A pergola that spans a path can be regarded as a series of arches. Build one to mirror the curves of the path beneath; linking the posts with sidebeams turns the pergola into a tunnel when climbing plants have covered the structure. Pergolas can be a practical means of providing shade in an extremely sunny spot, where trees and large shrubs may be inappropriate. They can be supported on one side by a house wall or a high boundary wall to give the feel of a covered area.

Arbours are covered, sheltered areas that usually contain a seat. They are open on one side only, so they do not form walkways in the manner of a pergola. They can be formed by hedging, masonry, posts or trelliswork, with crossbeams over the central area. The framework supports climbing or trained plants.

Obelisks are vertical columns that reduce in size towards the top, frequently in the form of an elongated pyramid. They can be used as frames for climbing or scrambling plants. Alternatively, they can be left unadorned, providing structure in a planted border. Simple tripods – informal alternatives – can be easily made from canes, tree stakes, or rustic poles.

CHOOSING BETWEEN WOOD AND METAL

Apart from cost implications, other factors affecting choice of materials are the dimensions and design of the structure, lifespan, relative 'weight', and appropriateness to the rest of the garden. For most small gardens, the choice will boil down to timber or metal in one form or another. In terms of installation and maintenance, coated steel is lighter and easier to handle. It requires little ongoing maintenance, but it may not suit the type of planting that you have in mind. For example, large climbing plants such as wistaria and vigorous growers like *Solanum* would soon be out of scale with the feature.

Steel scaffold poles have the extra weight useful for forming pergola posts. Using the same material for the crossbeams may be a little utilitarian for some tastes, but the resulting structure would certainly be rugged enough to support most climbers. A compromise may be reached by using scaffold posts with timber crossbeams.

All timber has an organic appeal and sits well in informal surroundings. For cottage-style and informal country gardens, choose a rustic pole structure. For timeless grace, nothing beats the patina of weatherworn oak. Timber is easy to work with if you decide to make your own pergola and arches.

MAKING YOUR OWN PERGOLA

Be sure to get the dimensions of the finished pergola right: nothing is more irritating than having something that is not tall or wide enough to accommodate plants and paths.

Any structure over a path should be wide enough to span it *and* allow at least 30cm for planting around each post. Pleasing proportions can be given to pergolas if you design them as a series of cubes, with height, width and space between posts being equal. The height should be at least 2.5m for plants to be trained over it and to allow enough room for walking beneath. If you plan to plant wistaria or trained laburnum, allow extra height for hanging blooms. You may want to create intermediary crossbeams, particularly if the structure is to provide instant shade.

D-I-Y TIMBER PERGOLA

Calculate how many posts your site has space for – you may have already done this when drawing up the plan. Timber uprights should normally be 75x75mm minimum, but if other features are larger-scale and the site can take extra weight, or you plan to grow larger climbers, increase this to 100x100mm. Choose pressure-treated softwood or hardwood. Main roof or crossbeams must be strong enough for the structure. You can use the same timber as the posts for a strong arch or series of them, or 150x150mm, which can be bought ready-notched for fitting the uprights, and finished at the ends.

Rose-covered arch.

Galvanised brackets and screws can be used to fix the crossbeams to the uprights, but the structure will be stronger and more visually attractive if carpentry joints are made. If side beams are included, these can be fixed with simple notched joints. If you plan to have a single crossbeam, fixed with a cross-halving joint on to the post, then the height of the posts will be whatever finished height you decide on. If you plan to make the crossbeams out of thinner timber and fit either side of the uprights, then the posts should be higher than the finished height of the pergola – allow a minimum of 100mm extra timber and shape the end to suit. All cut timber must be treated with preservative and stained to match.

The main crossbeams of a pergola must be capable of supporting the plant growth plus other weights such as snow that might collect there. They should also be able to support the weight of people if they are to play a dual role as part of a swing or other play equipment. If you are in any way unsure of its ability to take this kind of extra weight, tell your children

An arch creates a sense of mystery – what is around that corner?

firmly that they must not attempt to play on it. You may want to include secondary crossbeams made from smaller pieces of wood. Alternatively, wire can be stretched across to support climbing plant growth so that a roof is formed.

Whichever construction method you choose, it is usual for the crossbeams to be given a decorative finish to the ends. You can buy these ready cut, but you may want to design and cut your own to match other aspects of your garden.

PUTTING UP ARCHES AND PERGOLAS

Posts should be positioned and erected in the same manner as fence posts. Given the extra height and weight that these structures have to bear, it is a good idea to combine fence spikes with concrete for extra secure fitting. If the design includes side beams, these should be fitted next, and finally the crossbeams. Add round-headed vine eyes to the top and bottom of each face of the posts and stretch garden wire between to support climbing plants.

WATER FEATURES

Water was one of the first features introduced into the great Mogul and Islamic gardens, where great value was placed on its reflective qualities and cooling effects in a hot, dry landscape. It is just as desirable a feature for a garden in a more temperate climate, adding sound, light and texture. A water feature can provide a natural habitat for wildlife and plants. With modern technology, construction and maintenance are easier than ever before. Options range from a gurgle pond to a small formal pool with fountains and matching statuary: you do not need acres of space to include water in some shape or form that will blend in with the overall design of your garden.

DESIGN CONSIDERATIONS

● Water features should be in scale and character with the surrounding garden.

● Buy the best-quality butyl or PVC liner that you can afford – some butyl is guaranteed for up to 50 years, while cheaper PVC may deteriorate in as little as 5 years.

● To calculate how much liner you will need for any pond, add twice the depth of the proposed pond to its maximum length and width.

● Find a position on level ground that receives the sun for about two-thirds of the day, away from overhanging trees but sheltered from strong winds.

Above and above right: raised formal ponds.

Far right: informal pond.

MAKING A FORMAL POND

A formal pond is strongly geometric in shape and is best sited close to the house and patio. If you are making a raised-edge formal pool, make sure that the walls are strong enough to resist the pressure of the water. Formal ponds with raised edges can be more susceptible to frost damage than those that are sunk into the ground, but, in their favour, can be built to accommodate a space for sitting. If you plan to keep fish in the raised pool, allow a depth of 60cm.

The best method for building a raised formal pond is to construct double walls similar to cavity walls in a house. To keep costs down, use concrete blocks for the interior wall (unseen), and face the exterior with bricks or stones.

Mark out the shape of the pond and excavate for concrete footings. These should be 10-15cm deep and 38cm wide. Install the concrete foundation, remove all sharp stones from the central subsoil and compact this surface. Cover the subsoil with a layer of damp sand. Cover this with an underlay of geo-textile membrane or old carpet to further protect the butyl liner.

Build up the double walls to the required height and fix wall tie wires placed at intervals between the inner block wall and outer brick wall. Check that the walls and the base of the pond are level as you build.

To fit the liner so that an attractive band of brick is exposed on the inner wall above the surface of the water, an extra 1m on each dimension of liner will be required. Prior to laying the top two courses of blocks and bricks, fit the liner into the pool and take it over the inner wall into the cavity. It is a good idea to start filling before securing the top to ensure the liner fits snugly. Weight the excess liners down at the top with loose bricks and blocks. Fill with water from a hose and ensure that it fits smoothly into the rectangular form.

Finish the top two courses of the inner walls with bricks – dark engineering bricks are ideal. Mortar bricks into place using a mix to which a waterproofing agent has been added. Trim the excess liner off and mortar the coping slabs around the top of the pool, making sure that the edges of the slabs overhang the top of the pool at both sides.

The same principles apply if you want to create a formal pool that sits flush with the ground. Keep the pool rectangular, edged with stone at ground level, and sunk into a lawn, gravel or paving. It can be excavated and lined with butyl, but the supporting walls do not necessarily have to be constructed with blocks.

MAKING AN INFORMAL POND

Informal ponds are irregular in shape, sunk into the ground and better placed away from the patio and house. Their edges may be hidden by marginal planting.

Mark out the shape of the pond with a flexible hosepipe: peg it to the ground while you excavate. Mark out where the deepest part of the water will be and the position of shelves for marginal plants. Use levelling pegs to achieve accurate depths. The sides of the pond should slope by up to 20 degrees. At the edges, set datum pegs and check that the edges are level. Even if the ground slopes, the pond must be

level. Remove all sharp stones from the hole and spread damp sand, geo-textile membrane or old carpet over the base of the pond to provide a cushion underlay for the liner to a depth of 12mm.

Unfold the liner and fit it into the hole, weighting it down at the edges with bricks or stones. Fit it into the curves and different levels by hand. Then start to fill with water from a hosepipe. As it fills, the water will stretch the liner so that it fits into the contours of the hole. Fill to almost ground level.

Once full, trim off the excess liner with a sharp knife or scissors. Leave an overlap of about 15cm, which will be covered and held in place by an edging of stones or concrete slabs – these might be slabs preformed into curves. Lay the

stones so that they overhang the edge of the pond by 5cm, hiding the liner. The mortar should have a waterproof additive.

An alternative edging treatment for an informal pond might be a sloping 'beach' set with cobblestones. Place the cobblestones on the liner, bed into sand and secure with mortar. Loose pebbles can be added for an authentic finish. The pool might also form part of a rock garden edged with rocks in natural-looking outcrops and sunken groups.

POND PLANTS

FLOATERS
Eichornia (water hyacinth)
Hydrocharis (frog bit)
Stratiotes aloides (water soldier)
Trapa natans (water chestnut)
Utricularia vulgaris (bladderwort)

OXYGENATORS
Callistriche verna (water starwort)
Ceratophyllum demersum (hornwort)
Fontinalis antipyretica (willow moss)
Hottonia palustris (water violet)

MARGINALS
Acorus calamus (sweet flag)
Calla palustris (bog arum)
Caltha palustris (marsh marigold)
Carex stricta (sedge)
Iris laevigata (Japanese water iris)
Lobelia cardinalis (Cardinal flower)
Myosotis scorpiodes (water forget-me-not)
Schoenoplectus ssp. tabernaemontani 'Zebrinus'
Typha minima (reedmace)
Zantedeschia aethiopica (white arum lily)

WATER LILIES
Dwarf forms
Nymphaea candida – white
N. 'Paul Hariot' – yellow
N. laydekeri 'Lilacea' – pink

Small forms
N. 'James Brydon' – carmine
N. laydekeri 'Fulgens' – red
N. odorata 'Sulphurea' – canary yellow

MAKING A POND FOR WILDLIFE

Adding a pond to a wildlife garden (see pages 110-13) will increase the diversity of creatures attracted. The larger the pond the greater the variety, but even a small pond can support a surprising array of creatures if planted and maintained sympathetically.

Aim to create an organically shaped pool. Dig out the soil to a level 5cm deeper than the

Below: include plenty of native plants, but no fish, in a wildlife pond.

sloping area. Wait 48 hours before planting so that chlorine can evaporate.

You can plant native species in the margins of the pool and the area immediately surrounding the water to attract more wildlife, though some of these plants may become invasive. Include one or two ornamental plants to increase the visual appeal of your wildlife pond. A quick way to establish a variety of pond insects is to collect

depth of water required, to accommodate the liner and underlay. Make the deepest part of the pond at least 60cm to provide an ice-free area for hibernating frogs. Create shelves for marginal plants in the sides about 20-25cm deep, keeping the slope of the sides gentle. A gently sloping shoreline to one side of the pond will provide access for amphibians and other creatures such as hedgehogs which may fall in accidentally.

Take up and put to one side a 30cm strip of soil from the perimeter of the pond. Discard any stones from the base, put down a layer of damp sand or old carpet, then fit the liner. Weight down the edges. Fill the shape slowly with water, allowing it to smooth out the creases of the liner. Cover the edges of the liner with the turf strip and place gravel and pebbles on the

Bog garden enclosing small, informal pool.

a bucket full of water from an established pond. Fish should not be included, however, as they eat tadpoles, spawn and larvae.

MAKING A BOG GARDEN

Bog gardens fit naturally next to informally shaped pools and wildlife ponds, helping to disguise the fact that the pools are man-made. In wildlife gardens, they extend the variety of native plants that can be grown, thus increasing the number of creatures that will be attracted.

If you have a poorly drained area in the garden it is a good idea to work with nature and turn it over to the planting of moisture-lovers rather than trying to drain it. The soil of a bog garden should never dry out but neither should it stand waterlogged for long periods. If there is no naturally damp spot, create one by putting an

Above: cross-section of pond showing water plants submerged to different levels.

Below: you do not need to excavate a pond. Water plants will be happy in a half-barrel, provided you raise them to the appropriate height.

POND PLANTS

LARGE-LEAVED
Darmera peltata (formerly *Peltiphyllum peltatum*) the umbrella plant
Hosta sieboldiana 'Elegans'
Rheum palmatum ornamental rhubarb
Rodgersia aesculifolia

MEDIUM-LEAVED
Eupatorium cannabinum (hemp agrimony)
Filipendula ulmaria (meadowsweet)
Ligularia dentata 'Desdemona'
Lysimachia punctata (loosestrife)
Lythrum (purple loosestrife)
Mimulus cardinalis (monkey flower)

SMALL-LEAVED
Matteuccia struthiopteris (shuttlecock fern)
Onoclea sensibilis (sensitive fern)
Osmunda regalis (the royal fern)
Primula denticulata (drumstick primula)
Trollius (globe flower)

expanse of liner in a place that has been dug out to a shallow level. Puncture the liner with a garden fork to allow for drainage. The area created should not be too large, as it will be difficult to maintain.

You can ensure that an area designated as a bog garden does not dry out by laying capillary matting over the liner to act as a wick between an adjacent pool and the bog. Alternatively, build your bog garden joining the pond with a shallow threshold between the two just below water level.

Fill the area with soil, which should be mixed with a large amount of well-rotted manure, another aid to water retention. Hide the edges of the liner with soil and stones. Finally, add plants that flourish in moisture-retentive soil.

PLANTING

Water plants can be divided into six broad groups: floaters, bog plants, oxygenators, marginals, water lilies and deep-water aquatics. Planting should take place between May and September, not in the dormant season. Use open-sided plastic containers or baskets so that growth can be controlled and plants can be lifted, divided and repotted after a few years.

Floaters, so-called because they float freely near the surface of the water, include the water hyacinth (*Eichornia*) and water chestnut (*Trapa natans*). Frog bit (*Hydrocharis*) is a good plant for a small pond. Bladderwort (*Utricularia vulgaris*) is a carnivorous floater, available from specialist nurseries.

Bog plants will root in moist soil but do not like

Pond in summer with water lilies.

to be permanently submerged. Many large-leaved plants like boggy areas and so make a good choice. *Hosta sieboldiana* 'Elegans' has large blue-green foliage but is prone to slug and snail damage. Smaller-leaved and with feathery white fragrant flowers in summer, meadowsweet (*Filipendula ulmaria*) grows in the wild to about one metre. Some ferns are appropriate: *Onoclea sensibilis* can also grow in shallow water, while *Osmunda regalis*, one of the tallest hardy ferns and with rich bronze fronds in autumn, requires a lime-free soil.

The foliage of oxygenators, also known as waterweeds, is submerged or on the surface of the water and so releases oxygen into the pond, reducing the build-up of algae and providing egg-laying sites for many pond creatures. The water starwort (*Callitriche verna*) is suitable

for shallow ponds. By contrast, willow moss (*Fontinalis antipyretica*) likes moving water.

The roots of marginals are submerged, while the leaves and flowers grow above the surface of shallow water. They are ideal growing from shelves in the pond. Marsh marigold (*Caltha palustris*) is a popular marginal.

Water lilies are useful for keeping fish cool in summer, but you need to avoid varieties with too vigorous a growth rate for the size of pond. Dwarf forms include *Nymphaea candida*, *N.* 'Paul Hariot' and *N. laydekeri* 'Lilacea'. Deep-water aquatics can be placed in the deepest part of the pond. Their leaves float and flowers grow on the surface of the water. Water hawthorn and pond lilies such as *Nupharlutea* (yellow pond lily) fall into this category.

SAFE WATER FEATURES

Where there are young children around, standing water is always a danger: consider filling a pool temporarily with sand or pebbles and plants until the children are older. Alternatively, choose one of the closed systems that uses a pump to provide the sight and sound of running water. These water features are easy to construct and, because the reservoirs of water are securely covered, they are safe for young children and do not become clogged up with leaves and other debris. Algae are not a problem, because the water reservoir is not exposed to light.

USING PUMPS FOR RUNNING WATER

All of the following features are based on a small reservoir and submersible pump run from mains electricity. If you have no electricity in the garden or outbuildings, you may be able to pass the wire through the wall and plug the pump into a socket, using a residual current device (RCD). If you require an extension cable it is essential to use waterproof connectors. The water in the closed systems has to be topped up from time to time, so site the feature within reach of an outside tap, too. Central heating expansion tanks can be used, hidden, to contain the water, and the larger the tank the less topping up will be required. Tanks can be sited either above or below ground, depending on the style of the feature. The top should be covered with strong wire mesh and then cobbles, rocks or large pebbles which can all be bought from large garden centres.

For ground-level systems, dig a hole deep enough for the top of the tank to be 2-3cm below the surface of the ground. For large fountains (where spray falls outside the tank), the tank should be placed in the centre of the catchment area. This area should be given a slight gradient so that water drains back into the tank for recycling. Line this area with a pond liner and cover with a layer of pebbles.

When choosing a pump you need to know how much water it can pump (the flow rate) and how high (the head height). A small fountain or gurgle pond requires a flow rate of 450-900 litres (100-200 gallons) per hour. A wall fountain, which may deliver the water some distance above the pump, requires 675-900 litres (150-200 gallons) per hour.

BELL FOUNTAINS

Ideal for the tiniest of gardens, a bell fountain can be contained in a free-standing pot. The size of pot will be dictated by the size of the pump you want to use – 30cm is likely to be the minimum base size. If you want to use a terracotta pot, you will need to line it either with butyl or another plastic pot without drainage holes. The pot holds both pump and water. The 'bell' of water is created by the bell fountain attachment for the outlet pipe of the pump.

This type of feature can look good when placed on a low wall near a patio. It can also be grouped with other containers: for example, bog plants grown in half barrels. However, make sure that stray leaves and other debris does not fall into the pot and clog it up.

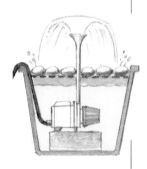

Bell fountain.

Right: water bubbles up through a hole in a rock to form a gurgle pond.

Above: you will need a powerful pump for a wall fountain.

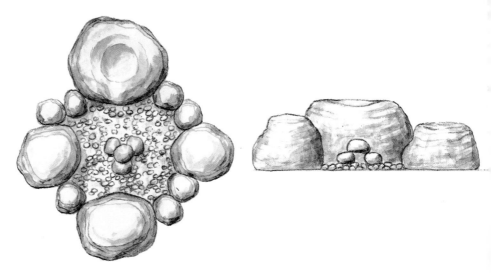

Right: bird's-eye view and elevation of a small Japanese water basin.

GURGLE PONDS

A gurgle pond circulates water up, through and around a large millstone or rock, which can be made flush with the ground or form part of a raised bed. The stone must have a hole through the middle large enough to take the outlet pipe from the pump. The stone is placed on strong metal mesh over the tank, and the area is covered with large pebbles to surround the feature stone. The pipe should finish about 2cm inside the hole so that it cannot be seen from above. The flow rate should be adjusted so that water gurgles out of the hole and runs over the central stone and pebbles back into the tank below. For stronger geyser effects, buy a special attachment for the pump.

To increase the feeling of cool tranquillity that a gurgle pond can bring to your garden, plant moisture-lovers amongst the large pebbles around it. Bold shapes of hostas, arum lilies (*zantedeschia*) and irises will all look attractive.

WALL FOUNTAINS

Wall fountains are suitable for formal gardens, courtyards and areas next to patios. This type of feature can make a good focal point, built to the right scale, at the far end of a small garden. Ornamental fountain heads can be bought in a range of styles and materials.Use recirculated water from a tank.

The outlet hose from the pump pushes the water up to and out of a wall-mounted spout or fountain to fall back into the tank below. The hose can be taken up the back of the wall, via holes drilled top and bottom, or it can be chased into a groove cut into the front of the wall. If building a new wall, install the feature at the time of construction.

Disguise the tank with a low decorative wall, wooden edging or mesh and pebbles. By building the tank wall to a height of 45-65cm and finishing it with a coping of 40-45cm you can provide an area of auxiliary seating at the top.

> *A fascinating aspect of Japanese water features is that some of them do not use water at all, rather pebbles are laid in patterns reminiscent of the flow of rushing streams. Many elements of Japanese gardens are directly related to Buddhist concepts of order and balance.*

The reservoir tank for a wall fountain can either stand on the ground in front of the wall or a smaller basin can be mounted on the wall itself. Choose the style that suits your garden.

JAPANESE DEER-SCARERS

A deer-scarer – *shishi odoshi* – is a Japanese-style feature that could be used to give a hint of the Orient in a corner where the surrounding planting and surfaces might continue the theme. The cascading sound of water is accompanied by the rhythmic tap of bamboo.

Excavate a hole for the tank and pump, and cover with mesh and pebbles. Water is pumped through the outlet tube hidden inside a thick piece of hollow bamboo placed vertically in the ground. It then travels down a gently sloping bamboo tube, supported by two pieces of bamboo tied together to form a V-shape. The stream of water flows into the end of another hollow piece of bamboo, which has been carefully positioned on a pivot to catch the flow.

The bamboo on the pivot is blocked so there is a limit on its capacity. As this limit is reached, the piece of bamboo overbalances and swings down, emptying the water back on to the pebbles and into the tank below. Having shed its load, the piece of bamboo swings back and the non-pouring end makes a 'thunk' sound as it hits the strategically placed rock beneath it. Metal studs can be fixed to both the piece of bamboo and the rock for extra emphasis of the sound.

JAPANESE WATER BASINS

A *tsukubai*, or water basin, is another Japanese feature that can be used in a Western garden (and made child-safe). Traditionally placed beside a path leading to a Japanese tea house, the water basin is used for cleansing prior to the tea ceremony. The basin stone looks best placed close to the ground, with a rocky hollow in front of it – this is the tank. Water from a hidden hose is fed into the basin via tubing placed in a length of hollow bamboo. Alternatively, water can be made to bubble up from the base of the *tsukubai* like a small spring. The natural spring effect can be enhanced by the surrounding planting. Over time, the rocks and basin will become moss-covered, adding to their Japanese aura. A *tsukubai* should never be left to stand full of water when children are nearby, and leaves should be cleared.

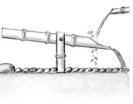

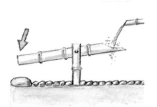

Above: the deer-scarer overbalances every few minutes, making a pleasant 'thunk' noise.

PLANTING

Lawns, trees, shrubs and herbaceous plants are best added after any hard landscaping has been completed. Try to create a harmonious scheme using plants that suit the specific conditions in your plot – aim for a permanent backbone of plants that both shapes the garden and complements plants providing seasonal interest.

PLANNING A SCHEME

Planting is for many people the most important element of a garden, yet it is difficult to plan because plants go through so many changes through the seasons and from year to year. Plants can perform many functions. They can divide space structurally in the same way that walls, fences and trellis can – screening ugly views and providing a backdrop for the rest of the garden. You can use them for ground cover in the case of grass and planting, say, between paving stones. Perhaps most obviously, plants provide ornamental interest, colour, height and texture – even scent and sound. For a successful scheme that provides interest all year round, follow our guidelines.

CREATING A BACKBONE STRUCTURE

Backbone planting comprises the plants that along with the hard landscaping are used to provide the main structure of a garden – the three-dimensional framework that gives the plot its shape and character. It is within this framework, which stays more or less permanent all year, that transient flowerings provide different zones of interest as the seasons pass. Gardens that do not have an overall structure can be very hit-and-miss affairs, often looking 'bitty' and relying too heavily on the appeal of lots of small features here and there.

There are several ways to achieve a successful planting framework. First and foremost, an overall shape should be established. For a formal look, your planting should rigidly follow a geometric pattern and be in symmetry with paths and boundaries. However, in informal small garden settings, planting that follows the lines of paths and boundaries can make the plot look even smaller. For example, the narrowness of a long, thin garden will be accentuated by long, thin borders on either side. As all parts of the garden are visible at once, there is no sense of mystery and so the garden will look dull – no matter how good the plants may be.

Opposite: this garden contains plenty of evergreens including conifers and grasses, which form the backbone of the design. There are plants in flower in every season. Careful juxtaposition of shapes, sizes, textures and forms shows off each element to the full.

- Balance the elements of lawn shape, hard surfaces and border shape with carefully positioned trees and shrubs to create a framework of sweeping curves, bays and spurs.

- Evergreens can be used as permanent backdrops at the back of borders, but don't use too many.

- Hedges form effective garden dividers and backdrops to borders but take up space.

- Train climbing plants up walls and fences. Gardens look bigger if the boundary is hidden.

- Taller plants positioned either side of a good view effectively frame it. An arching shrub or a tree can be used in the same way.

- Position a 'specimen' plant in front of a neutral, sympathetic backdrop.

- Create a focal point by positioning an 'architectural' plant among plants with softer shapes and more delicate leaves.

- Shrubs reaching eye level planted close to where screening is needed are more effective than large trees on a boundary.

Above: without the evergreen backdrop, much of the impact of these boldly shaped plants would be lost.

Above right: good backdrop shrubs, Prunus laurocerasus *'Otto Luykens' and* Euonymus fortunei *'Emerald 'n' Gold' (front).*

By extending parts of the border planting towards the centre, you can instantly soften the angularity. The shape of the lawn and borders is best delineated at the time of hard landscaping if you are completely overhauling your garden.

Simple, yet effective, shapes for lawns are circles, ovals, diamonds or oblongs set at angles to the boundaries. Two shapes could also be interlocked. If you opt for an irregular shape, sweeping curves are far preferable to wiggly lines. A sinuous curving lawn that leads the eye into the garden is an excellent starting point. As a kind of outdoor carpet, the lawn can unify the structure of the garden by providing a sympathetic floor and a foil to other planting. A mass of low-growing plants can also achieve this, say, in a front garden, where a lawn may be inappropriate or inconvenient.

A good principle for backbone planting in general is to create plant masses that shape the garden into bays and spurs without being too solid or blocklike. This adds depth and mystery without making the space seem smaller. To achieve this, a range of different heights of plants should be the aim. Trees and large shrubs are useful for backbone planting because of their height, shape and permanence. Climbers trained up fences and walls can also provide good backbones.

Evergreen shrubs play a crucial role in creating the basic framework as they provide colour and a constant point of reference throughout the year. Do not use too many, otherwise the effect could be rather static. One evergreen shrub to three deciduous ones is a good guide. You can use evergreens to frame views and to subdivide the garden into smaller areas, providing shelter, privacy and a screen for eyesores. Above all, they create an attractive backdrop for other garden plants, and as such are useful at the back of borders and on the boundaries of the garden.

Deciduous backbone shrubs help create mood as well as structure in the garden. For framing views, choose plants that have attractive winter outlines or coloured bark as well as looking good in summer. Like evergreens, deciduous shrubs can make a good foil for summer borders. Plant bulbs between them for colour while they are leafless.

You may already have plants in your garden that would function well as backbone planting if moved (see also 'Assessing Your Garden', pages 34-5). Established specimens will bring a look of maturity to a new design. If you need to obtain new plants for backbone areas, it is often worth paying extra for large plants, particularly for slow-growing types such as fastigiate yews and magnolias.

CHOOSING PLANTS FOR BACKDROPS

As a background for the rest of the garden, the plants should be restful on the eye, yet provide textural contrast to avoid looking too blocklike. It is possible to achieve this without using too many different plants, especially when you consider at the diversity of leaf shape and plant habit that even a small group can offer. For example, a satisfying group might consist of *Cotoneaster cornubia*, *Ligustrum lucidum* and *Prunus laurocerasus* 'Otto Luyken'. All of these are reliably hardy and evergreen, and will reach different heights.

Adding occasional plants with variegated evergreen foliage introduces diversity, but should

Above: good backdrop shrubs, Ligustrum lucidum *'Excelsium superbum' and* Skimmia japonica *'Rubella'.*

Left: Elaeagnus x ebbingei *'Gilt Edge'.*

not be overdone. Bright splashes year-round can be more valuable than short-lived flowers – think about the cheer given through the seasons by *Elaeagnus* x *ebbingei* 'Gilt Edge' or *Ligustrum lucidum* 'Tricolor'.

WAYS TO USE HEDGING

Evergreen hedging in particular makes an excellent backdrop to borders, statues and other objects placed in the garden as focal points. The fine texture of conifers is more effective than large glossy-leaved laurels – the latter require pruning with secateurs to avoid a mass of brown leaves.

PLANTS FOR HEDGES

Formal – can be clipped hard
Buxus sempervirens (e; box)
Carpinus betulus (hornbeam)
x *Cupressocyparis leylandii* 'Castelwellan Gold' or 'Robinson's Gold' (e; Leyland cypress)
Fagus sylvatica (beech)
Ilex aquifolium (e; holly)
Ligustrum japonicum (e; privet)
Thuja plicata (e; Western red cedar)
Tsuga heterophylla (e; Western hemlock)

e = evergreen

Informal – for flowers and fruit
Berberis darwinii (e; barberry)
Berberis x *stenophylla* (e)
Cotoneaster simonsii (e)
Rosa rugosa

Low-growing hedging and edging
Buxus sempervirens 'Suffruticosa' (e; dwarf box)
Lavandula angustifolia 'Hidcote' (e; lavender)
Santolina chamaecyparissus (e; cotton lavender)
Teucrium chamaedrys (shrubby germander)

Hedges are long-lived and if the right hedging plant is chosen need not be too onerous to maintain. They can be formal or informal, clipped and narrow or unclipped and open, whichever style suits the rest of your garden. Use hedging in the same way as trellis and fencing to screen off utility corners of the garden. A clipped hedge of any type makes an excellent wind filter, far better for shelter than a vertical wall or fence.

The drawback of all hedging is that it takes time to establish and needs more maintenance than walls and fences. A run of hedging will need to be cut at least once a season. The time this takes will be reduced if you choose a slow-growing plant. A maintenance path should be left in front of a hedge – allow about 50cm (20in), more for conifers. All hedges take a lot of water and nutrients from the soil adjacent to them, coniferous ones more than most.

cypress is that left to its own devices it will grow to the very large tree that it is naturally. Once out of control, it is very difficult to cut back to re-establish the appearance of the hedge. Slower-growing conifers that make good hedges include *Thuja plicata* and *Tsuga heterophylla*.

Box is a traditional form of hedging that can be clipped and formed into topiary. For low-growing edging, choose the dwarf variety *Buxus suffruticosa* 'Nana'. When the plants are put in about 20cm apart, this variety takes only a couple of seasons to form a good low hedge.

Informal hedges can produce both flowers and berries, making them a good choice for a small garden. Good varieties include *Cotoneaster simonsii*, *Berberis darwinii*, *B.* x *stenophylla*, *Rosa rugosa*. For country-style hedges,

Single planting a deciduous hedge.

Double planting a coniferous hedge.

If you plan a formal garden, some form of evergreen hedging will be very appropriate. Traditional yew has the reputation of being very slow, but with proper preparation and spacing plants 50cm apart, a hedge can begin to fill out after a few seasons.

Leyland cypress hedging is renowned for its fast growth – 50cm and above per season – which is the main reason it has been so widely planted in Britain. Try varieties such as 'Castelwellan Gold' or 'Robinson's Gold', which are slightly slower-growing golden forms. Provided that it is kept under control from the time of planting, a Leyland hedge will quickly provide an evergreen backdrop that can be cut to height and shaped. But the problem with Leyland

hawthorn and holly are good choices, but the latter can be very slow to establish.

Starting a hedge
It is important to prepare the site of the hedge thoroughly beforehand. Remove any perennial weeds from the area prior to digging. Double-dig a trench about 45-60cm wide, incorporating plenty of organic material with the soil to aid moisture retention, particularly important with yew. Allow four weeks for the soil to settle. Mark the position of the plants according to which planting system you are adopting – you can prepare the ground individually for each plant, or dig a trench, marking the plant spacings and backfilling with soil as each one is put in.

The timing of the planting will depend on your choice of hedging. Bare-rooted plants (deciduous hedging such as beech and hornbeam) should be planted in the dormant season – November to March. Root-balled specimens (some conifers including yew) should be planted in October or March. Container-grown hedging plants can be planted at any time, but remember that a new hedge will need careful watering in its first season to ensure survival. Encourage side branching of beech plants by cutting back after planting to within a few shoots.

Hedging plants are generally spaced around 60cm apart for quick close-knit effect. Increasing the spacing to 75cm can reduce costs slightly but it will take longer for the hedge to form. Plant one row or two, depending on the width of hedge you are aiming for.

To get hedges to establish on exposed sites, erect a temporary fence of windbreak netting around 1m high on either side.

USING WALL SHRUBS AND CLIMBING PLANTS

Clothing boundary walls or fencing with climbing plants is a good way to reduce the often overbearing presence of such structures in a small garden. Some plants will cling to the wall without assistance; others will need trellis or some other support. Make sure that the preservative treatment used on timber fencing and trellis is non-toxic to plants. Using the walls of the house to support plant growth helps to harmonise the house with the garden and give it an attractive anchor of vegetation. Scented climbers can be encouraged to grow round doors and windows. Having some expanse of wall free of plants can look attractive, too, so you may want to leave about a quarter to a half of the area uncovered.

Above: conifer hedge, right side clipped, left untouched.

Above: Vitis vinifera *'Purpurea'.*

Left: Clematis viticella *'Etoile Violette'.*

CLIMBERS AND WALL PLANTS

Sunny situations

Actinidia kolomikta
Carpenteria californica
Campsis (trumpet creeper)
Ceanothus (California lilac)
Clematis (large-flowered hybrids)
Cytisus battandieri (Moroccan broom)
Fremontodendron 'California Glory' (fremontia; irritant)
Itea ilicifolia
Passiflora caerulea (passion flower)
Piptanthus laburnifolius (evergreen laburnum)
Rosa 'Ena Harkness Climbing'
Solanum crispum (potato vine)
Trachelospermum jasminoides
Tropaeolum tuberosum 'Ken Aslett'
Vitis coignetiae (Japanese crimson glory vine)
Vitis vinifera 'Purpurea' (purple-leaved vine)

Shady situations

Chaenomeles speciosa
Chaenomeles japonica
Clematis alpina
Euonymus fortunei 'Emerald Gaiety' (winter creeper)
Garrya elliptica (silk tassel bush)
Hedera colchica 'Sulphur Heart' (Persian ivy)
Hydrangea petiolaris (climbing hydrangea)
Lonicera periclymenum 'Graham Thomas' (honeysuckle)
Parthenocissus quinquefolia (Virginia creeper)
Parthenocissus henryana (Chinese Virginia creeper)
Pileostegia viburnoides (climbing viburnum)
Pyracantha 'Mohave' (firethorn)
Tropaeolum speciosum (flame creeper)

The colour of any flowers should harmonise with the colour of the masonry behind them. Greens, blues, dark reds, purples and whites will look good against red and yellow bricks. Pale bricks and grey stonework will be a restful background for pinks, yellows, reds and blues. Variegated and golden foliage can be used to lighten a gloomy dark wall. You will have to strip away foliage to maintain your wall.

When choosing a plant, bear in mind the microclimate created at the base of the wall or fence, and consider whether you would prefer a self-supporting type or are prepared to train it against the wall or fence. All wall planting should be set about 30cm from the base: soil at the base of walls tends to be full of stones and rubble from building, and there may be a narrow area that does not catch rain. Plenty of organic material should be dug into the soil to help overcome this tendency. Leave at least 50-60cm space if the climber has a non-flowering, unattractive stem, so that some smaller subjects can be planted in front.

ASPECT

● South-facing walls and fences are best for slightly tender and exotic plants. The surface behind will hold heat and catch the maximum amount of sun creating a warmer microclimate and protecting the planting from cold north and east winds. Choose plants that can cope with dry summers.

● North-facing walls/fences are constantly cool, shady and moisture-retentative. Dense shaded areas under large trees are difficult.

● East-facing walls and fences can be cold and expose and yet thaw out quickly in the morning, damaging plants.

● West-facing walls and fences are favourable sites, receiving late sun and not subject to quick thaws that damage buds and shoots. They also benefit from warm, wet west winds, but still suffer rain shadow at their bases.

● Both north- and east-facing beds are affected by wind chill, which shortens the growing season. However, the moisture retained in the soil can be a benefit. South-west facing walls are most suitable for tender plants.

CHOOSING TREES FOR SMALL GARDENS

If your garden is very tiny – a roof or balcony perhaps – trees may be beyond the scope of appropriate planting, though you might want to use a tall tree-like plant for height and interest. By contrast, you may have one or two mature trees in the garden that will be retained due to legal restrictions or through choice, because of the air of maturity that they add.

Space limits in small gardens mean using fewer plants overall. It is well worth looking out for trees and shrubs that provide more than one season of interest. *Amelanchier lamarckii* can be an excellent choice for the small garden. It tolerates shade and damp soils and produces creamy white spring flowers followed by red berries in the summer. The pale green foliage is tinged salmon when young and turning into brilliant orange-red hues in the autumn. Similarly, both the maple (*Acer*) and crab apple (*Malus*) families offer a wide range of suitable trees and large shrubs, many of them with more than one season of interest.

When choosing a tree for the small garden, make sure that it will not outgrow its welcome, a very common problem and a real nuisance if you have to prune radically each year. Worse still, a tree that is encroaching on your house will affect it structurally. So, if you are considering planting a purple-leaved tree, for example, you could plant *Malus* 'Royalty' in preference to *Acer platanoides* 'Crimson King'. It is a much smaller tree with similar glossy purple leaves and has the added benefit of deep red flowers followed by dark red fruits in autumn.

New trees should not be planted closer to a house than the distance equivalent to their mature height. When considering the range of options open to you, consult a plant encyclopedia: they invariably give a guide to height and spread at maturity, though the actual size will depend a lot on local climate and soil conditions. It is also worth visiting arboretums and botanic gardens, where mature trees should be labelled, sometimes with the date of planting included.

Above: Acer palmatum *Atropurpureum.*

Left: Picea pungens.

Far left: Prunus *'Kiku-shidare-Sakura'.*

TREES

Deciduous
Acer griseum (paper bark maple)
Acer palmatum 'Senkaki' (coral bark maple)
Betula utilis 'Jacquemontii' (Himalayan birch)
Cornus controversa 'Variegata' (wedding cake tree)
Laburnum x *watereri* 'Vossii' (golden chain tree; poisonous)
Malus 'Golden Hornet' (crab apple – yellow fruit)
Malus ' Red Sentinel' (crab apple – red fruit)
Sorbus (rowan)

Evergreen
Chamaecyparis lawsoniana 'Pembury Blue' (Lawson's cypress)
Cryptomeria japonica 'Elegans' (Japanese cedar)
Ilex aquifolium 'Pyramidalis' (holly; conical cultivar)
Picea pungens 'Koster' (Colorado spruce; blue form)
Pinus mugo (mountain pine)
Taxus baccata 'Fastigiata' (Irish yew)

Small weeping trees
Betula pendula 'Youngii' (weeping birch)
Cotoneaster salicifolius 'Pendulus'
Malus 'Red Jade'
Prunus 'Kiku-shidare-sakura' (Cheal's weeping cherry)
Pyrus salicifolia 'Pendula' (weeping ornamental pear)
Salix caprea 'Pendula' (Kilmarnock willow

Coloured foliage
Acer (maple – golden and purple types)
Catalpa bignonoides 'Aurea' (golden Indian bean tree)
Gleditsia triacanthos 'Sunburst' (golden honey locust)
Malus 'Royalty' (purple-leaved crab)
Prunus cerasifera 'Pissardii' (purple-leaved plum)
Prunus x *cistena* (purple-leaved sand cherry)

Trees can be used to good effect as focal points. Some shapes of tree lend themselves to this use, the habit add emphasis to the position the tree occupies in the garden. Trees with weeping habits are natural focal-point subjects, as are conifers with a conical shape. However, too many plants with a definite architectural shape in a planting scheme they will lose their value as points of emphasis.

USING SPECIMENS AND FOCAL POINTS

Some large plants may have a feature of such outstanding beauty, such as magnificent foliage or flowers, that they merit positions where they can be viewed on their own. These are known as specimen plants. With just a small selection of specimens you can create constantly changing scenes around the garden. For maximum impact, group the specimens with other plants that complement their distinctive features. For example, *Magnolia stellata* underplanted with crocuses and *Primula* 'Wanda' could form the focus of attention in springtime; a witch hazel could scent the air in a section of the garden devoted to winter-flowering plants such as hellebores, snowdrops and winter aconites.

Some plants have a strong architectural shape and naturally create strong focal points. For example, a spiky plant such as *Phormium tenax* has sword-like leaves which will punctuate border planting and give an immediately exotic flavour. For stemmed spikes, include *Cordyline australis* and *Yucca filamentosa* in borders with well-drained soil. They are all evergreen and reasonably hardy in most areas once established. Focal plants can be man-made too: topiary shapes are useful in both formal and informal planting schemes.

If well-positioned, specimens and focal plants can form the most attractive part of your garden and direct attention away from eyesores. Careful placing of a specimen plant in a border can further reinforce its shape, providing a visual full stop at one end, for instance, or emphasising the climax of a curve.

ARRANGING THE BORDERS

When planning a border, a good starting point is to think of it as three layers – foreground, middle ground and background – though you will not necessarily adhere to this throughout. The back layer usually includes the boundary wall, fence or hedge and should provide a sympathetic backdrop to the middle and front layers. For example, adding an informal core of evergreen planting in front of a *Lonicera nitida* hedge might include *Mahonia* x *media* 'Charity' with *Euonymus fortunei* 'Emerald Gaiety'. Each plant has a different height, form, leaf shape and texture, the variegation of the *Euonymus* providing an added highlight.

If a border is backed by a fence or wall, this can be partially obscured with climbers, so providing good textural contrast to planting in front. Many ivy varieties make good border backdrops, some of them variegated. *Hedera helix* 'Buttercup' has golden leaves that turn green as they age. *Hedera helix* 'Goldheart' has dark green leaves with yellow hearts. Both of these have small foliage. For greater impact, the larger-leaved ivies include some classics such as *Hedera colchica* 'Sulphur Heart', which has yellow-splashed foliage that can grow to the size of dinner plates.

Do not rely on climbers alone to clothe the back of the border otherwise the effect will be very

LATE SPRING

WINTER

flat. Include some taller shrubs that will break the line of the fence.

With the middle row of planting, you could aim for pockets of colour that will keep going all year and take over when the surrounding plants are past their best. Ideal in this situation are plants that have either a very long season of interest or several seasons of interest. Plants with brightly coloured foliage can also be used in the middle. The border will look stark in winter if it has large areas of bare soil at the front. The easiest way to overcome this is to plant low-growing evergreens, either as an edging or in groups of three or five around other plants. Box, hebes and heathers are ideal for this.

Arranging borders from back to front in decreasing height enables all plants to be seen. On the other hand, breaking regularity by bringing taller plants forward will lend added depth to the tapestry effect of planting. If you have borders that can be seen from more than one side you will need to adopt a similar technique and plan the highest point of the border. Good effects result from creating a high point at one end and balancing this at the other end with a lower group of similar plants. A good choice of plants to bring to the front of borders are columnar subjects such as the yew *Taxus baccata* 'Fastigiata' and tall herbaceous plants with feathery foliage or frothy flowers – such as bronze fennel or the ornamental seakale (*Crambe cordifolia*) with its giant heads of tiny white blooms – which allow a view of plants behind. Some plants such as mulleins (*Verbascum bombyciferum* and varieties) grow into spires from a rosette base and prefer to be exposed to sunlight in free-draining soil at the front of a sunny border.

LOOKING AT HOW NATURE DOES IT

Plant growth occurs naturally in layers, or tiers, resulting in combinations of plants that do not compete for food, light and moisture. For example, bluebells will thrive in a bluebell wood beneath a canopy of deciduous trees, flowering in early spring before light levels are diminished by the foliage of the next wave of lower growth – bracken, brambles, ferns and foxgloves – and the upper canopy of trees. Relating this to your own garden, underplant deciduous shrubs with a mix of spring bulbs, low evergreen plants and herbaceous material that will take over as the season progresses.

To simplify your decision-making, choose subjects that normally grow together – plants that originate from the same natural environment. For example, lavender can look ill at ease when bordering a bed of rhododendrons but completely at home with herbs and sun-loving herbaceous plants. Include repetitions of plants and planting in groups to avoid the somewhat speckled look of numerous single specimens, which do not really occur in nature. Aim for a harmonious balance of groupings. Plant odd numbers of plants to avoid regimentation and create a drift effect.

As a starting point, think about the harmony of one shrub combined with three medium to tall herbaceous plants and five smaller ground-covering specimens.

CREATING COLOUR SCHEMES

Colour is not static. Light, shadows and texture will all alter the visual effect of pigments in plants. Dark colours produce a feeling of closeness – a solid evergreen hedge enclosing a small garden will make the plot feel even

Below: the architectural shape of Yucca filamentosa *creates a focal point against a backdrop of softer-leaved plants.*

Border on opposite page: designed to give spectacular display in late spring, but with no regard to the rest of the year. Background – Forsythia x intermedia; *middle –* Ribes sanguineum, Pieris japonica *and* Viburnum carlesii; *foreground – dwarf hybrid azaleas and* Spiraea x arguta *'Bridal Wreath'.*

Border on this page: designed for year-round interest. Background – Osmanthus burkwoodii; Berberis stenophylla; *middle –* Daphne odora *'Aureomarginata',* Potentilla fruticosa *'Tangerine',* Hypericum patulum *'Hidcote'; foreground –* Helianthemum nummularium.

LATE SPRING

WINTER

Right: grey-theme garden.

Below: yellow-theme garden.

Far right: the flowers of Daphne odora have a glorious scent, but deter children from trying to eat them.

COLOUR

● Soil type can affect colour. The colour of hydrangeas, for instance, will vary according to the pH level.

● Blue retreats visually.

● White planting draws the eye. Use pale tints rather than pure white to lighten borders unless you want to focus attention.

● Use complementary colours for harmonious schemes, e.g. red and green; yellow and purple; orange and blue.

smaller. 'Extend' the dimensions of a garden by using cool colours further away from the house – blues, violets, greys and dull browns. Use plants combining cool colour with fine texture at the end of a long path, particularly one covered by a pergola, to create an impression of greater length.

Hot colours – reds, yellows, oranges – foreshorten distances. To make your small garden appear larger, keep hot colours close to the house or patio and emphasise the effect by choosing plants with large, textured leaves.

Colour schemes using pinks, lilacs and blues lightened with creams and whites have come to represent the typical planting style in the UK, probably due to the quality of soft light at this latitude. In parts of the world with brighter light – the Mediterranean or California, for example – much stronger colours tend to be used. However, there is nothing to stop you using hot tones to create excitement. Linked to a good framework of green foliage, the occasional burst of intense colour will work: for example, Scottish flame flower (*Tropaeolum speciosum*) against an evergreen hedge. Whatever your preferences, using a limited palette is often more satisfying than using every colour on offer. Allow the colour emphasis to shift throughout the year (see 'Seasonal Interest').

PLANNING FOR FRAGRANCE

Fragrance can be actively planned. Scent is provided in two distinct ways: from flowers and from aromatic foliage. With the latter, essential oils are released when leaves are crushed,

brushed or heated. Plants with fragrant flowers include roses, honeysuckle, philadelphus and mahonia; plants with aromatic foliage include rosemary, chamomile, artemesia and lavender. Many aromatics are also evergreen.

Spring and summer fragrance is so abundant that it can be used throughout the garden, but you may want to put winter fragrance close to the house – perhaps *en route* to front or back doors – where it can be appreciated in comfort. A sheltered site can encourage scent to linger on the air. Obvious spots for scent planting are

doors, windows, pergolas and arches, which will bring the fragrances up to nose level. An arbour over a seat will become a romantic bower with the addition of a fragrant climber. Honeysuckle (*Lonicera periclymenum*) varieties are excellent for this purpose, as are, of course, climbing roses – choose *Rosa* 'Zéphirine Drouhin' for scent without thorns or 'The New Dawn' for strong scent on a plant with good resistance to disease.

Fragrant plants can be included at every level of your garden. Thymes, chamomile and pennyroyal happily grow between paving slabs, releasing their scent when trodden. Put evening-scented plants near areas where you sit to enjoy the late sun – night-scented stock, nicotiana and evening primrose, for example. Scent can also be used as a hidden 'focal point' to lure the visitor deep into the garden.

As an evergreen backdrop, the climber *Clematis armandii* has good spring fragrance, too. However, do not bother to find scented climbers and shrubs for walls at the back of large borders. Summer-scented planting should be included at the front of borders, within brushing distance if an aromatic plant is used such as lavender, sage or origanum. Also bear in mind that to appreciate scented water lilies to the full a raised pool will be needed.

As with colours and flavours, people experience scent in different ways. Box (*Buxus sempervirens*) and flowering currant (*Ribes atrosanguineum*) both produce leaf aromas that you either love or hate. The odour of *Clerodendrum bungei* and the aptly named skunk cabbage (*Lysichiton americanus*) are definitely an acquired taste. Note that a link may exist between scent and some allergic complaints such as hay fever and asthma.

Classifications of plant scent range from herbal/balsam to spicy/musk, and through the true citrus oranges and lemons to the peppery muskiness of nasturtiums (*Tropaeolum majus*). Scent associations can be created: the aroma of the cistus family instantly conjures up the Mediterranean even in the slightly cooler climes of the average British summer. Heat reacts with scent and can produce overpowering effects – take care when planning where to place pots of *Lilium regale* and other pollen-heavy subjects.

FRAGRANCE

Trees with scented flowers
Magnolia x soulangiana
Magnolia denudata
Malus hupehensis (crab apple)
Malus transitoria (crab apple)
Prunus padus
Prunus x yedoensis

Trees with aromatic foliage
Clerodendrum
Eucalyptus gunnii
Eucalyptus pauciflora niphophila

Shrubs with scented flowers
Chimonanthus praecox (winter sweet)
Cytisus battandieri (Moroccan broom)
Daphne odora (poisonous)
Daphne cneorum (poisonous)
Elaeagnus commutata
Hamamelis mollis (witch hazel)
Lonicera fragrantissima
Lonicera purpusii (shrubby honeysuckles)
Mahonia japonica
Osmanthus delavayi
Philadelphus coronarius (mock orange)
Rhododendron luteum
Sarcococca humilis (Christmas box)
Viburnum carlesii

Scented roses
'Fantin Latour'
'Fruhlingsgold'
'Madame Isaac Pereire'
'Cecile Brunner'
'The Fairy'

Shrubs with aromatic foliage
Artemisia abrotanum
Caryopteris x *clandonensis*
Choisya ternata (Mexican orange blossom)
Helichrysum italicum (curry plant)
Laurus nobilis (bay)
Lavandula (lavender)
Myrtus communis (myrtle)
Perovskia atriplicifolia
Rosa eglanteria
Rosmarinus officinalis
Salvia officinalis

FRAGRANCE

***Perennials with
scented flowers***
Erysimum (perennial
wallflower)
Dianthus 'Mrs Sinkins'
(pink)
Dictamnus albus
(burning bush)
Hemerocallis citrina (day
lily)
Hesperis matrionalis
(sweet rocket)
Paeonia (e.g. 'Duchesse
de Nemours')

***Fragrant annuals
and bulbs***
Cheiranthus cheiri
(wallflower)
Convallaria majalis (lily
of the valley: poisonous)
Dianthus barbatus (sweet
william)
Hyacinthus orientalis
(hyacinth)
Lathyrus odoratus (sweet
pea)
Lilium regale (regal lily)
Matthiola bicornis (night-
scented stock)
Matthiola incana (ten-
week stock)
Narcissus (daffodil)
Nicotiana affinis
(tobacco plant)
Oenothera biennis
(evening primrose)
Tropaeolum majus
(nasturtium)

Fragrant climbers
Clematis armandii
Clematis montana
'Elizabeth'
Jasminum officinale
Lonicera periclymenum
(honeysuckle)
roses (e.g. 'Compassion',
'The New Dawn')
Wistaria sinensis

Trees with scented flowers include the larger magnolias and crab apples such as *Malus hupehensis* and the less common *Malus transitoria*. There are also trees whose foliage exudes scent – the leaves of *Cercidophyllum japonicum* release the pungent smell of burnt sugar when they fall. Shrubs with scented flowers include *Daphne odora* (poisonous), flowering in early spring, and *Hamamelis mollis*, with the lovely but curious shaped flowers of the witch hazel, providing reliably fragrant flowers in the depths of winter but preferring a slightly acid soil.

DRAWING UP A PLANTING PLAN

For inexperienced gardeners, making a planting plan may seem arbitrary or overly technical. However, doing so will help you in grouping plants that like similar conditions (e.g. sun or shade), assess the year-round interest and work out how many plants you will need. Refer to plant encyclopedias and nursery catalogues to shortlist plants that you like and are suitable for different areas in the garden.

You do not need to work out your whole planting plan at once, but aim to get all the backbone planting in. For gaps, you could simply say 'annuals' and 'bedding', later to be replaced by herbaceous plants and bulbs.

Your survey plan of your garden, which you will have made for the hard landscaping, may be too small for detailed planting notes. It is often easier to redraw individual beds on a larger scale or to use an enlarged photocopy, either of the whole plan or just the areas to be planted. Work out your plants in pencil or on tracing paper over an inked-in drawing of the other features in the garden. As shown in the chapter 'Mapping Out Your Plans' (pages 114-23), simple sketches in elevation help you visualise effects.

It is always worth marking in pen where shade will be cast by solid features and large plants already in situ – shade is one of the most significant factors affecting plant choice. Also mark in pen any notes relating to climate, aspect and other general planting require-

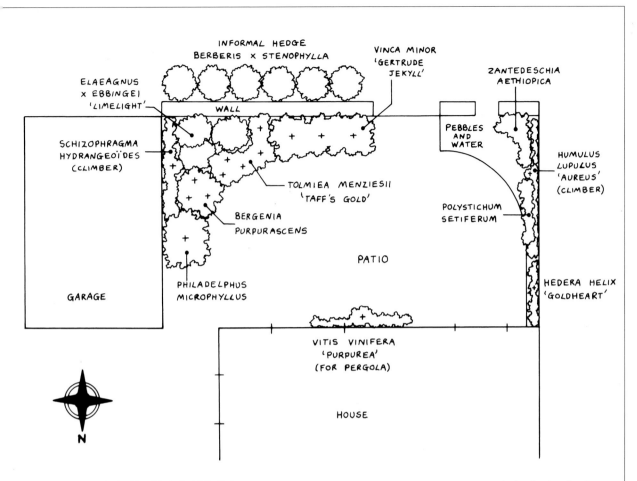

INFORMAL HEDGE
BERBERIS × STENOPHYLLA

VINCA MINOR
'GERTRUDE
JEKYLL'

ZANTEDESCHIA
AETHIOPICA

ELAEAGNUS
× EBBINGEI
'LIMELIGHT'

WALL

PEBBLES
AND
WATER

HUMULUS
LUPULUS
'AUREUS'
(CLIMBER)

SCHIZOPHRAGMA
HYDRANGEOÏDES
(CLIMBER)

TOLMIEA MENZIESII
'TAFF'S GOLD'

BERGENIA
PURPURASCENS

POLYSTICHUM
SETIFERUM

PATIO

GARAGE

PHILADELPHUS
MICROPHYLLUS

HEDERA HELIX
'GOLDHEART'

VITIS VINIFERA
'PURPUREA'
(FOR PERGOLA)

N

HOUSE

DRAWING UP A PLANTING PLAN

● Make a large-scale plan or an enlarged photocopy of the beds to be planted.

● Always mark the plants in pencil as you are likely to make a lot of changes.

● Start with backbone plants, trees and larger shrubs, climbers, hedges and edges.

● Mark single plants as a simple circle to show the likely spread of the plant. Groups of the same plants can be drawn as drifts. Use 'X's to show how many plants are in each drift.

● Group smaller plants together for more impact, i.e. allow for at least three of most herbaceous plants.

● Use cuttings from catalogues around the plan to give you a better idea of what the plants look like.

● Check out your plan for seasonal interest by colour-coding the plants according to their main season of interest.

● Use your plan as a guide. When it comes to planting, it will be a lot easier to see what actually works and what doesn't.

ments. The planting plan does not have to be complicated: circles or approximate shapes with suggested plant names will suffice, as shown in the layout plans in this book. A good idea is to place crosses indicating how many plants you will need for each area. These marks can be transferred on to the ground using canes when it comes to putting the plants in.

As the plan needs to be to scale, allow 45-60cm for each herbaceous plant and around half the ultimate spread for trees and shrubs. A circle guide, available from specialist stationers, map out the plan to scale. Once you have done a rough plan, it is a good idea to check it by using a simple colour coding system. For example, to check on year-round interest, colour evergreens green, spring flowers yellow, summer flowers red, autumn plants purple and winter interest blue. This will give you an idea of the balance through the seasons in your plan. Similarly, you can use the same idea to work out colour schemes and avoid clashes at certain times of the year.

In the planting plan shown here, following the same garden design as shown on pages 115-23, a group of shrubs has been sited to block off the view beyond the corner of the garage. With the climbers on the wall of the garage behind, this group represents the tallest part of the border. The rest of the planting is for foliage effect. With the north-facing border, the plants chosen should provide an attractive view from the house and patio without obscuring the rest of the garden. They will be in relative shade cast by the garage and the new hedge.

Opposite page: the scent of Matthiola incana *may make your head spin!*

SEASONAL INTEREST

Your backbone planting should provide some structure throughout the year, so your garden should never look dull. The next phase of planting is to add seasonal highlights so that your garden becomes an ever-changing tapestry of flowers and foliage. In a small garden, it is often a good idea to plant concentrated pockets of colour in different areas that come to a peak at different times of year.

Another simple approach is to include plants that have more than one season of interest. Such plants can be scattered through the garden to provide incidental highlights or they can be grouped together for more dramatic focus at particular times of the year. In these ways you will never get bored looking at the same view because the focus will shift around.

SPRING

March to May is a time of great optimism in the garden, with a plethora of plants getting into gear. *Malus floribunda*, the Japanese crab apple, is an excellent choice of small tree (or large shrub) for the small garden. One of the earliest crab apples to flower, the plant's dark crimson buds open to a white or blush tint. It has the added bonus of producing small red and yellow fruits in the autumn. The climber *Clematis armandii*, an evergreen, can produce flowers as early as the end of March in warm years. Its dark foliage enhances its white blooms. Choose the variety 'Apple Blossom' for blush pink buds. To grow happily, this clematis will need a sunny wall that will help to dissipate its sweet scent. Train it before the leaves mature.
One of the best spring-scented shrubs is

Above: white and blue scilla with narcissus.

Above right: Viburnum *and* Prunus tenella.

In summer, when you spend more time outdoors, you can allow for interest in all parts of the garden. By contrast, in winter when the nights draw in, it pays to concentrate on areas near the house, so colour and texture can be viewed from indoors. A small group of winter-flowering heathers with a few hellebores and a red-stemmed dogwood, for example, can do a lot to brighten up your winter days.

What you include for seasonal highlights is very much down to personal taste. On the following pages we suggest a number of plants to consider for each of the seasons.

Osmanthus delavayi, another evergreen with narrow dark leaves. Its flowers may look small but they are held all along the branches in great numbers and produce one of the sweetest scents of any shrub. Ideal for a small spring corner, it also produces flowers from an early age and can be pruned.

Forsythia and *Ribes sanguineum*, the flowering currant, are enduringly popular. The flowering currants come in a range of colours – plant 'Pulborough Scarlet' for deep red blossoms or 'Album' for a white form. A common cause of disappointment with forsythia is its failure to

Above: early spring border.

Left: tulips and muscari.

flower after incorrect pruning – try cutting back about a third of the old wood immediately after flowering. Camellias can be covered in blooms in the early part of the season. They need acid soil to thrive, so grow them in containers and raised beds. Remember to plant or place the containers where the buds of these plants will not receive the early morning sun – this causes them to become damaged, and the plant will not flower.

At low levels of the garden, underplant low-growing perennials, deciduous trees and shrubs with spring bulbs. Examples to include are scillas, narcissus and grape hyacinth. *Cyclamen coum* may be on the winter side of early spring, but consider *Cyclamen repandum* for a flush of purple-red flowers just above ground level. Some of the low-growing herbaceous plants get into their flowering stride early: try cheerful combinations of *Aubrieta deltoidea* and *Alyssum saxatile*. Pulmonarias provide low-level colour at a time when most branches around them are still bare – many of them have attractive markings or variegated leaves.

Perhaps the best-value plants for spring interest are hellebores and some of the euphorbias.

Hellebores are available in a wide range of shades, some now with double flowers. These flower for a long period, sometimes from winter to spring. The evergreen foliage of *Helleborus argutifolius* has architectural qualities; choose varieties of *H. orientalis* for plum- and purple-toned drama. *Euphorbia characias* throws up its typical inflorescent bract-style flowers in early spring and looks good year-round in a border with its upright 'bottle-brush' leaves.

SUMMER

By the end of May, the well-planned garden is really beginning to fill out. All the trees will have unfurled their leaves; one of the later ones to produce foliage is *Robinia pseudoacacia* 'Frisia', but it retains a bright spring freshness throughout the summer months by virtue of its golden foliage. This tree can reach heights of around 10m at maturity, putting it beyond some small gardens, but its rate of growth can be held in check by cold winds and frost or judicious pruning. From May through to September many herbaceous plants are at their best, and if you are planning a mixed scheme this is the time of year when the tapestry of colour and texture will be at its peak. Out of many fine shrubs with which to fill a border for summer impact, one of the most memorable is the Moroccan broom, *Cytisus battandieri*. This can be grown as a free-standing shrub in warmer areas and against the protection of a south- or west-facing wall in cooler regions. It can also be trained as a single-stemmed tree. The foliage is a pleasing silver-grey, an attraction in itself, but the star quality of *Cytisus battandieri* is in its upright, pineapple-scented, yellow flowers.

Silver foliage is a useful linking colour in any border scheme, cooling down hot colours and providing a light foil against darker foliage behind. A good silver foliage plant to include in a border would be the butterfly bush, *Buddleia davidii*, which is well-known and genuinely attracts butterflies. For striking variegated leaves go for the variety 'Harlequin'. *Buddleia* x *weyeriana* has scented, dome-shaped yellow flowers and grey-tinged foliage.

Roses are well to the fore at the height of summer. In a small garden, you will probably want to concentrate on types that produce more than one flush of flowers. It is best to obtain types that are not too prone to mildew, blackspot, aphids and other problems. *Rosa*

Summer border with white dianthus and white Tanacetum parthenium.

'The New Dawn' is an excellent shell-pink climber that flowers all summer. The larger shrub roses do not require much maintenance, and many have attractive foliage also. *Rosa glauca*, for instance, has excellent blue-grey leaves and small pink flowers in summer, followed by hips in autumn. In the case of smaller shrub-type roses, gardeners with small gardens have greatly benefited from recent

Herbaceous border with (from right) penstemmon, hydrangea, delphinium, calceolaria and ground-cover rose.

introductions such as the English roses produced by David Austin, which have all the qualities of old-fashioned roses. 'Mary Rose' and 'Graham Stuart Thomas' are among the best varieties of this type.

With regard to medium-sized summer shrubs, the two plants that stand out from the rest are fuchsias and hydrangeas. The hardy forms of fuchsia range in size from the diminutive 'Tom Thumb' to 'Mrs Popple' and the much larger *Fuchsia magellanica*, all of which will produce their distinctive flowers over a long period of time. The genus covers a wide range of choice and flower colour, with the hardy forms not given to the showiness of bloom that the tender varieties often sport. For impressive foliage effects, plant *F. m.* 'Versicolor', renowned for its silver-grey foliage edged with white and pink. This is a good subject to plant as a group for full summertime effect. 'Genii' has striking golden leaves.

The flowers of hydrangeas on a soil with a pH level of 5 or below, which is very acid, will be blue; they will be pink on any soil with a pH of 6 and upwards. However, if your soil is slightly acid or neutral (up to pH 7), you can get blue flowers by applying a blueing agent (aluminium sulphage). Soil-testing kits give information on how to treat soil. The range of hydrangeas suits most situations and colour palettes; they come into their own from summer right through to autumn. Mophead types are common, but larger forms such as *Hydrangea aspera* ssp. *sargentiana*, which requires woodland conditions, are excellent from late summer onwards. Hydrangeas are hardier than they might appear, surviving temperatures down to –10° C. Walls clothed with *Hydrangea petiolaris* will enjoy the splendour of its large, white, lace-capped flowers – even after fading they can provide a wonderful backdrop for dew-encrusted spiders' webs, through to the effects of winter frosts. For white *Buddleia*-style flowers, plant *H. paniculata* 'Grandiflora'. The flowers borne by the lace-cap forms are as showy as any perennial. For cool hues try *H. macrophylla* 'Blue Wave'. The variety *H. m.* 'Lanarth White' has similar pink central flowers on limey soils, varying to blue on acid. The outer florets are a pure creamy white on any soil.

Some herbaceous perennials will produce repeat flowerings if cut back after the first crop. Some of the hardy forms of geranium fall into this category. Choose plants with firm stems, or site stragglers next to upstanding neighbours and plant closely so that any tendency to sprawl is not obvious. If you plan to use herbaceous plants at the front of a border, either choose low mat- or mound-forming varieties, such as *Polygonum affinis*, *Stachys byzantina*, *Sedum spectabile* and *Dianthus* 'Mrs Sinkins', all of which will provide a well-behaved edging.

The old standard *Alchemilla mollis* is an undemanding plant that will grow almost anywhere, but its propensity for self-seeding can make it almost invasive. Many herbs are appropriate subjects for the front of borders. In this position they can be reached for culinary use and will release their scent when brushed or crushed. *Origanum vulgare* 'Aureum', the golden form of marjoram, is a superb edging plant and has the added bonus of blue-lilac flowers in high summer. The sages are also good value in this respect. For extra interest use *Salvia officinalis* 'Purpurascens', the downy purple-leaved form, or 'Icterina' with its lemon yellow and green variegated foliage. The rest of the salvia family provides useful perennial plants for sunny situations, flowering well into autumn. However, many are only half-hardy.

For grass-type foliage at the front of a border, *Kniphofia* 'Little Maid' provides small yellow pokers late in the season. By contrast, a true grass such as *Festuca glauca* gives summer-long silver-blue tufts that can be a stunning foil for many other colours.

Taller summer herbaceous plants include the day lily, with lots of colours available; some produce scent as well. The cottage-style plants – lupins, delphiniums, hollyhocks, poppies and daisies – are all popular but may present problems. *Papaver orientale* flowers once in early summer; its value is then reduced to distinctive seed-heads from early June onwards. Similarly, lupins produce their early bright spires in June and then dwindle into seed-heads. Good planning will take these kinds of factors into account; if you can, arrange for them to be obscured by plants with later flowerings. Summer bulbs and bulbous-rooted plants include the *Agapanthus* family, alliums (the ornamental onions) and the regal lilies. These last specimens can be grown in pots and dropped into spaces as required.

AUTUMN

Autumn planting is all about fiery colours, as woodland takes on the appearance of an Oriental carpet laid out with gold, tawny, red, orange and crimson hues. There is evidence that the most vivid blazing colours occur on acid soils. Colder nights of autumn bring changes in the way that deciduous plants photosynthesise, causing a build-up of soluble colouring pigments in leaves before they decay. Areas with a low pH produce vivid scarlet hues, while chalky soil produces lower-toned purple colourings.

A large space is not vital for creating a good autumn display. Starting with the upper canopy of plant growth, trees such as *Sorbus* 'Joseph

Top: Hydrangea macrophylla 'Lemmenhof'.

Bottom: Hydrangea petiolaris.

Autumn flowers include these sedums and chrysanthemums.

Rock' and *S. hupehensis* produce excellent colour. The smaller members of the horse chestnut family such as *Aesculus parviflora* are worth considering as large shrubs or small spreading trees. It produces candle-like flowers in summer, and attractive yellow autumn leaves – it looks good in spring, too, when the young leaves glow bronze. For good autumn fruits, *Malus* 'Red Sentinel' manages to hold its crab apples until well into winter. The autumn colour of Virginia creeper (*Parthenocissus quinquefolia*) and Boston ivy (*P. tricuspidata*) is a fairly common sight on walls. *Parthenocissus henryana* has palm-shaped leaves strikingly veined with silver and with reddish backs. The vigorous *Vitis coignetiae*, with its very large leaves, produces a spectacular crimson scarlet show in autumn and should suit most small gardens, but not tiny gardens.

Among the shrubs, the deciduous azaleas offer good autumn tones if you have acid soil. *Rhododendron luteum* is also one of the sweetest-scented spring-flowering shrubs. The spindleberry produces vibrant colours on any soil. *Euonymus alatus* (poisonous) has the added bonus of corky-tipped wings on its branches, a feature to admire in winter.

Berries are a sign of autumn activity – some cotoneaster and pyracantha varieties will produce red, orange or yellow fruits, some of which even escape the attention of birds. *Cotoneaster cornubia* is a large form with an impressive show of berries. *Callicarpa bodinieri* 'Giraldii' brings something different to the autumn border; small lilac flowers in summer are followed by small violet berries – choose the variety 'Profusion' for the best show of berries.

Cornus alba in autmn.

There is also a cooler side to the autumn colour palette. *Ceanothus* 'Autumnal Blue' flowers from August onwards and has evergreen value as well. Caryopteris produces late, long-lasting blue flowers, as does plumbago (*Ceratostigma willmottianum*). The latter needs to be planted in a sunny position and will reward you with good foliage colour. The Michaelmas daisy family includes varieties with blooms in a range of magenta, purple and lilac tones and also some wonderful blue hues. *Aster* x *frikartii* 'Mönch' flowers from July to October, its lavender blue daisy heads blending with many other plants. For a taller, later daisy, use *A. novi-belgii* 'Climax'. Hot spots can still flicker in the autumn border at herbaceous level with chrysanthemums, crocosmias, dahlias, heleniums, heliopsis and red-hot pokers. Autumn planting could include *Kniphofia triangularis* and *K. uvaria*, the aptly named *Helenium autumnale* for yellow-brown ochre shades, and the dahlia 'Bishop of Llandaff', with its suitably dark purple foliage, and 'Bloodstone'. Although in southern parts of the British Isles dahlias can be regarded as hardy perennials, it can still be a good idea to lift them after the first frosts.

Many plants die down gracefully, their lingering seed-heads another symbol of autumn. Be selective about the big autumn clear-up in the garden, as seed-heads of all types offer food for birds through the winter. For vertical interest, *Clematis tangutica* produces yellow bell-shaped flowers in late summer, followed by fluffy seed-heads in autumn. After its succulent growth has died back, the large flat seed-heads of *Sedum spectabile* look good at the front of the birder. Astilbes combine feathery seed-heads with bronze foliage. *Deschampsia cespitosa* is commonly called tufted hair grass and looks good in a group or singly as a specimen; it needs a slightly acid soil to thrive. From midsummer, tall flower stems add airy plumes to its dense base tussock, which turn bronze or gold depending on the variety. *Molinia caerulea* 'Variegata' is one of the best variegated grasses – green and cream leaves with feathery plumes, and all suffused with buff tones in autumn. For caterpillar-shaped flower heads, plant *Pennisetum orientale* or *P. villosum*. Both have very fine leaves and downy seed-heads in autumn, although the latter may be worth protecting from winter cold.

At bulb level, it is easy to confuse autumn-flowering colchicums (poisonous) with the crocuses of spring: their flowers are similar shades. *Nerine bowdenii* is hardy except in the coldest areas, where it might need a protective mulch. This plant has bright pink flowers in September and October. Schizostylis provide good flowers for late cutting and the spiky shape is similar to gladiolus, but daintier. The toad lily, *Tricyrtis*, gives wonderful late, purple, lily-type flowers and is happiest in light.

WINTER

Winter in the garden need not be dull. A large number of plants continue from autumn producing flowers and fruits, or have attractive bark or stems. It is a testing time for the success of your design, though, the framework of the plot stripped bare of the padding of deciduous ornamental foliage and the bulk of flowering material. Good backbone planting comes into its own in winter, with evergreen subjects and conifers providing specimen planting and a backdrop to winter performers. A good one of these is *Betula utilis* 'Jacquemontii', with its bright white-barked trunk combined with typical birch habit. This is a good tree for a small garden, perhaps forming a year-round focal point as well as winter magnificence – if it is planted in front of a dark green backdrop, the paleness will contrast all the more.

As good dark evergreens, *Aucuba japonica* and holly are excellent value – choose a self-fertile variety for a crop of berries and lighten planting groups by including variegated forms. The acer family offers a range of possibilities for winter interest, most notably *A. griseum* (paperbark maple), *A. davidii* (snakebark) and *A. pensylvanicum*. For a polished mahogany look, *Prunus serrula* and *P. maackii* are worth growing for their attractive bark but are not as spectacular in flower as other cherries.

Witch hazels are hard to better as winter-flowering trees, combining fragrance and autumn hues earlier in the year, the only drawback being that they prefer acid soils. *Prunus subhirtella* 'Autumnalis' reliably produces flowers from November to March.

Plants with an architectural shape take on a new significance in winter. For instance, the curious contorted branches of *Corylus avellana* 'Contorta' arguably look better without their

Above: birch trunks in snow.

Above: Helleborus foetidus, Cornus alba *'Sibirica' and* Cornus stolonifera *'Flaviramea'*.

droopy leaves. Fatsias, yuccas and conical conifers have extra value at this time of year. The foliage of *Cryptomeria japonica* 'Elegans', a variety of Japanese cedar, also takes on a different russet hue in winter.

The choice of climbers providing winter interest would surely include the stalwart ivies for their evergreen reliability and also colour options. Winter-flowering jasmine (*Jasminum nudiflorum*) is a common sight; it requires some encouragement to scramble up walls. The scope of the clematis group is wide, including *C. cirrhosa* var. *balearica*, which combines feathery evergreen leaves with waxy red-freckled flowers in early or late winter. Choose the variety 'Freckles' for a heavy

Winter can provide effects not seen at any other time of year. The polished black stems of *Cornus alba* 'Kesselringii', and the red- and yellow-stemmed *C. a.* 'Sibirica' and *C. stolonifera* 'Flaviramea' look particularly stunning with snow on the ground, or if there is a good covering of snowdrops beneath and a pale background for contrast. *Rubus cockburnianus* produces ghostly white-bloomed stems and so needs a dark backdrop for maximum effect; like most of the rubus clan, it can be invasive. Try *Salix acutifolia* 'Blue Streak' for black-purple stems beneath a pronounced blue-white bloom. *Salix gracilistyla* 'Melanostachys' produces outstanding black catkins with brick-red anthers prior to leaves. Good alternatives to witch hazel include *Cornus mas* and *Chimonanthus praecox*, the aptly named winter sweet. This shrub can be trained on a wall or grown in front of a sunny one, where the heat radiated by the wall will help to waft its scent around the garden, though the plant may take some time to produce flowers. Care may be needed with winter colour combinations – some people may find the pink viburnums (*V.* x *bodnantense*, *V. farreri* and *V.* x *burkwoodii*) discordant when in close proximity to flowering mahonias, witch hazels and winter jasmine.

At a lower level, winter-flowering heathers – *Erica carnea*, *E.* x *darleyensis*, *E. erigena* – can be grown in areas where there is some lime, but not on thin chalky soils. They are, perhaps, seen to best effect in large swathes, but can be a useful plant for the front of the border in a small garden. The earliest of the hellebores, *Helleborus niger*, may require the protection of a cloche to ensure Christmas Day blooms in cold winters; the rest of its family takes winter planting well into spring. All the hellebores provide valuable winter evergreen foliage.

Snowdrops emerging from the soil bring cheer with the end of winter in sight. Dramatically contrast their whiteness with the dark foliage of low-growing evergreens such as *Ophiopogon planiscapus* 'Nigrescens' and the dark-leaved viola (*Viola riviniana* 'Purpurea'). Finish off the winter garden with pools of crocuses and the early-flowering small daffodils – *Narcissus* 'February Gold' – planted in drifts to flower before the spring growth of perennial plants.

Top left: Euonymus *and* Cornus alba *stems against snow.*

Bottom left: Eranthis hyemalis.

scattering of maroon speckles. *Lonicera fragrantissima* is not a true climber, rather an untidy shrub that can be trained against a wall or fence in the small garden. Its pale flowers in the middle of winter release a typically sweet scent. Delicate tracery is formed on a supporting surface by deciduous plants such as the climbing hydrangea and the fishbone branches of *Cotoneaster horizontalis*.

LAWNS

The temperate climate of the British Isles encourages the cultivation of lawns. The best conditions for lawn-growing are found in the west of England and Scotland, and the whole of Ireland, where winters are mild and moist and summers are not too hot. The ideal soil for growing a good lawn is a sandy one with a slightly acid pH – conditions in coastal regions are near-perfect. Clay soils are not ideal for producing fine lawns because of poor drainage.

Most lawns consist of a mix of different grass types, ranging from fine to coarse, with the ratio of the mix affecting the look and durability of the lawn. Any indigenous grass types will try

to take over, particularly if a lawn is neglected over a period of time. Having a lawn means accepting the chore of ongoing cutting and maintenance (see also 'How Much Maintenance?', pages 18-20). Frequent cutting encourages the growth of fine grasses, keeping coarser, vigorous forms at bay.

RENOVATING A LAWN

If you have inherited an unkempt patch of grass, try to renovate it. This is better than starting from scratch, unless the area is hopelessly uneven or has been totally overrun with weeds and moss. An old lawn can be given a new shape to fit your new scheme.

Opposite: cross-section of fine lawn showing moss.

Right: coarse grass is suitable for hard-wearing family gardens.

Your tolerance of lawn weeds such as daisies and speedwell (*Bellis perennis* and *Veronica filiformis*) will depend on whether you are aiming for a fine sward of turf or a utility family patch. Broad-leaved weeds such as plantain, dandelion, and self-heal may have to be controlled even in family lawns. This can be done by cutting or digging them out by hand. An organic (non-chemical) method of dealing with tap-rooted specimens is to shake a small amount of kitchen salt in the centre of the weed. Stubborn perennial weed pests can be dealt with using an appropriate chemical or a combination of manpower and organic solutions. Moss in any quantity is an indication of poor drainage, and always a bad sign. It means that soil is compacted, its fertility lowered or with an extreme pH value. Mowing grass too close also causes moss to grow. To rid a lawn of moss, use either a proprietary weedkiller or lawn sand, and then scarify to remove the dead growth.

Renovation is best undertaken in early spring, giving the grass the chance to grow through the peak growing period of May and be well on the way to recovery by the end of the first season. The grass should be mown in the early part of spring using a rotary mower with blades set at approximately 5cm. The clippings should be removed as they will contain weed growth. A week later, mow again but with the cutting height set to its highest. Any bare patches should be re-seeded at this point, using an appropriate seed mix for the type of lawn and location. Over the next few weeks, the grass should be mown weekly, with the clippings collected and the blade height being gradually lowered.

ALTERNATIVES TO GRASS

Low-growing plants provide an alternative way of achieving green ground cover. They will not stand up to the heavy wear that grass does but may be a better option for areas of pure ornament. Mix some of these plants to create a tapestry effect.

Acaena (sandwort; forms burrs)
Arenaria balearica chamomile (use 'Treneague', the non-flowering form)
Leptinella squalida
Mentha requienii (Corsican mint; for moist shade)
Silene acaulis (campion)
Soleirolia soleirolii (baby's tears; or mind-your-own-business; for moist shade)
Thymus (thyme – creeping types)
Gallium odoratum (woodruff; for shade)

The lawn should be fed with either a liquid or granular fertiliser, combined with a weed preparation as necessary. Scarifying, aeration and other annual maintenance procedures will also be necessary to stimulate new growth of finer grass species in the lawn. When these reach a healthy level they will cover up the soil

Chamaemelum nobile (chamomile) is a good alternative to grass.

allowing less space for weeds to encroach. The lawn can be altered to the shape required by your design. Unwanted turf can be placed grass-side-down to form an excellent soil additive after it has composted.

CREATING A NEW LAWN

If you decide your grass is too far gone to make renovation a worthwhile option, or there is no grass on site, there are two ways to create a lawn – seeding or turfing. Seeding is cheaper but it may take a year before the lawn can be subjected to heavy wear. Turf gives instant aesthetic results and can be used after two or three months. Laying turf may be worthwhile if you have children waiting for somewhere to play, or pets who would disturb a seeded lawn.

Turfing

Turf should always be obtained from a reputable source. Check the condition before you buy to make sure that the grass quality is suitable and the soil is free-draining, not heavy clay. The turf should not be infested with weeds or dead organic matter. Always buy cultivated turf grown specifically for lawns rather than meadow turf cut from rough pasture. The unit of supply is usually the square yard.

Having marked out and prepared the site (see pages 131-3), lay the first row of turf along any straight edge – the path or patio, for instance. Each piece should be positioned flush with neighbouring turves. Work across the area using a plank to kneel on, placed on the first

row of grass. Stagger the joints of the next and subsequent rows to achieve a bond similar to brickwork. Cover the whole area and trim the edges to the required shape. Trim any straight edge along the string guideline, reinforced by using a plank as a cutting edge and a protected place to stand. For a curved edge, start by laying the turves along the outline, making nicks in them as necessary to form a curve. Once you have formed the outline, continue by laying the turf across the lawn as you would if it were a rectangle, trimming the edges flush with the curve.

The surface should be tamped down with the back of a garden rake at regular intervals. This removes air pockets. A light roller can be used for this job. Any gaps between the turves are filled by a top dressing of sandy loam. This should be brushed well in. During dry spells, the new lawn should be watered in with a fine rose on the watering can or a sprinkler and hose. To avoid shrinkage, the turves should be kept watered until they have become rooted into the topsoil.

Seeding

Grass seed mixes for lawns in temperate areas, known as cool-season grasses, commonly contain a mix of fescues (*Festuca*), bents (*Agrostis*), meadow grasses (*Poa*) and perennial ryegrass (*Lolium perenne*). Each grass has different qualities. Fescues are reasonably hard-wearing and tolerate low cutting. Bents are naturally low-growing and can be closely mown. Meadow grasses are hard-wearing but do not like low mowing and some will have coarse leaves. Ryegrass grows quickly, is hard-wearing and tolerant of a range of soil types but is coarser-textured and resents close mowing.

Most modern grass cultivars are bred for good green colour and mowing qualities. When sowing a lawn, choose a ready-mixed seed mixture appropriate to the type of lawn you are aiming to create and the conditions in your garden. For quality lawns, the mix will probably contain modern cultivars of species of fine-leaved bents and fescues – browntop and highland bent (*Agrostis tenuis* and *A. castellana*), with Chewing's fescue and creeping red fescue (*Festuca rubra*).

For a family lawn, the mix will invariably include perennial ryegrass with red fescue, smooth-

Above left: use a straight edge to guide your first row of turf.

Above right: stagger the joints of each row.

Left: water the new lawn thoroughly on dry days.

stalked meadow grass, and browntop or highland bent. The main reason for perennial ryegrass is its hard-wearing characteristic and fast germination time – 7 days as opposed to 21 for other varieties. But because ryegrass is such a fast grower, it may be worth looking for mixes that do not include it but remain drought-tolerant, stay green and, above all, are low-growing, so you have less mowing to do. For

example a mix of smooth-stalked meadow grass (Kentucky blue grass – *Poa pratensis*), Chewing's fescue and browntop.

Seed can be sown by hand or with a spreading machine. Using a machine, sow half of the mix in one direction at the rate recommended by the seed suppliers. Then spread the other half working in the opposite direction. The machine should be taken right up to the end of each row. By hand, mark out the new lawn into a one metre grid. Weigh seed for each area at the given rate and sow in two directions.

Using a garden rake, lightly rake over the site. In dry periods, keep watering the area to ensure germination, and make sure the area is not disturbed by humans or animals. You may need to net the area to prevent birds from eating the seed. After 7-14 days the seed should germinate (if ryegrass is included). Let the grass grow to a height of about 50-75 cm, then make the first cut using a rotary mower with the blades set to take off 12cm.

Above: mechanical scarifier.

Right: using a lawn aerator.

Opposite left: Primula obconica is allergenic.

Opposite right: Ruta (rue) can cause severe blistering.

MAINTAINING A LAWN

All of the following procedures promote aeration of the lawn to counter soil compaction. Some remove excess thatch – dead material which collects on the soil's surface. Some thatch is beneficial to a lawn as it helps to counteract the effects of drought and wear. But encouraging air, water and nutrients to reach the roots of the grass stimulates the growth of finer species to promote a healthy lawn of any type – formal or informal, family or ornamental. As these procedures can make a lawn more vulnerable to drought, it may be best to carry them out in autumn when there is more moisture in the air. Mow the lawn to the required summer height first. After maintenance work, a low nitrogen feed should be applied and the lawn left to recover for a couple of weeks.

Scarifying – rake the grass to remove the build-up of thatch and enable more air to reach the roots. Small areas can be scarified by hand using a spring-tined rake but it can be extremely hard work – the raking must be vigorous to be effective. Hiring a machine will make the job easier. To remove the maximum amount of debris, scarify in two different directions over the whole surface. Any moss should be treated with a moss killer or lawn sand prior to scarifying, as it can spread living spores.

Aeration – do this by using a machine which punctures the soil surface or by hand using a hollow-tine fork (both from hire shops).

Slitting – only effectively achieved using a machine with knife-like blades that cut into the soil to a depth of about 10cm. These air channels aid healthy grass growth.

Spiking – opening small holes to let more air into the topsoil by inserting a garden fork into the ground vertically and gently easing it back without breaking up the surface. For larger areas, use a hand spiker or hire a mechanical one.

Hollow tining – to aerate, relieve soil compaction and remove thatch. The tiner removes small cores of the lawn topsoil, which include grass, thatch and soil. The lawn is tined at regular intervals resulting in a series of holes about 10cm deep all over the surface. The small cores are removed and the lawn top-dressed with a sandy mixture as described below.

Top-dressing – apply to a lawn immediately after the procedure above, on a dry day. A sandy mixture of six parts medium sand, three parts sieved soil and one part peat, coir or leaf mould should be suitable for most lawns. Apply at a rate of 1kg per square metre after scarifying, but if the lawn has been hollow-tined, increase to 3kg per square metre. Apply by hand and brush into the surface with a besom or use a hand-pushed lawn weed and feed application, which can be hired.

PLANTS TO BE WARY OF

See pages 30-1 for poisonous plants.

Of the many thousands of plants in the British Isles, only a few are potentially harmful. On pages 30 and 31 is a list of plants that are poisonous when eaten – a risk mainly for young children and pets. The poisonous plants that seem to cause most problems are yew, deadly nightshade, woody nightshade, monkshood, laburnum, cherry laurel, daffodils and euphorbias. Horse chestnuts have killed horses, and rhododendrons have poisoned dogs and goats in the past. Poison ivy (*Rhus*

next to paths, where it can brush against skin and cause an increased sensitivity to the sun and blistering rashes. Allergic reactions include skin rashes, swellings, eye problems and breathing difficulties. Plants that cause allergic reactions are poison primula (*Primula obconica*), ivy (*Hedera*), chrysanthemum (*Dendranthema*), mezereon (*Daphne mezereum*), Leyland cypress (x *Cupressocyparis leylandii*), *Alstroemeria* and *Schefflera*.

IRRITANT OR ALLERGENIC PLANTS

Arum (lords and ladies)
Alstroemeria (Peruvian lily)
x *Cupressocyparis leylandii* (Leyland cypress)
Daphne laureola (spurge laurel)
Daphne mezereum (mezereon)
Dendranthema (chrysanthemum, except dwarf types)
Dictamnus albus (burning bush)
Dieffenbachia (dumb cane, leopard lily)
Echium
Euphorbia (except poinsettia)
Ficus carica (fig)
Fremontodendron
Hedera (ivy)
Hyacinthus – bulbs
Lobelia tupa
Narcissus (daffodil and narcissus)
Primula obconica (poison primula)
Ruta (rue)
Schefflera
Tulipa – bulbs

These irritant plants are listed in the Horticultural Trades Association's code of practice for labelling of potentially harmful plants. See pages 30-1 for poisonous plants.

radicans, R. succedanea and R. *verniciflua*) is the only plant actively discouraged from sale by the Horticultural Trades Association. If you have poisonous plants in your garden, make sure pets cannot consume them. If old enough to understand, children can be taught not to eat such plants; it is best not to let very young children play near them.

Far more common than poisonings, however, are skin reactions to toxic plants. Even if your garden is adult-only, it is worth knowing which plants can cause rashes and other problems in humans. Rue, for instance, is best not sited

Asthma and hay fever flare up during the summer months, the main pollen season. Tree pollen in the air from February onwards and mould spores at their highest level in October and November can cause hay fever and breathing problems in some people. Symptoms can also be triggered by heavily scented flowers. Grass pollen is a common cause of hay fever.

Hedges attract dust and spores, and making compost involves disturbing spores, so you could ask someone else to cut a hedge or make compost for you.

OPTIONAL EXTRAS

Last, but not least, think about those special decorative items that can add so much character to your garden. Lighting, in itself, can completely transform the look of a garden at night. Even functional compost bins can be attractive features in their own right, and seats can be placed to form focal points. Follow some of our security tips, too, for a safe and burglar-free garden that does not feel like a fortress.

ORNAMENTS

One or two garden ornaments can do a lot to set off plants or create focal points in a small garden. There is a vast range of ornaments to choose from. Old statues can cost thousands of pounds but most garden centres stock reproductions in reconstituted stone at reasonable prices. Chimney-pots, staddle stones and clay drainpipes (from salvage yards) can look attractive in the right setting and are not that expensive. Large rocks or pieces of driftwood could be even cheaper alternatives.

USING ORNAMENTS

Plants with very intricate foliage can get lost among other leaves in the garden. Plain ornaments such as terracotta urns will highlight the fine detailing of the foliage and together they will make an impressive feature. Conversely, plants with large plain leaves make perfect partners for ornaments with an intricate shape or fine detailing, such as Grecian urns.

Ivies are useful for adding interest to shady corners but their mass of small leaves does little to grab the attention. A simple figurine set amongst the ivy instantly focuses the eyes and gives the leafy backdrop a new perspective. The same principle can be applied wherever there are a lot of small-leaved plants.

If you have a situation where a path turns a corner and then goes out of view, this is an ideal site for a garden ornament. A simple statue will draw your attention to the path in the foreground and then lead your gaze to the garden beyond. Not only will you notice the plants around the statue a lot more but the ornament will enhance the sense of mystery of the parts of the garden that you cannot see.

Ornaments can also make the entrance to the house appear a lot more welcoming. A pair of ornaments either side of the door will add a touch of formality and grandeur. A single ornament, such as a chimney-pot or an urn on a pedestal, creates a visual exclamation mark and can be especially effective when used to balance lush planting on the opposite side of the door.

Even the smallest gardens have potential vistas, perhaps a path framed by a tree or a pergola. However, if the end of the path simply leads to a fence or a hedge, you may never have realised this. By using an ornament at the end of the path to act as full stop, you can create a perfect vista in the grand garden style.

Ornaments are also useful for linking together disparate objects. For example, a collection of small pots can make your patio look a bit like a garden centre. However, a few large pebbles or a painted watering can placed among the pots can turn them into a co-ordinated feature.

AGEING EFFECTS

● Marble ornaments are not only expensive but will 'sugar' in the climate of the British Isles.

● Bronze and lead take on a good appearance with age.

● Check for frost resistance with terracotta; the material takes on interesting hues over time.

● Hardwoods or seasoned oaks will last longer than softwoods.

● Cast iron should be painted or treated against rust.

● Natural stone looks good and is extremely durable but expensive.

● Concrete and reconstituted stone can be 'aged' to good effect.

A carefully positioned boulder can be the perfect complement for an arrangement of containers.

*Above and left: the eye is not
drawn to the mass of small
leaves in the corner until
the ornament is added.*

*Right: seen from this angle,
the statue helps entice the
visitor into the garden.*

'AGEING' CHEAP MATERIALS

Many low- to mid-priced garden ornaments are made from concrete or some form of reconstituted stone. The latter is made by a process known as dry-casting, whereby a damp mix of cement and crushed stone dust is packed into a mould. The porous rough surface of this material will take on a pleasing appearance once moss, algae and lichen have developed. However, this takes years. Other ornaments made from a mix of cement and materials such as pea shingle have a much smoother surface that is impervious and does not encourage the growth of mosses and lichens.

Various methods of 'distressing' can be employed to help 'age' these materials, making them look more like old stone. Natural yoghurt and liquid manure applied to surfaces will encourage the growth of algae. With smooth concrete, the surface of the object may need to be given a key for growth to become

Bird baths are available at many garden centres. The one shown here could be 'aged' if so desired.

SAFE ORNAMENTS

Many garden ornaments at ground level are anchored safely by their own weight. If you need to raise an object, perhaps to give it more impact, avoid creating an unstable pile of base stones. A plinth should be wider than the widest part of the object, as much for proportion as stability. Solid concrete blocks may suffice as supports and can be finished to blend with the ornament they support. However, wherever possible, bolt down heavy items or set them in concrete. If children are using the garden avoid placing any ornaments close to paths, fronts of borders or anywhere near an area used for games: in these situations, young children may try to swing on them or will crash into them during play, breaking themselves and the ornament. Never place unsecured ornaments on the tops of walls.

established: sandblasting and sandpapering are two options. Placing the objects in a shady north-facing site and watering them is another simple method – in damper areas this can age the material quite quickly.

Alternatively, use paints to age a concrete ornament. Put a little white emulsion in a tin with a squeeze of acrylic raw umber. Paint a small area at a time, mixing small quantities as you need them to produce a slightly uneven result. Stippling with a larger soft brush or using a sponge can also work well. Mix in a dash of black for recesses, making sure to soften the line of this new shading. For additional authenticity, sandpaper off some of the paint from the raised parts of the object. These always age faster than the main body and recessed areas.

For a simple greenish hue, rub parsley over pale surfaces.

CONTAINERS

Opposite top: terracotta elephant laden with flowers.

Opposite bottom: why not consider dismantling the car and using parts for sensational pansy containers?

Ranging from pots and troughs to window boxes and hanging baskets, containers are useful for creating seasonal interest in different parts of the garden. Grow in them anything from herbaceous plants, shrubs, crops of fruit and vegetables to exotics that must be moved indoors for winter. Containers also allow you to grow plants with specific soil requirements, such as acid-loving rhododendrons and camellias, or alpines, which need free drainage. Containers can form an attractive part of the display in their own right or be utilitarian and remain completely hidden by plants. The only real drawbacks of using them are the watering needs of the plants and the possibility of frost damage with some materials. Raise terracotta

line them with polythene, remembering to make drainage holes at the bottom to prevent the compost from drying out too rapidly. Use a loam-based compost such as John Innes no. 3 for plants that are going to remain in the same containers for years. An ericaceous compost or peat-based multi-purpose compost is suitable for acid-loving plants. Line concrete containers first if using them for ericaceous plants. Adding a slow-release fertiliser such as Osmacote at planting time will reduce your need to feed.

ENHANCING PLANTS AND CREATING FOCAL POINTS

A well-arranged group of containers often makes more impact than does a casual

Use Versailles tubs for a formal look.

containers off the ground in winter to avoid cracking. Glazed earthenware is more resilient. Grecian urns and pots with narrow tops are not ideal for planting as it will be impossible to get the roots out without breaking the container.

PLANTING UP

Two-thirds plant growth to one-third pot height is a fair proportion to aim for most of the time. Ensure good drainage by adding a layer of stones or old crocks (e.g. smashed terracotta pots) at the bottom. If using terracotta pots,

'scattering' around the garden. Balance your arrangement by placing a star performer – such as a hot spot of plant colour or architectural specimen – at the centre.

Even when left unplanted, a carefully positioned container can form a very effective focal point in exactly the same way as garden ornaments (see page 208). Collections of containers can also be used to create different effects. For example, a set of matching terracotta pots in different sizes planted with drought-resistant plants such as

STYLES

● Period urns and cisterns etc are in keeping with older houses.

● Wooden Versailles tubs are ideal for the formal garden with clipped topiary planting.

● Stone containers have good weathering properties resulting in a pleasing patina and are essential for the formal garden.

● Re-constituted stone (concrete that looks like real stone) will need ageing or distressing for totally authentic look.

● Use old household utensils and wooden half barrels in a very informal garden.

yuccas, echeverias and pelargoniums will create a Mediterranean effect. Half-barrels in different sizes planted with bog plants such as gunneras, rodgersias and ligularias can be used to create a small-scale jungle effect.

You may want to give containers extra height when using them singly as focal points or in groups – stand them on a slab or make a plinth from treated timber, stained to match any other timberwork. However, be sure to secure a container safely.

Above: containers need not necessarily contain anything at all.

Left: sink garden with succulents.

GARDEN FURNITURE

PORTABLE FURNITURE

If you plan to move tables and chairs around a lot, perhaps to catch the evening sunlight or to escape the scorching midday sun, choose furniture that is relatively lightweight. Moulded plastic tables and chairs fall into this category, but because they are so light-weight do need to be taken in over winter. Such furniture is easy to clean and quick to dry after summer downpours so long as water does not puddle in the contours. For lounging, deckchairs are always popular. More comfortable, but also more expensive and less weatherproof, are the padded types of folding chairs, some of which have detachable upholstery.

Check before you buy that the furniture will fit in your shed or house for storage, and also on

Above: hosta and bamboo resting on sturdy wooden seat.

Right: white furniture will nearly always form a focal point and sometimes makes a space seem larger.

the patio itself – remember that you need space for pulling chairs out from tables. If you do not have plenty of storage space there is little point in buying portable garden furniture.

Seats for eating need to be higher than those for relaxation. Ideally, your knees should be at the same level as your thighs for good sitting posture, though deckchairs are always popular. Table tops need to be flat, not prone to warping or splintering, and the corners should be rounded. Slats should be narrow enough to shed water rather than cutlery and food. Avoid items

with narrow grooves, which can be hard to clean. Parasols, either free-standing or table-covering, should be firmly secured in a weighted base to withstand gusts of wind. If you plan to eat outside a lot, it may be worth investing in a dining canopy or sideless tent – useful for both shade and rain protection.

BUILT-IN FURNITURE

If you take al fresco dining seriously but have limited storage space for garden furniture when not in use, it may be worth building some permanent outdoor seating and storage, perhaps as part of a built-in barbecue complex. As the furniture becomes part of the overall garden design, its appearance needs more careful consideration. Wooden chairs, tables and benches are the most popular, but metal (and even stone) furniture is available for the purpose. Metal components of wooden furniture, including nails and screws, should be made of brass; if made of steel either galvanised or coated with paint or acrylic. Wooden picnic tables with built-on benches are sturdy and last for a long time but require some agility and are not comfortable for long periods of sitting.

Simple seats can be made from timber slats set between brick walls, and a brick or block central plinth can support a timber tabletop. The most durable material is brick; it is possible to buy tables and bench seats in brick kit form. If possible when building permanent barbecues, include cupboard space for charcoal, utensils, parasols, outdoor games and other equipment. For instance, build a hinged bench with storage space below.

As with any other permanent feature, check and double-check dimensions as you build.

Left: brick-built barbecue and work top.

Far left: metal seat.

FEATURES AND FOCAL POINTS

As well as being functional items, chairs and benches can be used to focus the view in particular parts of your garden. Most people appreciate having something solid behind them when sitting, such as a wall, fence or hedge for shelter and security – an appropriate backdrop of plants also helps to 'anchor' a seat into a garden. Enclose a seat with a bower or arbour structure to make it a larger feature, a secret haven from which to enjoy a pleasant vista, scented planting trained over the arch and dappled shade all at once. A good solution is to site one in a sheltered spot at the end of a path so that the visitor can enjoy either the view back along the path or another vista that opens up.

The scale and colour of any seat placed as a focal point should be in keeping with its surroundings. Green garden furniture can be surprisingly discordant sometimes. A white seat has more visual emphasis and can create an illusion of depth, too. Seating built around the trunk of a tree, or a raised structure covered with chamomile, which releases its scent when sat on, are excellent ways of integrating furniture with the rest of the garden.

LIGHTING

Lighting a path to help you find your way.

Right: up-lighting a pergola.

LOW-VOLTAGE LIGHTING versus MAINS

Night-lighting adds an extra dimension to the garden. For maximum brightness – e.g. security spotlights and floodlights – mains electricity at 240V will be required. A 300W bulb mounted at 2.4m on a wall will easily light an area of 30 square metres. Cables taking electricity from the mains through the garden must be protected by an armoured conduit and laid at least 50cm deep: do this during other excavation work. Outdoor plugs and switches must be waterproof and should be fitted to walls or concrete posts, never to fences. Consider including switches both indoors and out. The circuit must be protected by a RCD (residual current device) and a fuse or miniature circuit-breaker (MCB) which is separate from all household wiring. Never attempt to wire into the mains supply if you are not sure what you are doing – get an electrician to do the work.

Low-voltage systems are a cheaper option, available in kits and far easier to install. They operate with a transformer that converts mains voltage from 240V to a 12V supply. Some also incorporate a timer, which is useful for security purposes. The transformer is kept inside the building and plugs into a normal household mains socket. Low-voltage lights have the great advantage of being movable, so it is possible to change the look or mood of your garden. As the cable carries only 12 volts, if cut accidentally during other gardening activities it will not result in an electric shock.

Low-voltage lights give out very little illumination compared with the mains lights, but as they are used mainly for decorative effect and are suited to areas close to the house this is not necessarily a drawback. Some kits have cable only 7.5m long with 15m the maximum length. Easy to install, the kits are perfect for tiny gardens and may form part of a lighting scheme in larger small gardens where decorative effects are required.

UTILITY LIGHTING

Finding your way to your own front door in the dark can be surprisingly difficult if your house is not right next to a street lamp. Installing security lighting can help overcome this and is also useful for deterring unwanted visitors to the house and garden. Simple bulkhead or porch lights fixed to walls are one option in small town gardens. A halogen spotlight at the front of the house makes a good security light. Country-dwellers may have enough land to warrant halogen spotlights both back and front. It is worth considering one with a fitted PIR (passive infrared detector), which detects changes in temperature as a person approaches and activates the light. You can buy these to fit on to other garden lights. Other priority areas for utility lighting are steps which are used regularly in the dark and paths next to steep slopes.

LIGHTING YOUR PATIO

For good overall light on your patio you will need a spotlight or series of bulkhead types fitted to the wall of the house. These are all mains-powered. Spots for outdoor use must be sealed PAR 38 bulbs, but globe, post and wall-mounted bulkhead lights can take ordinary bulbs as they are protected from the weather by their casing.

Wall-mounted spots are relatively easy to install on a house wall. The lights are wired into an existing house lighting circuit and the switch should be placed in a convenient spot – by the back door or sliding door from a living room. A hole is drilled through the wall at a slight downward angle and should be filled immediately with mastic to keep moisture out. If the light fitting is double-insulated, the earth should be terminated with an insulated connector.

LIGHTING INDIVIDUAL FEATURES

Floodlighting everything will add a little drama to the garden at night but pounds to your

LIGHTING EFFECTS

● Produce different effects by experimenting with the direction and placement of lights. Varying light intensity, positioning at different heights and using colour appropriately can produce fantastic lightscapes.

● *Up-lighting:* light source placed below to shine up through plants. Creates drama. Use with statues, facades, trees and plants with a striking shape, e.g. weeping trees, yuccas and birches – especially good in winter.

● *Up-/down-lighting:* combines light sources both above and below. Will disguise true source of beam. Use for trees, terraces, patios.

● *Down-lighting:* source above subject gives good general illumination; creates a pool of light around a plant and indicates perspective. Use for plants, overhanging verandahs and balconies.

● *Shadowing:* beam of light projects outline of plant on to a surface behind. The light is placed in front, on the ground and angled up through the branches. Use for trees and large shrubs with interesting shapes.

● *Grazing:* light positioned to one side of a surface with good texture: light is directed across the surface. Use for rough stone walls and textures such as flint.

● *Accent:* use small spots for highlighting low-level objects such as small statues, decorative containers, striking plants such as phormium, grasses etc.

● *Silhouetting:* use wall or other vertical surface to position hidden light source to illuminate plant group or object from behind. Use for individual or groups of trees or ornaments with pleasing shapes.

● *Border:* low-level lighting along the border of drives and pathways that throws the edge into relief, highlighting joint between hard surface and ground cover.

● *Mirror:* use standing water to create a night-time mirror. An area behind the pool is lit and the water left dark. Up-light large trees or other features to create an image.

Above: lights positioned behind plants.

electricity bill, so concentrate instead on picking out plants and features here and there. In general, avoid coloured light, as reds and purples do not work well with foliage colours. Experiment with complementary colours – if you have a purple-leaved tree or hedge, bathe it with a yellow beam. Large-flowered plants and subjects with very architectural shapes tend to show up best when lit.

COMPOST BINS

Above: palisade box compost bin.

A pile of rotting vegetation and grass cuttings at the back or side of the garden can be an eyesore, even if hidden by the shed or garage. Compost heaps and bins are normally regarded as functional rather than decorative items. In a small garden, however, a compost bin could be made into an attractive feature.

Garden compost is decayed organic matter that can be returned to the soil as a moisture-conserving mulch and incorporated into planting holes. The composting process generates heat which in turn encourages the various decaying materials to break down. During this process weed seeds and some garden pests and diseases are killed. Home-made compost is ready to add to the soil when the materials have turned into a dark, crumbly non-odorous mixture.

other soil organisms to invade the materials and assist in aerating and breaking them down.

Allow room near the bin for wheelbarrow access. Don't leave gaps between the pieces of wood when making up the sides of the bin, otherwise the edges of the compost will dry out and heat will escape. Give heaps and bins a waterproof cover, either a purpose-built lid, a thick piece of carpet or a scrap of roofing felt. This prevents both drying out and waterlogging.

The interior of compost bins should either be painted with a rubberised paint or lined with heavy-duty polythene. For the exterior, use a water-based preservative as, once dry, this will not harm the plants within the immediate surroundings.

Right: window-box-style bin.

Far right: wicker-style surround.

The best size for a compost bin is 1 cubic metre, though this may be too big to fit in a small garden; 0.75 cubic metres is usually a more convenient size. The highest temperatures will be registered two or three weeks into the cycle and the debirs should have metamorphosed into a rich-looking mixture after about three months. Turn the ingredients over with a fork to aerate the heap and speed up the breaking-down process. Layering manure alternately with organic material will also help.

Compost bins and heaps should be placed directly on the soil, not on a paved or concrete surface. This enables earthworms, insects and

COMPOST-MAKING

- Do not discard cooked foods and meats on the heap. This will attract rats and other vermin.

- Keep the proportion of grass clippings down as they can prevent air from circulating.

- Burn any older weeds about to set seed and perennial weeds. Add as ash to the compost.

- Add materials in layers of at least 15–23cm.

- Using a timber compost bin will help to speed up the composting process by conserving and concentrating heat within the heap.

GARDEN SECURITY

Thieves strike both town and country gardens: from antique lead statuary and gardening tools to entire hedges, conservatories and ponds complete with fountains and fish, nothing escapes their attention. Security is likely to be more lax in the grounds of a house than in the building. In fact, it is estimated that about £70 million worth of garden items are taken each year in the UK. To compound the misery, household insurance policies rarely cover items outside, and from outhouses like sheds only if there is evidence of forced entry. Plants and greenhouse contents are rarely covered, though plants are very frequently targeted.

It is worth keeping a note of serial numbers of machinery and marking garden tools and valuable items with your postcode and house name or number with an engraving kit or

ultraviolet pen: when large hauls of machinery have been uncovered such markings have been used to trace owners. More expensive plants can also be electronically tagged.

Most garden crimes are committed by the opportunist thief, and taking only a few precautions may be enough to deter them. But by using as many preventive measures as possible to create an obstacle course, you will put off even the more cunning of garden intruders. You do not have to make your garden look like a top-security prison to achieve this, though, since measures like the ones mentioned here are subtle but effective.

1. Well-placed security lights with built-in passive infrared detectors (PIDs) can be enough to deter unwanted visitors at night – this is the time when your garden is most at risk of losing bulky items that take some shifting.

2. Secure a shed by replacing external hinges with internal ones and installing locks on door and windows. Screen the view of the contents from prying eyes with curtains or even trellis and climbers outside.

3. If you have a house burglar alarm system, extend it to the outbuildings. If there is no mains electricity supply, obtain a battery-operated portable type. Brief neighbours so that they can recognise the sound.

4. Do not leave garden tools lying about. Even if they have little intrinsic value, they can be used by thieves to force doors, break windows, lift plants or cause general damage.

5. If you cannot store items away, use wall anchors with a length of chain and lock attached.

6. Shrubs and trees near the house can screen the activity of a thief from neighbours. Keep them pruned, removing lower limbs that might also facilitate a burglar's entrance to an upstairs room. Plant prickly specimens on your boundary and beneath windows.

7. Use gravel for front paths and drives; it makes a quiet entry and exit impossible.

8. Weight precious items down and use bolts where feasible. Place bricks in large tubs and containers, and padlock exposed hanging baskets. Use a marking or electronic tagging system on valuable items.

9. Attach trelliswork extensions to boundaries; they allow an open view of the garden but make burglary hard work.

10. Screen valuable plants so that they cannot be identified from the road, and remove labels of new valuable planting to make them less obvious.

Plant a Berberis *on your boundary or underneath a window; its long, fine spikes will deter intruders.*

INDEX

Acaena 59, 201
Acanthus 28, 63
Acca sellowiana 82
Acer 92, 183, 184
A. davidii 196
A. griseum 184, 196
A. negundo 85
A. palmatum 86, 183, 184
A. pensylvanicum 196
A. platanoides 67, 183
A. pseudoplatanus 59
Achillea 59
Aconitum 30, 33
Acorus calamus 169
Actinidia kolomikta 182
Aesculus 30
A. parviflora 195
African marigold 111
Agapanthus 194
'ageing' garden ornaments 209
Agrostemma githago 30
Agrostis 202
A. castellana 202
A. tenuis 202
Ajuga reptans 72
Alchemilla mollis 23, 53, 63, 64, 194
alder 111
allergenic plants 205
alliums 23, 194
alpines 30, 102, 154
Alstroemeria 205
Althaea rosea 53
alum root 63, 99
Alyssum saxatile 53, 99, 111, 191
Amelanchier lamarckii 183
Anemone
A. x hybrida 59
A. japonica 63, 98, 99
angels' trumpet 30
annuals, fragrant 188
Anthemis tinctoria 97
Aquilegia 30
A. vulgaris 53, 99
Arabis 53
Aralia 92
arbours 15, 165
arches 15, 119, 164, 166, 167
Arenaria balearica 66, 201
Artemisia absinthium 51
A. abrotanum 187
Arum 30, 205
arum lily 169
Arundinaria 85
Aster 111
A. x frikartii 35, 196
A. novibelgii 196

Astrantia major 53
Atropa 30
Aubretia deltoidea 53, 111, 191
Aucuba japonica 196
autumn crocus 30, 111
autumn planting 194-6
azalea 99, 152

baby's tears 201
balcony gardens 48-51
bamboo 28, 51, 59, 85
barbecues 37, 119, 123, 213
barberry *see Berberis*
bark mulches 12, 24, 25
bay 51, 55, 187
bear's breeches 28, 63
beauty bush 55
bedding plants 21
bee balm 111
bee hives 53, 55
beech 180
beech hedging 23
begonia 99
bellflower 53
Berberis 51, 59, 69, 85
B. darwinii 112, 180
B. x stenophylla 23, 99, 180, 185
B. thunbergii 97
bergamot 111
Bergenia 99
B. cordifolia 59
Betula
B. jacquemontii 77, 111
B. pendula 59, 184
B. tristis 111
B. utilis 184, 196
birch *see Betula*
bird baths 209
bird pests 44
bladderwort 169, 171
bleeding heart 53, 99
blind people, planting for 28
bluebell 185
bog arum 169
bog gardens 40, 112, 170-1
borders
  design 20-1, 184-5
  herbaceous 23
  mixed 23
  shrub 23-4
boundaries 11, 134-41
  front gardens 69
  options 11
  ownership 46
  planning permission 46
  in tiny gardens 104
  see also fences; hedges; walls

box *see Buxus*
brick
  paving 146-7
  raised beds 153
  walls 138-9
Briza 28
broom *see Cytisus; Genista*
Brugmansia 30
Brunnera macrophylla 98, 99
buckthorn 31
Buddleia
B. alternifolia 111
B. davidii 35, 55, 63, 111, 192
B. x weyeriana 192
buildings, garden 156-9
bulbs
  fragrant 188
  spring 191
burning bush 188, 205
busy lizzie 98, 99
butterfly bush *see Buddleia davidii*
Buxus
B. sempervirens 55, 180, 187
B. s. suffructicosa 55, 99, 180

calico bush 30
California lilac 85, 196
Calla palustris 169
Callicarpa bodinieri 195
Callitriche verna 169, 172
Calluna 111
Caltha palustris 30, 169, 172
camellia 99, 191
Campanula carpatica 53
campion 201
Campsis 182
candytuft 53, 111
caper spurge 44
Cardinal flower 169
Carex 63
C. hachijoensis 70
C. stricta 169
Carpenteria californica 182
Carpinus betulus 55, 180
Caryopteris 25
C. x clandonensis 51, 187
castor oil plant 31
Catalpa bignonoides 184
Catharanthus roseus 30
catmint 32, 53, 63
Ceanothus 85, 196
Ceratophyllum demersum 169
Ceratostigma willmottianum 111, 196
Cercidiphyllum japonicum 28, 188

Chaenomeles
C. japonica 182
C. speciosa 111, 182
C. superba 85
Chamaecyparis lawsoniana 51, 59, 184
Chamaemelum 28, 52, 53, 66
chamomile *see Chamaemelum*
checker berry 30
Cheiranthus cheiri 188
cherry *see Prunus*
cherry laurel *see Prunus laurocerasus*
children
    play areas 29-31
    safety 30, 173, 209
    young gardeners 30, 31
Chimonanthus praecox 187, 199
Choisya ternata 21, 63, 187
chrysanthemum 205
circles, marking out 131
Cistus 25, 51
Clematis 182
C. alpina 51, 182
C. armandii 28, 187, 188, 190
C. cirrhosa 198
C. montana 36, 51, 188
C. tangutica 196
C. viticella 181
Clerodendrum 28, 187
C. bungei 187
climate 40-2
climbing plants
    aspect 182
    backbone planting 179, 181, 182
    for balconies 51
    for cottage gardens 53
    fragrant 188
coastal gardens 58
Colchicum autumnale 30, 111
columbine *see Aquilegia*
compost bins 37, 123, 216
compost making 216
concrete paving 10, 35, 143-4, 146
conservatories 16-17, 159
container gardening 17, 48, 51, 210-11
Convallaria majalis 30, 188
Cordyline australis 184
Coreopsis verticillata 59
corncockle 30
corners, marking out 131
Cornus
C. alba 59, 198, 199
C. controversa 92, 93, 184
C. mas 199
C. stolonifera 198, 199
Coronilla glauca 55
Corsican mint 201
Corydalis flexuosa 99
Corylus
C. avellana 196

C. maxima 59
costs, assessing 8-17
Cotinus coggygria 59, 63, 85
Cotoneaster 35, 59
C. cornubia 112, 179, 195
C. dammeri 22-3, 73, 103
C. horizontalis 59, 85, 199
C. microphyllus 103
C. salicifolius 23, 184
C. simonsii 180
cottage gardens 18, 52-7
cotton lavender 25, 180
crab apple *see Malus*
Crambe cordifolia 185
Crataegus
C. x lavallei 82
C. monogyna 55, 58, 59
Crocosmia 63
Crocus nudiflorus 111
crown imperial 98-9
Cryptomeria japonica 184, 198
x *Cupressocyparis leylandii* 35, 180, 205
curry plant *see Helichrysum*
curves, marking out 116, 131
Cyclamen
C. coum 191
C. repandum 191
Cydonia oblonga 55
Cytisus
C. battandieri 182, 187, 192
C. x kewensis 51
C. x praecox 55

daffodil *see Narcissus*
Dahlia 53, 196
Daphne 30
D. cneorum 187
D. laureola 30, 205
D. mezereum 55, 205
D. odora 28, 185, 186, 187, 188
Darmera peltata 28, 171
Datura 30
day lily 188
dead-heading 23
dead nettle 98, 99
deadly nightshade 30
decorative features 14-15
Delphinium 30, 53
Dendranthema 205
Deschampsia cespitosa 196
designers, garden 122
Deutzia 35, 55, 63
Dianthus
D. barbatus 53, 111, 188
D. 'Mrs Sinkins' 188, 194
Dicentra spectabilis 53, 99
Dictamnus albus 188, 205
Dieffenbachia 30, 205
digging 132, 133
Digitalis 30
D. purpurea 53, 98, 99

disabled people, gardens for 26-8
dividing structures 12-13
dog deterrence 32, 69
dog runs 32
dogwood *see Cornus*
Doronicum 111
drainage 46
    containers 210
    paved areas 133
    raised beds 152-3
drainpipes, disguising 162, 163
driveways 69-71
dry-stone walls 141
dumb cane 30, 205
dustbin screens 37

Echinops ritro 59
Echium 205
Eichornia 169, 171
Elaeagnus
E. commutata 85, 187
E. x ebbingei 28, 97, 179
E. pungens 82
electrical supply 173, 214
elephant's ears 59
Epilobium angustifolium 97
Epimedium 63, 99
E. perralderianum 103
Erica
E. carnea 85, 199
E. x darleyensis 199
E. erigena 199
Erigeron karvinskianus 53
Erysimum 53, 111, 188
Escallonia 63
Eucalyptus
E. gunii 28, 187
E. pauciflora niphophila 187
Euonymus 30
E. alatus 195
E. fortunei 51, 178, 182, 184
E. japonicus 84, 85
Eupatorium cannabinum 171
Euphorbia 30, 205
E. amygdaloides 98, 99
E. characias 82, 192
E. lathyris 44
evening primrose 187, 188
exposed gardens 58-9
eyesores, screening 36-7

Fagus sylvatica 180
false helleborine 31
family gardens 60-3
Fatsia japonica 51, 82, 84, 85, 198
fencing 11, 134-7
    acoustic fencing 84
    closeboarded 134, 136
    decorative finishes 137
    erection 134-7

fence panels 134, 135-6
gravel boards 135
palisade and picket fencing 137
planning permission 46
sources 12
trellis 11, 12, 13, 50, 104, 109, 137, 160-3
fennel 185
ferns 99, 102, 172
Festuca 202
F. glauca 70, 194
Ficus carica 205
fig 205
Filipendula ulmaria 171, 172
firethorn *see Pyracantha*
flame creeper/flame flower 98, 182, 187
fleabane 53
flowering currant *see Ribes*
foam flower 99
Fontinalis antipyretica 169, 172
forget-me-not 111
formal gardens 64-7
Forsythia 85, 185, 190-1
fountains 173, 174, 175
foxglove *see Digitalis*
fragrant plants 28, 187-8
fremontia 182, 205
Fremontodendron 182, 205
French marigold 111
frog bit 169, 171
front gardens 68-73
frost 40
fruit trees 78-9
fruit and vegetable growing 18, 21, 54, 78-9, 133
Fuchsia 99, 193
F. magellanica 193-4
F. 'Mrs Popple' 55
F. 'Riccartonii' 58
F. 'Versicolor' 99

Gallium odoratum 201
garden furniture 212-13
garden 'rooms' 74, 75, 104
Gardening Which?: Capel Manor gardens 56-7, 60-3, 74-8, 80-3, 86-7, 88-93
Garrya elliptica 182
gates 46
Gaultheria 30
Genista 51
G. aetnensis 97
G. lydia 79
Gentiana asclepiadea 99
Geranium 53, 59, 63
Geum 63
Gleditsia triacanthos 184
globe flower 171
globe thistle 59
Gloriosa superba 30
glory lily 30

gold dust 111
golden chain tree 55, 184
golden honey locust 184
golden hop 104
gorse 59
grape hyacinth 98, 111, 191
grass-grid paving slabs 70-1
grasses 70, 202-3
gravel beds 22
gravel boards 135, 155
gravel drives and paths 10, 12, 25, 30, 52, 147
gravel mulch 24
greenhouses 15, 25, 36, 123, 158-9
Griselinia littoralis 58, 85
groundcover plants 22-3
Guelder rose 55
gum tree 28
Gunnera 28
G. magellanica 93
gurgle ponds 174, 175

Hakonechloa macra 23
Hamamelis mollis 187, 188
hard landscaping 8, 9, 134-75
hawthorn *see Crataegus*
hazel *see Corylus*
heartsease 53
heathers 70, 111
Hebe 55, 72, 85, 111
Hedera 30, 51, 55, 85, 205
H. colchica 182, 184
H. helix 53, 99, 106, 184
hedging
cottage gardens 52, 55
evergreen 179, 180
formal 180
informal 180
low-growing 180
starting 180-1
trimming 23
Helenium autumnale 196
Helianthemum 25
H. nummularium 185
Helianthus annuus 53
Helichrysum
H. italicum 28, 187
H. petiolatum 155
Helictotrichon sempervirens 23
Helleborus 30, 191
H. argutifolius 192
H. foetidus 198
H. niger 199
H. orientalis 192
Hemerocallis citrina 188
hemp agrimony 171
henbane 30
herbaceous plants 23, 63, 194
herbs 194
Hesperis matronalis 111, 188
Heuchera 63, 99

holly 55, 85, 98, 99, 180, 184
hollyhock 53
honesty 98
honeysuckle *see Lonicera*
hornbeam 55, 180
hornwort 169
horse chestnut 30
Hosta sieboldiana 171, 172
Hottonia palustris 169
Humulus lupulus 104
Hyacinthus 205
H. orientalis 188
Hydrangea 85
H. aspera 194
H. macrophylla 194
H. paniculata 194
H. petiolaris 51, 98, 182, 194
Hydrocharis 169, 171
Hyoscyamus 30
Hypericum
H. patulum 185
H. perforatum 30
Hyssopus officinalis 111

Iberis sempervirens 53, 111
iceplant *see Sedum*
Ilex aquifolium 55, 85, 98, 99, 180, 184
Impatiens 98, 99
Indian bean tree 184
Indian currant 93
insect pests 43
Ipomoea 30
Iris 30
I. foetidissima 98, 99
I. laevigata 169
Itea ilicifolia 182
ivy *see Hedera*

Japanese anemone 59, 63, 98, 99
Japanese cedar 184
Japanese deer-scarers 175
Japanese water basin 174, 175
Jasminum 53
J. nudiflorum 55, 79, 198
J. officinale 28, 53, 188
Jew's mallow 63
Juniperus
J. communis 51
J. sabina 30
J. 'Skyrocket' 51

Kalmia 30
katsura 28
Kentucky blue grass 203
Kerria japonica 59, 63
Kniphofia
K. 'Little Maid' 97, 194
K. triangularis 196
K. uvaria 196
knotweed 63
Kolkwitzia amabilis 55

Laburnum 30, 59
L. x *watereri* 55, 184
lady's mantle 23, 53, 63, 64, 194
Lamium 99
L. galeobdolon 98, 103
L. maculatum 98
landscape architects 122
landscape contractors 8, 9, 10,
  122, 124, 125
Lantana 30
Lathyrus
L. latifolius 53
L. odoratus 188
Laurus nobilis 51, 55, 187
laurustinus 55
Lavandula 25, 53, 111, 180, 185,
  187
L. angustifolia 35, 53, 111, 180
Lavatera 35
lavender *see Lavandula*
lawns 200-4
  alternatives 66, 201
  easy-care 20
  maintenance 204
  mowing 19-20
  mowing strips 20, 80, 82
  new lawns 20, 30, 131-3, 202-4
  renovating 17, 200-2
  seeding 202-4
  shapes 178
  sloping 102
  specialist products 27
  turfing 202
Lawson's cypress 51, 59, 184
leopard lily 30, 205
leopard's bane 111
Leptinella squalida 66, 201
Leyland cypress 35, 180, 205
lighting 214-15, 217
Ligularia dentata 171
Ligustrum 23, 30
L. japonicum 85, 180
L. lucidum 179
L. ovalifolium 55
lilac *see Syringa*
Lilium regale 187, 188
lily 99, 187, 188, 194
lily of the valley 30, 188
lime 111
Limnanthes douglasii 53
Liriope muscari 99
Lobelia 99, 111
L. cardinalis 169
L. tupa 30, 205
log paths 150, 151
log rolls 150, 153
Lolium perenne 202
long, thin gardens 74-9
Lonicera 23, 51
L. fragrantissima 28, 187, 199
L. nitida 55, 184
L. periclymenum 53, 182, 187, 188

L. pileata 99
L. x *purpusii* 55, 187
loosestrife 171
lords and ladies 30, 205
low-maintenance gardens 80-3
Lunaria annua 98
lungwort 99
Lupinus 30, 194
lyme grass 58
Lysichiton americanus 187
Lysimachia punctata 171
Lythrum 111, 171

Magnolia
M. denudata 187
M. x *soulangiana* 187
M. stellata 85, 184
Mahonia 55, 69, 85
M. aquifolium 59, 99, 112
M. japonica 28, 187
M. x *media* 184
M. pinnata 97
mail-order design services 122
maintenance 18-25
  mowing 19-20
  plant care 20-1
  watering 25
  weed control 24-5
Malus 183
M. floribunda 82, 190
M. 'Golden Hornet' 55, 184
M. hupehensis 187, 188
M. 'Red Jade' 184
M. 'Red Sentinel' 93, 184, 195
M. 'Rev. W. Wilks' 55
M. 'Royalty' 183, 184
M. sylvestris 55
M. transitoria 187, 188
maple *see Acer*
marjoram 111
marsh marigold 30, 169, 172
masterwort 53
Matteuccia struthiopteris 171
Matthiola
M. bicornis 188
M. incana 188
meadows 111
meadowsweet 171, 172
Mentha requienii 201
Mertensia maritima 58
metal panels 12
Mexican orange blossom 21, 63,
  187
mezereon 55, 205
Michaelmas daisy 35, 111, 196
microclimates 40
mignonette 53
Milium effusum 70
Mimulus cardinalis 171
mirrors 107-9, 162
Miscanthus 70
M. sinensis 'Gracillimus' 23

mock orange 28, 55, 187
moles 44
Molinia caerulea 196
Monarda didyma 111
monkey flower 171
monkshood 30, 33
montbretia 63
morning glory 30
moss 201
mulches 24-5, 80
  bark 12, 24, 25
  grass clippings 20, 25
  gravel 24
  pebbles 80
mulleins 185
Muscari 98, 111
Myosotis 111
M. scorpiodes 169
myrtle *see Myrtus communis*
Myrtus communis 28, 55, 187

Narcissus 31, 190, 191, 199, 205
nasturtium 51, 53, 187, 188
Nepeta 32, 53, 63
Nerine bowdenii 196
Nerium oleander 31
Nicotiana 28, 187
N. affinis 188
noisy gardens 84-5
Nupharlutea 172
Nymphaea
N. candida 169, 172
N. 'James Brydon' 169
N. laydekeri 169, 172
N. odorata 169
N. 'Paul Hariot' 169, 172

obelisks 15, 165
Oenothera biennis 188
oleander 31
Omphalodes cappadocica 99
Onoclea sensibilis 171, 172
open-plan front gardens 71
Ophiopogon planiscapus 199
Origanum vulgare 111, 194
ornaments 206-9
Ornithogalum 31
Osmanthus 63
O. burkwoodii 185
O. delavayi 187, 190
Osmunda regalis 171, 172
oxygenating plants 169, 172

Pachysandra terminalis 66, 67,
  70, 103
paddling pools 29, 30
Paeonia 188
palisades 137, 153-4
pampas grass 70
Papaver orientale 194
parking and turning areas 69
parterres 66, 67

Parthenocissus 51
P. henryana 182, 195
P. quinquefolia 182, 195
P. tricuspidata 195
Passiflora caerulea 182
passion flower 182
paths
  design considerations 142
  dimensions 119
  edgings 52
  foundations 143
  front gardens 69
  gravel 25, 30, 52, 147
  log paths 150, 151
  paving, laying 144-7
  repairs 35
  safety 28
  siting 38
  stepping stones 150-1
patio gardens 86-7
patios
  dimensions 119, 142
  foundations 143
  lighting 215
  paving, laying 9, 144-7
  repairs 35
  paving
  block and slab splitters 9
  brick 146-7
  clay pavers 146
  concrete 10, 35, 143-4
  concrete blocks (pavers) 146
  curves and patterns 148
  drainage 133
  edgings 10-11
  foundations 11, 128, 143
  granite setts 10
  grass-grid paving slabs 70-1
  gravel 10, 12, 25, 30, 52, 147
  keeping costs down 10
  laying 144-7
  plant pockets 52
  site preparation 133
  slabs 9, 11, 52, 144-5
  sources 12
  steps and stepping-stones 148-51
  versus lawns 106
  see also driveways; paths; patios
pear, ornamental 55, 184
Pennisetum
P. orientale 196
P. villosum 196
perennials
  for cold hillsides 59
  for cottage gardens 53
  fragrant 188
  for shady gardens 99
pergolas 15, 119, 164, 165, 167
periwinkle see *Vinca*
Pernettya 31
Perovskia atriplicifolia 187
Persian ivy 182

Persicaria 63
P. affinis 59
Peruvian lily 205
pests 43, 44-5
pets in the garden 32-3
Philadelphus 28, 35, 85
P. coronarius 55, 187
Phlox 59
Phormium tenax 82, 184
Photinia 63
Phuopsis stylosa 111
Phytolacca 31
Picea pungens 183, 184
Pieris japonica 99, 185
Pileostegia viburnoides 104, 182
pine see *Pinus*
pink see *Dianthus*
Pinus
P. aristata 51
P. mugo 97, 184
P. nigra 58, 59
P. sylvestris 58, 59
Piptanthus laburnifolius 182
planning a garden
  budget 8-17, 124
  contractors 8, 9, 10, 122, 124, 125
  existing features 34-8
  legal matters 46-7
  maintenance 18-25
  professional designers 122
  scale plans 114-23
  setting priorities 29-33
  soil and climate 39-42
  wildlife 43-5
planning permission 46-7
plans
  measuring up 114-16
  mistake avoidance 123
  planting plans 188-9
  scale models 119, 121, 122
  schedule of works 124-7
  useful measurements 119
  working to scale 117-23
plant-lovers' gardens 88-93
plantain 201
Plantex 154
planting
  backbone planting 176-82
  borders 184-5
  colour schemes 185-7
  companion planting 56
  costs 17
  for fragrance 28, 187-8
  groupings 185
  mature plants 34-5
  plant care 20-4, 25
  planting plans 188-9
  seasonal interest 190-9
  site preparation 10, 133
  specimen and focal points 184
  times for 133

trees 183-4
  for wildlife 111-12
  see also lawns
play areas 29-31
plumbago 111, 196
Poa 202
P. pratensis 203
poached egg flower 53
poison ivy see *Rhus*
poisonous and irritant plants 30, 31, 33, 205
poke weed 31
pollution 84
Polygonatum 31
Polygonum affinis 194
ponds 168-75
  formal ponds 168-9
  gurgle ponds 174, 175
  informal ponds 169
  liners 169
  plants 169, 171-2
  pumps 173
  wildlife 43, 112, 170
Portuguese laurel 85
potagers 54
Potentilla fruticosa 24, 59, 185
Pratia pedunculata 70
Primula 98, 102
P. denticulata 171
P. obconica 205
P. 'Wanda' 184
privet see *Ligustrum*
Prunus 55
P. cerasifera 184
P. x cistena 184
P. 'Kiku-shidare-sakura' 183, 184
P. laurocerasus 31, 85, 178, 179
P. lusitanica 85
P. maackii 196
P. padus 187
P. serrula 196
P. subhirtella 196
P. tenella 190
P. x yedoensis 187
Pulmonaria officinalis 99, 191
purple loosestrife 111, 171
Pyracantha 23, 66, 85, 112
P. 'Mohave' 182
P. rogersiana 104, 106
Pyrus
P. calleryana 55
P. salicifolia 184

quaking grass 28
quince 55, 111

railway sleepers 14, 154-5
rainfall 40, 41
raised beds 14, 26, 27-8, 106-7, 152-5

reedmace 169
Reseda odorata 53
retaining structures 14
Rhamnus 31
Rheum palmatum 28, 92, 171
Rhododendron 98, 99, 152
R. *luteum* 187, 195
rhubarb forcers 55
rhubarb, giant 28
rhubarb, ornamental 28, 171
Rhus
R. *radicans* 31
R. *succedana* 31
R. *verniciflua* 31
Ribes 28
R. *atrosanguineum* 187
R. *sanguineum* 55, 111, 185, 190
Ricinus communis 31
rights of way 47
Robinia pseudoacacia 192
rock cress 53
rock gardens 18, 101, 102
rock rose 51
Rodgersia aesculifolia 171
roof gardens 94-7
rootstocks 78, 79
Rosa 18, 23, 35, 85, 188, 192-3
R. 'Angela Rippon' 22, 23
R. 'Easter Morning' 23
R. *eglanteria* 55, 187
R. 'Ena Harkness Climbing' 182
R. 'Fountain' 23
R. *glauca* 112, 192
R. 'Little Flirt' 23
R. 'Penelope' 23
R. *rugosa* 23, 180
R. 'Starina' 23
R. 'The New Dawn' 187
R. 'Zéphirine Drouhin' 68, 187
  scented roses 187
  shrub roses 23
rose periwinkle 30
rosemary *see Rosmarinus*
Rosmarinus 25, 28, 51, 53, 98
R. *officinalis* 28, 187
R. *repens* 53
rowan *see Sorbus*
royal fern 171, 172
Rubus
R. *cockburnianus* 199
R. *tricolor* 98
Rudbeckia 57
rue 205
Ruscus aculeatus 99
Ruta 205

safety
  children 30, 173, 209
  garden chemicals 30, 33
  garden ornaments 209
  poisonous and irritant plants
    30, 31, 33, 205

sage *see Salvia*
Salix 63, 111
S. *acutifolia* 199
S. *caprea* 111, 184
S. *gracilistyla* 199
Salvia 97
S. *officinalis* 28, 51, 187, 194
sandpits 29-30, 62
sandwort 201
Santolina 25
S. *chamaecyparissus* 180
Sarcococca humilis 99, 187
Saxifraga 53, 99
Scabiosa atropurpurea 111
scabious 111
Schefflera 205
Schizostylis 196
Schoenoplectus 169
Scilla 31, 190, 191
scree gardens 101
seakale 185
seats 107, 119, 213
security 69, 217
sedge 169
Sedum 53
S. *spectabile* 110, 111, 194, 196
Senecio viravira 97
sensitive fern 171, 172
shady gardens 98-9
sheds 15, 16, 36, 156-8
shrubs
  backbone planting 179
  borders 23-4
  for cold hillsides 59
  for cottage gardens 55
  deciduous 179
  evergreen 179
  for family gardens 63
  fragrant 187
  for shady gardens 99
shuttlecock fern 171
Silene acaulis 201
silk tassel bush 182
site preparation 8-9, 125-6, 127,
  128-33
  corners, circles and curves,
    marking out 131
  lawns 131-3
  levelling the site 128-9
  marking out 130-1
  paved areas 133
  planting, preparing for 133
  site access 125, 126
  site clearance 128
  slopes, creating 129-30
Skimmia japonica 179
skip hire 125-6
skunk cabbage 187
slopes 116, 120, 129-30
  measuring up 116
sloping gardens 100-3
Smilacina racemosa 99

smoke bush 59, 63
snowberry 99
snowdrop 199
soft landscaping *see* planting
soil
  acidity and alkalinity 39
  pH figure 39
  rainfall and 41
  in raised beds 154
  subsoil 39
  topsoil 39, 125
  types 39
  water table 40
soil-testing kits 194
Solanum
S. *crispum* 182
S. *dulcamara* 31
Soleirolia soleirolii 201
Solomon's seal 31
Sorbus 59, 111, 184
S. *hupehensis* 195
S. 'Joseph Rock' 194-5
S. *thibetica* 'John Mitchell' 93
Spartium junceum 59
Spiraea 63
S. x *arguta* 185
S. *japonica* 59
spring planting 190-2
spurge laurel 30, 205
Stachys byzantina 194
star of Bethlehem 31
starting a garden *see* site
  preparation
statuary 206, 208
stepping stones 150-1
steps 119, 148-50
stinking gladdon 98, 99
Stipa gigantea 23, 70
stock 187, 188
stone walls 140-1
stonecrop *see Sedum*
Stratiotes aloides 169
summer planting 192-4
summerhouses 15, 159
sunflower 53
sweet briar 55
sweet flag 169
sweet pea 53, 188
sweet rocket 111, 188
sweet william 53, 111, 188
sycamore 59
Symphoricarpos 99
S. *orbiculatus* 93
Syringa
S. x *josiflexa* 93
S. *vulgaris* 55

Tagetes 111
Taxus 31
T. *baccata* 51, 55, 59, 184, 185
Tellima grandiflora 99
terracing 100-1, 129

Teucrium
T. chamaedrys 180
T. fruticans 97
Thuja 31
T. plicata 180
Thymus 28, 52, 53, 66, 70, 111, 201
T. vulgaris 53, 111
Tiarella cordifolia 99
tick seed 59
timber decking 9, 58, 111
timber and metal structures 35-6
Timbron 160
tiny gardens 104-9
toad lily 196
tobacco plant 28, 187, 188
topiary 55, 66
topsoil 39, 125
Trachelospermum jasminoides 182
Trapa natans 169, 171
tree pruning and felling 46
tree stump removal 128
trees
    for cold hillsides 59
    coloured foliage 184
    for a cottage garden 55
    deciduous 34, 184
    evergreen 184
    fragrant 187, 188
    fruit trees 78
    for small gardens 183-4
    small weeping trees 184
    specimen and focal points 184
    for wildlife gardens 111
trellis 11, 12, 13, 50, 104, 109, 137, 160-3
Tricyrtis 196
Trollius 171
trompe l'oeil 109, 162
Tropaeolum
T. majus 51, 53, 187, 188
T. speciosum 98, 182, 187
T. tuberosum 182
trugs 55
trumpet creeper 182
Tsuga heterophylla 180
Tulipa 205
Typha minima 169

Ulex europaeus 59
umbrella plant 28, 171
underplanting 191

untidy gardens 47
utilities 15-17, 123
Utricularia vulgaris 169, 171

Valeriana officinalis 111
vandalism 69
vegetable gardens 18, 21, 54, 67, 133
Veratrum 31
Verbascum bombyciferum 185
Verbena bonariensis 111
Viburnum 35, 59, 63, 85, 190
V. x bodnantense 93, 199
V. x burkwoodii 88, 199
V. carlesii 28, 55, 185, 187
V. davidii 99
V. farreri 199
V. opulus 55
V. tinus 55
Vinca 85
V. major 99, 103
V. minor 51, 98, 99, 103, 111
vine *see Vitis*
Viola
V. cornuta 53
V. riviniana 199
V. tricolor 53
violet *see Viola*
Virginia creeper 51, 182, 195
vistas 38
Vitis
V. coignetiae 53, 182, 195
V. vinifera 181, 182

Waldsteinia ternata 103
wall fountains 174, 175
wallflower 53, 111, 188
walls 11
    brick walls 138-9
    crib walling (gabions) 14
    damp-proof course 138
    dry-stone walls 141
    planning permission 11, 46
    retaining walls 14, 101, 152
    screen block walls 139-40
    stone walls 140-1
    terminology 140
washing lines 37, 54, 62
water chestnut 169, 171
water features 15, 106, 168-75
    bell fountains 173
    bog gardens 40, 112, 170-1
    child safety 173

gurgle ponds 174, 175
Japanese deer-scarers 175
Japanese water basin 174, 175
ponds 168-75
pumps 173
wall fountains 174, 175
waterfalls 102
water hawthorn 172
water hyacinth 169, 171
water lilies 169, 172, 187
water plants 169, 171-2
water soldier 169
water starwort 169, 172
water table 40
water violet 169
waterfalls 102
watering 25
wedding cake tree 92, 93, 184
weed control 22, 47
    in lawns 201
    mulches 24-5
    organic gardening 133
    polythene sheeting 25, 80
    systemic weed killers 24
Weigela 63
Western hemlock 180
Western red cedar 180
whitebeam 93
wildlife 43-5, 111, 112, 170
wildlife gardens 20, 110-13
willow *see Salix*
willow gentian 99
willow and hazel hurdles 12, 55
willow moss 169, 172
wind effects 40, 42, 48, 58
window boxes 50
winter planting 196-9
winter sweet 187
Wisteria 31
W. sinensis 188
witch hazel 187, 188
wood spurge 98, 99
woodbine *see Lonicera*
woodruff 201
woody nightshade 31
wormwood 51

yarrow 59
yew *see Taxus*
Yucca filamentosa 97, 184, 185

Zantedeschia aethiopica 169

ACKNOWLEDGEMENTS

Photographs from *Gardening Which?* library, The Gardening Picture Library, Jerry Harpur/Elizabeth Whiting Associates, Richard Davies/Elizabeth Whiting Associates, Jean-Paul Bonhommet/Elizabeth Whiting Associates, Jay Patrick/Elizabeth Whiting Associates, Peter Woloszynski/Elizabeth Whiting Associates, Spectrum, Brian Rogers/Biofotos, John Glover, Pat Brindley, Heather Angel.

Illustrations by Peter Harper, Kuo Kang Chen, Peter Serjeant, Linda Waters.